World of Salads

World of Salads

by

ROSALIE SWEDLIN

Book Club Associates
London

This edition published 1980 by
Book Club Associates
By arrangement with Elm Tree Books Ltd

Illustrations by Pamela Dowson
Photographs by Bill Richmond

Filmset by Pioneer
Printed and bound in Great Britain by
Redwood Burn Ltd, Trowbridge and Esher

Contents

Acknowledgements

Among the many people who encouraged this first act of authorship, I am exceptionally grateful to June Hall and Kate Dunning, my original editors who commissioned this book; and to Susan Fletcher and Connie Austen Smith, whose gentle persistence and editorial guidance took me over the many hurdles along the way to completing the manuscript. To Carmen Callil I owe special thanks for her not-so-gentle but effective insistence that I not abandon the book when the obstacles seemed insurmountable.

To my colleagues at Anthony Sheil Associates who sampled the salads, to Sandy McCulloch who typed, metricated and made some sense of the more obscure recipes, and to the many greengrocers whose friendly advice transformed those innumerable shopping expeditions into happy learning experiences, I am warmly grateful.

My publishers and I would also like to thank the Inside Out Shop, Long Acre and Frida Marketing Services Ltd., Long Acre, London WC2 for their assistance in providing props for the photography. Also many thanks to Bill Richmond, the photographer for his painstaking care and expertise.

Permissions

The author and Elm Tree Books would like to thank the following
publishers for permission to quote:

A selection from *Oranges* by John McPhee. Copyright 1966, 1967 by
John McPhee. Reprinted by permission of Farrar, Straus and Giroux Inc.

A selection from *Fruit and Vegetables* by Erica Jong. Published by Secker
& Warburg, 1973.

A selection from *Middle Eastern Food* by Claudia Roden. Published by
Nelson, 1968.

from the *Artists Cookbook*, published by the Museum of Modern Art,
New York. Copyright 1977 by Madeleine Conway and Nancy Kirk.

from *Italian Food* by Elizabeth David. Published by Macdonald & Jane,
1954.

from the *Israeli Cookbook* by Molly Lyons Bar-David. Published by
Crown Publishers, Inc. 1964.

from *The George Bernard Shaw Vegetarian Cookbook*, ed. K. J. Minney by
Mrs. Alice Laden. Published by Garnstone Press.

from *Far Eastern Cookery* by Robin Howe by kind permission of Michael
Joseph Ltd., London 1969.

from *Alice B. Toklas Cookbook*. Published by kind permission of Michael
Joseph Ltd., London 1954.

from *The Mushroom Feast* by Jane Grigson, copyright 1975 by Jane
Grigson by kind permission of David Higham Associates Ltd., London.

from *Good Things* by Jane Grigson, copyright 1979 by Jane Grigson, by
kind permission of David Higham Associates Ltd., London.

Introduction

I have always been fascinated by salads. While, as Gertrude Stein might have said, a roast chicken is a roast chicken is a roast chicken on almost any dinner table in any country, a salad is a highly unpredictable combination of cold vegetables and herbs — and a multitude of other ingredients including meats, fish, pasta, beans, cheese, eggs and rice — which may be chopped, sliced, diced, boiled, blanched, shredded, grated, mashed or puréed and dressed in an equally various and unpredictable fashion.

Although the first salad recipe was recorded in England in 1390 by Richard II's master chef, it is John Evelyn's *Acetaria*, published in 1699, that undoubtedly makes the most important early contribution to the discussion of salads. 'Sallets in general', he wrote, 'consist of certain esculent Plants and Herbs, improv'd by Culture, Industry and Art of the *Gard'ner*; Or, as others say, they are a composition of *Edule* Plants and Roots of several kinds, to be eaten Raw or Green, blanch'd or Candied; simple, and serfe, or intermingl'd with others according to the season'. And for their composition he recommended a balance of ingredients which should 'fall into their places, like the *Notes* in *Music,* in which there should be nothing harsh or grating'.

Both Evelyn and his contemporary Gervase Markham, author of *The English Housewife*, placed salads into three groupings: simple, compounded, and those to decorate the table. Markham added a fourth group by combining those 'both for use and adornation'.

The French classical repertoire includes two kinds of salad: the simple salad — a bowl of tossed greens or another single vegetable, served as an accompaniment to the main course of after, for the purpose of refreshing the palate, and the combination salad — a separate and special course, most often served as an hors d'oeuvre or as a meal in itself.

During the years since John Evelyn first inspired the English homemaker with tips on preparation and the choice of ingredients for the salad bowl, the English seem to have neglected his valuable legacy. While the French perfected the art of salad-making with as much high purpose and flair as might be devoted to a soufflé or sauce mousseline, the English turned out such uninspired creations that one hardly finds surprising the remark by a nineteenth century traveller that, 'The salad is the glory of every French dinner and the disgrace of most in England.'

This statement has a certain truth even these days, if not in the English home, most certainly in the average restaurant throughout the country. Not too long ago, the *Sunday Times* colour magazine ran an article called 'Sad Salads', rating the taste, freshness and appearance of salads served in a variety of London restaurants. All too often the critic had recourse to such comments as 'limp hot house lettuce', 'soggy potato salad', 'sour cole slaw', 'insignificant and over vinegary dressing', and 'cucumber, thick and skinny'.

I hope my salad passion is infectious. As an American who has lived in London for many years, I miss the wonderful selection of salads available in the U.S.A. from the simplest drug store to the finest four-star establishment. But even salad-sophisticated Americans may find in many of the international recipes in this book new and delicious ways of enhancing or adding to their favourite dishes.

Or in the words of the great French philosopher of the palate, Brillat-Savarin, 'The discovery of a new dish does more for the happiness of mankind than the discovery of a star'.

Equipment List

Cheesecloth (for straining and herb bouquets)
Chopping board (unfinished wood)
Chopping bowl and crescent chopper with handle
Colanders and sieves
Cruet — for oil and vinegar
Electric blender or food processor
Enamel or stainless steel cookware
Food mill, Garlic press
French salad basket or salad dryers*
Jars
Juicer
Knives — paring, chopping, serrated, etc
Mortar and pestle
Mouli grater or drumlike revolving grater
Nutmeg grater
Pepper and salt mills
Potato peeler, Scissors, Slotted spoon
Salad bowls — glass, ceramic and wood — and Salad servers
Scales, Spice rack, String
Wire whisks (a birch whisk is also useful for whipping dressings)
Wooden spatulas

---

* These include everything from the simplest mesh salad basket to the plastic spin-dryers operated by centrifugal force: an inner perforated basket containing the greens spins and forces the water into a solid outer basket.

Measurements

Quantities are given in both metric and imperial measures, and occasionally U.S. cup measures – *in that order*. It is essential to follow one system of measurement throughout a recipe. They are *not* interchangeable.

The conversion table generally applied throughout the book is:

Liquids

Imperial	Metric	Cup
2½ fl oz	75 ml	¼ cup
5 oz (¼ pt)	150 ml	½ cup
10 oz (½ pt)	300 ml	1 cup
20 oz (1 pt)	600 ml	
1½ pt	900 ml	
1¾ pt	1 litre	
teaspoon	5 ml	
dessertspoon	10 ml	
tablespoon	15 ml	

A British standard measuring cup is equivalent to 10 fluid ounces.
An American Standard measuring cup is equivalent to 8 fluid ounces.

U.S. Cup Measures	British Equivalents
¼ cup	2 fl oz
1/3 cup	2 2/3 fl oz
½ cup	4 fl oz
2/3 cup	5 1/3 fl oz
1 cup (½ US pt)	8 fl oz
1¼ cup	10 oz (½ Imp pt)
2 cups (1 US pt)	16 fl oz
2½ cups	20 oz (1 Imp pt)

Solids

British and American solid weights, which are equivalent, are given below
with *approximate* metric equivalents.

Imperial	Metric
1 oz	25 g
2 oz	50 g
4 oz	100 g
8 oz	225 g
12 oz	325 g
14 oz	400 g
16 oz (1 lb)	450 g

Oven Temperature Chart

°C	°F	Gas mark
110	225	¼
130	250	½
140	275	1
150	300	2
170	325	3
180	350	4
190	375	5
200	400	6
220	425	7
230	450	8
240	475	9

Green Salads

For most people, a salad means lettuce. And why not? Lettuce has been cultivated for food since the earliest civilisations.

Our modern word lettuce derives from the Latin *lactuca,* but lettuce was known to the Greeks as *tridax* and features in Herodotus' accounts of the feasts served to Persian kings in the sixth century B.C. Throughout the ancient world, the green salad appeared as a standard feature on the banquet menu. The Hebrews served cress and lettuce with just a sprinkling of salt, the Greeks dressed their salads with honey and oil, and the Romans prepared a more elaborate dish with oil, spices, hard-boiled eggs and other garnishes.

The many varieties of lettuce cultivated today came from a wild, prickly lettuce of Asian origin. During the reign of Elizabeth I, lettuce was introduced to England; it was liked so much that within thirty years, no less than eight varieties existed and it became an important early crop in the American colonies.

Admired for its delicate taste and colourful adornment of the dinner table, lettuce has been equally appreciated as a rich and freely available source of vitamins and minerals, and as a useful aid to digestion. The Roman physician Galen praised it for curing his youthful stomach disorders and in old age he claimed that it brought him a good night's sleep. In the sixteenth century, *Gerard's Herball* advised readers that 'lettuce cooleth the heate of the stomache, called the heart-burning and helpeth it when it is troubled with choller'; and John Evelyn even went so far, while commending the many 'soporiferous' qualities of lettuce, to praise its salutory effect upon our 'Morals, Temperance and Chastity'. Early in our own century, C. H. Ellwanger wrote in *The Pleasures of the Table,* 'the mission of the salad is to correct the too liberal ingestion of rich and fatty substances, to prepare for the dessert, to stimulate and divert the taste and to promote stomachic harmony at a time when the appetite has begun to flag and the palate is impatient of a long delay between the roast and the *demi-tasse*'.

Perhaps it was the medicinal virtues of lettuce that prompted the still unresolved question as to when during the meal a green salad should be

1

served. In the first century A.D., the Roman poet Martial recorded his confusion when the Emperor Domitian changed the well-established custom of serving the salad course last: 'How comes it that this food which our ancestors ate only as a dessert is now the first that is put before us?' The answer, appropriate even today, is that the salad is such a versatile dish it can be served whenever it best accommodates with the rest of the meal — as a first course or an hors d'oeuvre; with the main dish; before the cheese; with the cheese; after the pudding; or as a whole meal in itself!

My own preference is to serve a green salad as a first course or following the entree with some cheese, if the main dish is a roast or a rich casserole. However, for suppers, light luncheons, and summer meals, a green salad makes a suitable and refreshing accompaniment to the main course.

Mastering the Perfect Green Salad

The mixing of the salad is too important an operation to be trusted to a servant. As we are here, Madame does not like to leave her visitors, but I see Gabrielle peep from behind the portières, and make a sign to Mademoiselle, about five minutes before dinner; and Mademoiselle goes into the *salle-à-manger,* and Madame rather loses the thread of her discourse, and looks wistfully after her daughter; for, if Monsieur is particular about anything, it is about his salads. Strictly speaking, Madame tells me, the vegetables ought to be gathered while the soup is on the table, washed and cleansed while we are eating the *bouli,* and sliced and dressed with the proper accompaniments while the *rôti* is being brought in. Madame's mother always mixed it at the table, she says, and I have no doubt Madame follows the hereditary precedent herself, when she has no foreign visitors staying with her.

French Life, Mrs. Gaskell

The perfect salad begins with the choice of greens. A basic salad can be made from one, or, a combination of greens — primarily lettuce — which complement each other in colour, texture and flavour.

There are four main varieties of lettuce generally available in Great Britain and North America: round (Boston), Webb's Wonderful (iceberg), cos (romaine) and curly endive. Many other types are seasonally available in the markets, along with greens not of the lettuce family. And don't forget the greens which can be picked wild; these tasty plants add wonderful variety to the salad bowl throughout the year.

2

Here is a basic selection:

Belgian Endive, called Witloof Chicory in the seed catalogues, is one of the loveliest delicacies for the salad bowl, but is often quite expensive. It has narrow, blanched leaves that grow in clusters and is at its best between May and October. Belgian endive need not be washed before serving. Simply remove any bruised outer leaves and wipe the rest gently with a damp paper towel.

Bibb Lettuce is not often found in British markets, but its crisp and pungent flavour is a great favourite with Americans. It has small heads with soft, pliable leaves and requires thorough rinsing or soaking to clean properly.

Butterhead (Round) Lettuce with its loosely packed, pale green leaves is popular on both sides of the Atlantic and is available throughout most of the year. The slightly bitter outer green leaves become soft, pale and mildly sweet in the centre. This is an excellent all-purpose lettuce, but should be washed with care to prevent the delicate inner leaves from bruising.

3

Chinese Cabbage looks more like a blanched cos (romaine) lettuce than a cabbage. It makes a most delicious, crispy salad ingredient and is now frequently stocked by the major supermarket chains, as well as specialist greengrocers.

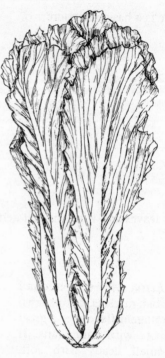

Cos (Romaine) has crisp, long leaves and a strong, sharp flavour. The outer, dark green leaves are often too coarse for salads, but they should be saved as decorative lining for platters. Both cos and romaine are usually available throughout the year.

Cress is a native of Persia which has been cultivated for salads since the sixteenth century. It is generally grown together with mustard and can be easily cultivated at home. Distinct in flavour, it should be used liberally to garnish salads.

Curly Endive or Chicory is a bushy, pale green plant — not related to lettuce — with tough, feathery leaves and a sharp, bitter flavour. It is mainly in season in winter and provides a wonderfully rich source of vitamins B and C and minerals, including iron. Because of its very strong taste, many people prefer it in combination with other milder greens, but it is also delicious

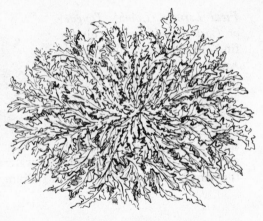

on its own with mustard vinaigrette or *à la Perigord*: with walnut oil, vinegar, a garnishing of sliced hard-boiled eggs, and a *chapon* (toast rubbed with garlic and placed in the bottom of the salad bowl).

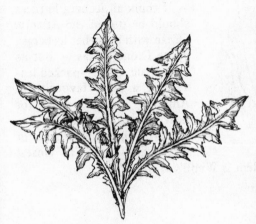

Dandelion Greens provide free food for the salad bowl. Older leaves may be somewhat tough, so choose only fresh young leaves for the salad bowl. Their thin, arrow-shaped leaves have a sharp, bitter flavour which can be reduced by blanching, i.e. covering the plant with an inverted flower pot for several days before using. These greens, long prized for medicinal virtues, are rich in iron and minerals, as well as vita-

mins A and C; and one cup of cooked greens has only 60 calories.

Escarole (Broad Leafed Endive or Batavia) is much like chicory but less bitter with heavier, broader, fan-shaped leaves. The centre is pale and yellowish, turning dark green at the edges and outer leaves.

Field Lettuce (Lamb's Tongue or Corn Salad) is difficult to find in Great Britain and America, but this tangy lettuce is extremely popular in France and Italy. Its dark green leaves resemble spinach, although milder in flavour, and are suitable for mixing with stronger greens, such as dandelion and watercress. It grows well throughout the winter and is a rich source of sodium and vitamin C.

Iceberg has its many detractors — 'I think all iceberg lettuces should be put in the Atlantic Ocean with the other icebergs', wrote Dione Lucas — but its crisp, pale, tightly-packed leaves are a great favourite in America and are ideal for heavy dressings such as Roquefort, Thousand Islands or Green Goddess. The closest widely available British equivalent is Webb's Wonderful.

Leaf Lettuce, of which salad bowl and green ice are popular varieties, is a delicate, loose-leaf lettuce that does not form heads. Its soft-textured leaves provide a pleasant contrast in combination with coarser greens like cos (romaine) or curly endive. Leaf lettuces wilt easily and should not be stored for too long.

6

Purslane, like dandelion, is a weed that can be picked free for the salad bowl. Its pleasantly acidic flavour and crisp texture provide a nice complement to milder greens.

Radicchio is a popular Italian chickory available in its native country throughout the year. A red variety, *Rosso di Treviso,* is now sometimes sold here at specialist markets during the early winter months. They are expensive and the heads are

often so small that they are only worth buying to add a bit of colour to your salad bowl. However, radicchio has a wonderfully distinctive flavour and its cabbage-like, crispy leaves are superb when dressed with mustard and garlic flavoured vinaigrette.

Rocket — *ruchetta* to the Italians, *rokka* in Greece and also known under its Italian-American name, *arugala*, is a native of southern Europe. It is difficult to find in England, but quite popular in America. Characterised by a very sharp, peppery flavour, it should be used in moderation as 'seasoning' for the salad bowl.

7

Sorrel, both wild and cultivated, has an unusual lemon-like flavour. It is more widely used in continental Europe than in Britain or North America, but can easily be grown from seed in the garden. It thrives in sandy soil and can often be found wild near beaches.

Spinach leaves have become increasingly popular as salad bowl greens. Mix them with lettuce or serve them on their own with garnishes of sliced raw mushrooms, hard-boiled eggs, bacon bits or grated cheese. Spinach leaves must be washed thoroughly to remove all the dirt.

Watercress has been used as both food and medicine for over two thousand years. The Greek general Xenophon included it in his soldiers' diet and it is still appreciated as a rich source of iodine and vitamin C. Its peppery, spicy taste combines well with many other greens, but watercress perishes easily and should be used within two days of purchase. Sort out the bad sprigs immediately, wash the rest, drain and store in a plastic bag in the refrigerator.

A bowl of fresh, tender leaves from any of half of a hundred kinds of garden lettuces, unadorned except by the simplest possible mixture of oil, vinegar and seasoning, is a joy to the palate.

The Cooking of Provincial France, H.F.K. Fisher

When selecting salad ingredients, always look for fresh, crisp greens. These should be washed carefully ahead of time so that the leaves are absolutely dry when placed in the salad bowl (accumulated water will dilute the flavour of the dressing and cause the leaves to wilt). Tightly packed greens — cos (romaine), Webb (iceberg), Belgian endive, etc — can be left intact when washing; however, loose-leaf lettuces which tend to accumulate dirt at their centres should be carefully separated before washing and storing.

There are several good ways to wash greens: some people soak the greens in cold, lightly salted water (which is meant to kill any possible germs or bugs); or you can simply rinse leaves under a cold, running tap. Yet another method involves cutting a core out of the centre of the lettuce and running water into the hollow with enough force to split the head apart, forcing the dirt from the centre.

After washing, gently tear the leaves into appropriate-sized pieces (according to your recipe), and allow excess water to drain by placing leaves in a lettuce basket, colander or sieve. There are now several mechanical dryers on the market which operate by centrifugal force. These are wonderful for preparing last-minute salads, when quick drying is essential.

To crisp and store lettuce, the leaves should be placed between layers of paper towelling or cloth towels, then gently rolled or folded, and finally, placed into a plastic bag or directly into the salad compartment of the refrigerator. Make sure the temperature is not too low or the lettuce will become translucent and wilt.

In spite of much that has been said against the wooden salad bowl — e.g. oil and garlic turn the wood rancid; washing leaves a wet wood taste — I still believe it is the ideal bowl for a tossed salad. A large, deep bowl made of unvarnished wood is least likely to bruise the leaves and its depth makes for easy tossing and requires less dressing. Do make sure to clean a wooden bowl with warm soapy water after each use, drying it straight away with a cloth towel; otherwise it will indeed become rancid!

With glass and ceramic bowls there is positively no danger of lingering after-tastes from previous dressings and glass bowls have the added advantage of showcasing your mixture of greens from top to bottom.

A green salad should not be dressed until just before serving, but the dressing can be prepared well in advance, in a separate dish or actually mixed in the bowl in which the salad will be served. With the latter method, the greens can be piled loosely on top of the dressing and allowed to stand in the fridge until just before serving. Sometimes the dressing is made *on* the salad: the oil is poured on first and the leaves carefully tossed until they glisten; then the other ingredients are added and the salad is tossed lightly once again. I recommend this method only to experienced salad makers as it is not so easy to correct a mistake.

In general, the bowl should be no more than half full and the leaves should be tossed just enough times so that they glisten with oil. Wooden salad tossers come in all shapes and sizes, including James Beard's novel 'salad hands' which allow the tosser to get easily to the bottom of the bowl where the dressing tends to accumulate.

No salad is complete without a suitable garnish. This need be no more than a sprinkling of fresh herbs or something which adds colour, a seasonal touch or a subtle accent of flavour. The list opposite may be used for inspiration, but developing your own favourite garnishes is part of the aesthetic pleasure in salad making.

Remember, to excite the good opinion of the eye is the first step towards awakening the appetite.

The Cook's Oracle (1821)

For dressing recipes see pages 19-41.

Garnishes for Green Salads

Vegetables and Pulses

Shredded carrots
Chopped pimento or red pepper
Thinly-sliced rings of green
   pepper
Slivers of radish
Small tomatoes or tomato wedges
Thinly-sliced onion rings
Sprinkling of cooked green peas
Sliced raw mushrooms
Sprinkling of garbanzo beans
   (chick peas)
Fluted cucumber slices
Diced avocado
Rings of fresh fennel
Chopped shallots or spring onions
Thin rings of raw leek
Tinned artichoke hearts,
   quartered; or artichoke bottoms
Palm hearts, cut into thin strips
Julienne slices of pickled beetroot
Shredded red cabbage

Fruits

Sections of fresh grapefruit,
   orange, or satsuma
Thin slices of unpeeled red apple
   or pear
Sprinkling of raisins or currants
A few pitted green grapes
Pomegranate seeds
Julienne strips of orange or lemon
   rind
Finely chopped dried fruits —
   dates, figs, apricots, etc.

Fresh Herbs

Parsley
Coriander leaves, chopped
Basil
Mint
Chives
Caraway seeds
Fennel leaves
Dill leaves

Miscellaneous

Hard-boiled egg slices
Crisply fried bits of bacon
Capers
Olives
Croutons
Grated parmesan cheese
Crumbled blue, Roquefort or
   Feta cheese
Chopped anchovies
Minced spicy sausage
Chopped or flaked nuts
Thinly-sliced water chestnuts
Toasted sesame seeds

Flowers*

Petals of both yellow and white
   chrysanthemums
Marigold petals
Nasturtium leaves and flowers
Rose petals
Violet flowers

*Use lemon juice, rather than
vinegar dressing if flowers are used
for garnish.

11

Green Salad with Egg Sauce   *Serves 4*

This recipe, from Mrs Alma McKee, formerly cook to H.M. Queen Elizabeth II, was a favourite at royal picnics.

> *1 large head round, cos or Webb lettuce*
> *2.5ml (½ tsp) dry mustard*
> *30ml (2 tbs) wine vinegar*
> *4 hard-boiled eggs*
> *2 raw egg yolks*
> *1 small bunch fresh chives, chopped*
> *150ml (¼ pt/½ cup) single cream*
> *salt, freshly ground pepper and a pinch of sugar*

Mix the mustard with the vinegar, pepper, salt and sugar to form a smooth paste. Sieve the hard-boiled egg yolks into a small basin and slowly add the raw egg yolks, lightly beaten, and half the quantity of cream. When smooth, add the vinaigrette paste, stirring all the time. Finish by adding the remaining cream.

To make the salad, break the washed and well-dried lettuce into small pieces and add the fresh chives. Pour on the dressing, toss and garnish with the chopped hard-boiled egg whites.

A richer variation of the recipe, called Normandy Lettuce Salad, requires 2 fresh egg yolks, 150ml (¼ pt/½ cup) double cream or sour cream and 45ml (3 tbs) vinegar. Blend until smooth then pour over the lettuce and serve.

Zelena Salata Sa Kiselim Mlekom   *Serves 6-8*

Yugoslavian Green Salad with Sour Milk dressing

> *2 heads of cos lettuce with outer leaves removed*
> *salt, freshly ground pepper and a pinch of sugar*
> *30-45ml (2-3 tbs) olive oil*
> *300ml (½ pt/1 cup) yogurt*

Wash the lettuce thoroughly, removing the outer bruised leaves and tear the remainder into small pieces. Drain and dry well before putting the leaves into the salad bowl. Sprinkle the lettuce with salt. To the yogurt, add sugar, salt and pepper to taste and gradually stir in olive oil; pour the mixture over the salad and toss the leaves gently until they glisten with dressing. Chill and serve.

Salade Verte aux Anchois   *Serves 5-6*

> *½ head of cos lettuce*
> *1 head of Belgian endive (chicory)*

½ *head of escarole (batavia)*
8 anchovy fillets, chopped
15ml (1 tbs) fresh parsley, chopped
10ml (2 tsp) fresh tarragon, chopped
200ml (7 fl oz/4/5 cup) mayonnaise (see recipe page 30)

Wash the cos and escarole, removing any bruised outer leaves. Drain and allow to dry thoroughly. Clean the endive with a damp paper towel. Each of the greens should be broken into similar, bite-sized pieces.

In the bottom of a large salad bowl, put the chopped herbs, mayonnaise and the anchovies. Stir well. Add the greens on top of dressing and toss gently until all the leaves are covered. Serve cold.

Salade Quercynoise   *Serves 4*

The Dordogne is the largest walnut growing region of France, and walnut oil is traditionally used in the preparation of salad dressings. The walnuts themselves, when not cracked for oil, are sun-dried in the autumn on slats of wood and stored for winter and early spring use.

1 head of curly endive
12 walnuts, roughly chopped
90ml (6 tbs) walnut oil
salt and freshly ground pepper
30ml (2 tbs) wine vinegar
a chapon (a slice of French bread toasted and rubbed on both sides with a
*   piece of cut garlic)*
optional
2 hard-boiled eggs, sliced

The lettuce should be very thoroughly washed (endive collects a lot of dirt at its centre), then broken into pieces and shaken dry in a lettuce basket. Wrap lettuce in a tea towel, pat dry and place in the refrigerator to crisp. The dressing is made by slowly adding the oil to the vinegar, salt and pepper.

Place the *chapon* in the bottom of a wooden salad bowl. Add the lettuce, walnuts and sliced hard-boiled eggs, if desired. Pour over dressing and toss gently.

Salade des Champs   *Serves 4-5*

Antoine Alciatore opened his New Orleans restaurant in 1840. Many of his dishes — pompano en papilotte, pommes soufflés, oysters à la Rockefeller — became world-renowned favourites. This delicate salad was specially created at Antoine's for the Chevaliers du Tastervin.

1 large bunch of watercress

3 good-sized heads of Belgian endive (chicory)
1 large pink-fleshed grapefruit
1ml (¼ tsp) dry mustard
60ml (4 tbs) olive oil
15ml (1 tbs) white wine vinegar
a dash of Tabasco or chilli sauce
a dash of Worcestershire sauce
salt and freshly ground pepper

Wash the watercress and remove any damaged stalks. Drain off excess moisture and allow to dry. Wipe the endive with a damp paper towel and remove any bruised leaves. Cut off the bottoms of the endive and separate into individual leaves. Place in a wooden salad bowl and add the watercress.

Cut the grapefruit in half and remove the pips. With a serrated-edge knife, separate the segments and add to the salad.

Prepare the dressing from the remaining ingredients, pour over salad and toss gently. Serve immediately.

Delmonico Salad   *Serves 4-5*

This salad was created at one of New York's smartest restaurants.

1 large head of cos or escarole
90-120ml (6-8 tbs) olive oil
30ml (2 tbs) wine vinegar
30ml (2 tbs) single cream
salt and freshly ground pepper
30-45ml (2-3 tbs) crumbled Roquefort cheese
a dash of Tabasco sauce
1 hard-boiled egg, finely chopped
2 rashers of streaky bacon, cooked, dried and finely crumbled
optional
a handful of garlic-flavoured croutons

Wash and drain the lettuce. If using cos, break the leaves in half; the leaves of escarole need only be separated from the core. Place the leaves in a tea towel, gently fold and place in the refrigerator to crisp until ready to use.

To prepare dressing, combine the olive oil, wine vinegar, cream and crumbled Roquefort cheese in a small bowl and whisk until smooth. Add the freshly ground pepper and Tabasco to taste, followed by the finely chopped egg and crumbled bacon.

Arrange the lettuce in a salad bowl and pour on dressing just before serving. Garlic-flavoured croutons make an excellent optional garnish.

Salade de Pissenlits au Lard

French Dandelion Salad

> *450g (1 lb) of young dandelion leaves*
> *1 clove garlic, peeled and cut in half*
> *15ml (1 tbs) wine vinegar*
> *1 small knob of butter*
> *salt and freshly ground black pepper*
> *225g (½ lb) pork fat or unsmoked bacon, cut into small pieces*
> *yolk of 1 hard-boiled egg, finely chopped*

Wash the leaves thoroughly to remove all the dirt and any chemical spray. Sort through the leaves and remove any brown or bruised bits. Drain and dry on paper towels or a clean tea towel.

Rub a large wooden salad bowl with the cut garlic clove and add the leaves. Sprinkle with wine vinegar and toss once or twice.

Soften the pork or bacon by cooking in the butter over a low heat for approximately 10 minutes.

Pour the butter and pork or bacon over the leaves. Toss well and garnish with the egg yolk.

An early American variation of this salad is known as Wilted Lettuce Salad and dates back to the pioneering days of the nineteenth century, being the sort of dish so easy to prepare it could be managed in the back of a covered wagon! In his *American Cookbook*, James Beard gives a recipe with a dressing made from equal parts of sugar and vinegar, to which are added some dry mustard, salt and chopped onion. This is poured over the greens with the hot bacon and bacon fat, but I would advise reducing the quantity of sugar unless the salad is to be served as a kind of relish with cold meats or sausages.

Caesar Salad

This American classic, created in Tijuana in the 1920s by restaurateur Caesar Cardini, is now an international favourite. Most recipes for Caesar Salad call for anchovies, but according to Julia Child, who consulted Caesar's daughter on the ingredients in the original recipe, Caesar never used anchovies. The addition of a small amount of Worcestershire sauce to the dressing — as this has a drop of anchovy — may account for the fairly standard deviation from Caesar's original salad.

Ms Child also discovered Caesar's method for making croutons — well worth the extra effort: 'Cut homemade-type unsweetened white bread into half-inch dice and dry out in the oven, basting them as they brown with olive oil in which you have steeped fresh crushed garlic for several days'.

The following recipe uses one, instead of the two eggs recommended by Rosa Cardini and if you do have a passion for anchovies, eliminate the Worcestershire sauce from the dressing and add 6-8 anchovy fillets, drained and thinly sliced, to your salad. A dishonour to the memory of Caesar Cardini, but they are undeniably delicious in combination with the dressing and Parmesan cheese!

2 heads of cos (romaine) lettuce
8 slices white bread, crusts removed and cut into small dice
60ml (4 tbs) olive oil
2-3 cloves garlic, crushed

Dressing
120ml (8 tbs) olive oil
30ml (2 tbs) fresh lemon juice
salt and freshly ground pepper to taste
1 egg, boiled (coddled) for exactly 1 minute
25g (1 oz) freshly grated Parmesan cheese
a few drops of Worcestershire sauce
optional
6-8 anchovy fillets (if used, eliminate the Worcestershire sauce)

Wash the lettuce and discard any bruised leaves. Remove the leaves gently from the stalks and break into pieces approximately 10-12cm (4-5 in) long. Drain and dry well. Wrap loosely in a clean tea towel and refrigerate until ready to use.

The croutons can be made Caesar's way or more quickly, by sauteing the diced bread in a little olive oil with crushed garlic. Turn frequently to avoid burning and remove when the bread is a delicate brown colour. Drain on paper towels.

Just before serving, place the lettuce leaves in a large wooden or glass bowl. Put the remaining ingredients in small individual bowls to be brought to the table with the lettuce; and chill the appropriate number of large, flat dinner plates on which the salad will be served.

First pour on the oil and toss well so that each leaf is thoroughly coated. Next add the lemon juice, a sprinkling of salt and several grinds of black pepper. Now break the egg into the salad, add a few drops of Worcestershire sauce and toss well again, making sure to get down to the leaves at the bottom of the bowl. Sprinkle on the cheese, add the croutons and toss once or twice more. Serve on the chilled plates.

Note Caesar left the lettuce leaves whole so that they could be picked up by the stem and eaten with the fingers.

Flemish Chicory Salad   *Serves 4-6*

6 good-sized Belgian endive (chicory)

225g (8 oz) thick rashers of bacon
oil for frying bacon
2 hard-boiled eggs, finely chopped
100ml (4 fl oz) olive oil
25ml (1 fl oz) white wine vinegar
salt and freshly ground pepper
30ml (2 tbs) fresh parsley, chopped

To reduce the saltiness of the bacon, cut each piece into small strips and place these in boiling water for approximately 5 minutes. Drain the bacon on paper towels and when thoroughly dry, fry the pieces in a little oil until crisp.

Wipe the endive with a damp cloth and remove any bruised leaves. Cut each head into pieces approximately 13mm (½ in) long, place in a glass salad bowl and add the chopped egg.

Make the dressing with oil, vinegar, salt and pepper. Pour over the salad and garnish with bacon and parsley. Toss thoroughly and serve immediately.

This salad can also be made with watercress instead of Belgian endive, or use both for an attractive blend of flavours and colour.

These salads are made with cooked greens to be chilled before serving:

Salade d'Endives à l'Orange   *Serves 4-6*

Endive Salad with Orange Dressing

6 good-sized Belgian endive (chicory)
2 oranges
60ml (4 tbs) olive oil
salt and freshly ground black pepper
parsley or mint and slivers of orange peel to garnish

Remove any bruised leaves from the endive heads and wipe with a damp paper towel. Cook them whole in gently simmering water for approximately 15-20 minutes or until tender. Drain carefully and allow to cool completely. The dressing is made by combining the juice of the oranges with the olive oil, salt and pepper. (If the oranges are very sweet, add a dash of lemon juice to taste.) Arrange the endives on a flat dish, pour on dressing and garnish generously with chopped fresh parsley or mint, and a sprinkling of shredded orange peel.

Horta Vrasta Ladolemono

Boiled Greens with Lemon and Oil Dressing

This traditional Greek salad is served the year round, varying with the

17

availability of seasonal vegetables. Allow about 225g (8 oz) of vegetables per person, as this amount will be substantially reduced with the loss of water in cooking. Choose from courgettes, chicory, dandelion greens, curly endive, escarole, kale, mustard tops, spinach or any other seasonal greens — which may be used singly or in combination.

Wash the vegetables thoroughly in several waters and drain. The courgettes can be cooked whole in a small amount of gently boiling, salted water. The spinach should also be cooked in a small amount of water, but the leafy greens are best fast-boiled in large quantities of water, and in an uncovered pot to prevent them from changing colour. When cooked, drain well and cool. Dress with oil and lemon juice (in 3:1 proportions), lots of freshly ground pepper and additional salt, if required.

Dressings

To make a good salad is to be a brilliant diplomatist; the problem is entirely the same in both cases — to know exactly how much oil to put with one's vinegar.

Oscar Wilde

The dressing is the crowning glory of a salad: it should enhance the flavour of the salad's components, complement the other foods with which it is to be served, and refresh the palate with its mildly piquant taste.

The classic worldwide favourite is vinaigrette — a basic combination of oil and vinegar, salt and freshly ground pepper, varying in proportions to accommodate regional and personal preferences. Variations on this standard theme include ingredients such as dry mustard, garlic, sugar, chopped herbs, shallots, Dijon mustard, cream, eggs and crumbled cheese. Often, too, lemon juice is used to soften the flavour, in combination with or in place of vinegar.

Before considering the preparation techniques and different types of dressings, a few words about the basic constituents:

Oil

'Smooth, light and pleasant upon the tongue', wrote John Evelyn of the perfect salad oil. Naturally he meant olive oil, long the acknowledged western favourite for dressing salads. But other plants yield oils of equal character and equal appeal.

Historically, flax and radish seeds provided oil for the Egyptians; the Greeks extracted oil from walnuts and opium poppies; while the richest earliest sources of oil for most Asian peoples were probably the soybean and the coconut. Groundnut, maize and sunflower are the traditional oils of Central and South America; and in West Africa the deep orange palm oil is most widely used, along with oils extracted from peanuts, sesame and corn.

19

Even where olive oil is widely available, many cooks prefer oils with blander tastes and less aroma. The lightest of all oils is safflower oil, an almost colourless oil with a very low cholesterol count. Other types recommended by the health conscious and natural food advocates are sunflower, sesame (*not* the dark Oriental variety), peanut and corn oils.

The versatility and value of olive oil was established early on, when the olive was first cultivated by the ancient civilizations of the eastern Mediterranean. Even then, the first pressing provided oil for cooking; the second pressing, oils for skin ointments, hair dressings and medicines; and further pressings yielded fuel for lighting and heat.

Like so many plants, the olive also has its niche in herbal folklore. Adam, according to B. A. Donaldson in *The Wild Rue*, was given an olive tree by the Angel Gabriel and told to extract the oil from its fruit as a tonic to cure all ills and pains; and St. Jerome's longevity was attributed to the addition of oil to his sparse diet of pulses, roots and herbs. In the Middle East today, oil is still consumed by the glass as an energy tonic.

La première pression à froid, the first pressing oil, extracted from the finest quality olives and crushed without application of heat, is still the connoisseur's most coveted dressing oil. George Ellwanger in *Pleasures of the Table* calls it 'A gift from the gods. The grape and the olive are among the priceless benefactors of the soil, and were destined, each in its way, to promote the welfare of man'. Vyvyan Holland, the great wine expert, even went so far as to say that the best *huiles vierges* were as rare as the best vintage wines and that the good vintages of the Sauternais were also good years for olive oil.

The flavour, character and quality of olive oil are affected as much by the country of origin as they are by the methods of extraction, harvesting and the degree of ripeness of the fruit when picked. The French oils — gold, fruity and light in colour — tend to be the most expensive: at around £2.00 a half litre, £3.50 a litre and £14.50 for a 5 litre can. (*Note* If you use oil in large quantities, it makes economic sense to buy the larger cans, which also provide the best method of storing the oil away from the light — like this, oil will keep for a year.)

Of the other Mediterranean varieties commonly available — Greek, Spanish and Italian — I prefer the Greek oils. They are not at all like the delicate French *huiles vierges*. Robust, thick, dark green and strongly aromatic, they are far more distinctive than the rather bland Italian or Spanish oils generally found in supermarkets. Greek oils make excellent dressings for all but the most delicate of salads.

Vinegar

The measure of vinegar in a classic vinaigrette tests the real expertise of the salad dresser. The basic formula in the traditional repertoires calls for

3 parts oil to 1 part vinegar, but many great cooks insist on more oil in the mixture. Equally, the palates of different nationalities dictate different proportions of vinegar to oil, as the recipes in this book amply illustrate.

The best salad vinegar, John Evelyn wrote, should be, 'perfectly clear, neither sowre, vapid or spent'. Red or white wine vinegar is most often used, although cider vinegar — a favourite of natural food devotees — is an acceptable substitute. Generally, malt vinegar is too tart for dressing but will do if no other vinegar is available. Distilled vinegar is best saved for pickling vegetables and rice vinegar, a delicate white Japanese variety, should be used in greater quantity than most vinegars to achieve a proper balance of piquancy.

The best wine vinegars are imported from Orléans in France, many with added herbs and spices. Flavoured and aromatic vinegars can also be made quite easily at home.

The simplest method is to steep the washed and dried herbs in vinegar (approx 100-150g (4-6 oz) herbs: 1 litre (2 pts) white wine vinegar) in a large tightly-sealed jar. Store, away from direct light, for about 6-8 weeks. Then strain the vinegar into smaller bottles containing 2 or 3 sprigs of fresh leaves and cork or seal securely. In the spring and summer, try this method with tarragon, thyme, mint, basil or chervil.

Another home-made technique requires boiling the vinegar. Use white wine or cider vinegar, approximately 1 litre (2 pts) to every 100-150g (4-6 oz) fresh herbs. Place the washed and dried leaves in the bottom of a heat-proof jar and crush lightly with a wooden spoon to release the flavour. Pour in the boiling vinegar and leave to cool. Seal tightly and store in a cool spot, away from direct light for 10 days — 2 weeks. Every now and then, invert the jar and replace right side up again. Taste to check the flavour, and when ready strain into smaller jars. Cork or seal securely and label for future use.

For a tasty garlic vinegar, peel and halve about a dozen cloves. Place these in a large heat-proof jar and pour in approximately 1 litre (2 pts) boiling cider vinegar. Cover and leave at room temperature for 24 hours. Then discard the garlic, strain the vinegar into smaller bottles, cover and label.

For an unusually pretty *fin de siècle* vinegar — lovely for dressing fruit salads — place 2 teacups of tightly packed, cleaned rose petals into a large jar. In a saucepan over a low heat, dissolve 50g (2 oz) caster sugar with 600ml (1 pt) white *distilled* vinegar. Remove from the heat and leave to cool. Pour over the rose petals, cover with a tight-fitting lid and allow to stand in a cool, dark place for 3-4 weeks. Remove the rose petals and strain the liquid in a clean jar. Cork and label for future use.

Dregs of the wine bottle can also be used to make an excellent wine vinegar. Mix equal quantities of wine with a cider vinegar (try 600ml (1 pt) of each to start), a couple of peeled and halved garlic cloves, 3 sprigs of fresh tarragon, a few peppercorns and a pinch — if desired — of dried basil or oregano. Pour into a bottle with a tight-fitting lid and store in a cool place for 2 weeks or so. Strain and use for dressing salads.

The Seasonings

Salt and pepper are the basic seasonings for vinaigrette, although some people prefer to leave the addition of salt to each individual eater. Pepper, mainly black, should always be freshly ground from the peppermill. 'It is a never to be omitted ingredient from our *sallets*', wrote John Evelyn, 'provided it be not too minutely beaten (as oft we find it) to an almost impalpable dust, which is very pernicious'.

Peppermills come in all shapes and sizes. Choose one with a good stainless steel or aluminium mechanism which allows the size of the grind to be adjusted. Salt mills are also widely sold, but most people happily use the traditional open dish. Fill it with sea salt, which has none of the chemical additives commonly found in ordinary table salt.

Mustard, sugar and garlic are the most popular optional constituents in the standard vinaigrette. Both dry mustard and prepared mustard (the French varieties, such as Dijon or moutarde de meaux, are better choices than the sharper English mustards) are suitable for salad dressings.

Sugar, to many, is a heresy but it seems to be used quite often, and for those who find even the slightest hint of vinegar too acidic, sugar is an acceptable antidote. Garlic, on the other hand, is widely favoured around the globe, but its advocates, as we shall see, disagree on the methods by which it is incorporated into the dressing.

Probably no seasoning has a richer folklore and literature than garlic. From Herodotus and Xenophon, to Rabelais, Bram Stoker and Lawrence Durrell, garlic has been noted, discussed, praised and abused. A plant native to the Siberian desert, garlic found its way via Asia Minor to Egypt and then, back through the trade routes to Eastern Asia, and westward to Europe. It played an important role in the diet and pharmacology of early civilisations; and was even valued as a medium of exchange in ancient Egypt: 15 pounds of garlic could purchase a healthy male slave.

Of its medicinal value, the Greek doctor Dioscorides, who lived in the 1st century A.D., had much to say and many of his prescriptions remained in use throughout the Middle Ages:

If eaten, it helps eliminate the tapeworm, it drives out the urine. It is good against snake bite with wine, or when crushed in wine. It is good against the bite of a rabid dog. It makes the voice clear, soothes continuous coughing, when eaten raw or boiled. Boiled with oregano, it kills lice and bed bugs. It doth clear the arteries. Burnt and mixed with honey, it is an ointment for bloodshot eyes; in case of

22

baldness it helps, too . . .

Greek Herbal of Dioscorides, translated by J. Berendes

In *The Book of Garlic,* Lloyd J. Harris quotes a tenth century Persian Herbal which advises: 'We should not be without it in any kitchen, nor leave it out of any food, nor despise it on account of its unpleasant odour . . . it drives away the toothache if you bruise it and lay it upon the tooth . . . it cures baldness by stimulating the growth of hair . . . it increases the natural heat of the body, and promotes digestion.'

Similar cures and remedies found their way into English medicinal lore and Culpeper's seventeenth century herbal commends the use of garlic for ailments as varied as animal bites, lethargy, skin blemishes, jaundice, piles or haemorrhoids.

But Culpeper's contemporary, John Evelyn, while acknowledging its medicinal virtues, '[forbids] it entrance into our salleting, by reason if its intolerable rankness . . . which made it so detested of old, that the eating of it was, (as we read) part of the punishment for such as had committed the horridest crimes. To be sure, 'tis not for Ladies Pallats, nor those who court them, farther than to permit a light touch on the Dish with a clove thereof . . .'. Or as Ford Maddox Ford wrote, 'Garlic is all very well on the bridge between Beaucaire and Tarascon or in the arena at Nîmes amongst sixteen thousand civilized beings . . . But in an *atelier de couture* in the neighbourhood of Hanover Square!'

There are many ways of adding a garlic flavour to salads. Rub a cut clove along the sides of the bowl; steep a peeled clove in the oil for an hour or so, and remove just before dressing the salad; or, as the French do, rub a piece of stale bread or toast with a cut clove, then place in the bottom of the salad bowl and toss with the chosen greens and dressing. Sometimes, a clove is put through a press or pounded with some salt in a mortar — this method makes a much stronger dressing, best suited to cold vegetable salads, dried bean or composed salads.

To avoid the persistence of a garlic smell on a knife or chopping board, sprinkle salt onto the board, then cut the clove in the salt; and to avoid odour on the hands, rinse them first with *cold* water after handling garlic.

Herbs can transform a simple vinaigrette into a seasonal delight. When available, always use fresh herbs — 2 or 3 carefully chosen kinds that complement your salad greens. Generally, 15-30ml (1-2 tbs) of finely chopped fresh herbs is the right amount for every 120ml (8 tbs) of dressing, but if dried herbs are substituted, use only 1/3 the amount. Dried herbs are sometimes soaked to restore their flavour before they are added to a recipe, but crushing them between the fingers as they are added to the oil works just as well. Whereas fresh herbs may be sprinkled directly onto the salad, dried herbs should be added to the oil well before the salad is dressed.

As there is an extensive literature on herb cookery, I have omitted a detailed description of the many other herbs which can be used in salads, but the following list includes various possibilities to invite experimentation and personal research.

Les Fines Herbes — the basic essentials

Chervil — warm and spicy, with a slight aniseed flavour.

Chives — use for a mild onion flavour.

Dill — a popular herb in northern and central Europe; especially tasty with cucumber and radish salads.

Sweet marjoram — its sweet spicy flavour resembles oregano, to which it is akin, but somewhat milder.

Mint — one of the oldest culinary herbs; used widely in Middle Eastern cooking.

Parsley — the universal herb; easy to grow and a rich source of vitamin C; the curly variety is most commonly available, but the flat-leaved Italian variety has greater flavour.

Sweet basil — this fragrant herb grows profusely throughout southern France, Greece and Italy and is widely used in cooking.

Summer savory — similar to, but more delicate than thyme.

Tarragon — true French tarragon is the chef's best bet, adding a delicate but distinct flavour to all sorts of foods.

Thyme — a strong flavoured herb native to southern Europe.

Other herbs

Angelica — more commonly eaten as a candied preserve, the stems may be chopped and added to salads.

Balm — when adding chopped balm leaves to salads, use slightly less vinegar or lemon juice in the dressing.

Caraway — these seeds add a spiciness to cabbage salads and also act as a digestive aid.

Coriander — the fresh leaves are popular in Indian and Middle Eastern recipes; the seeds are used for poaching vegetables *à la grecque,* in ratatouille and in many African and Asian recipes.

Fennel — the leaves may be substituted for parsley; a great favourite in France and Italy.

Hyssop — chopped young hyssop leaves add a sweet aroma and delicate peppery taste to salads; also suitable for fruit salads.

Lovage — the peppery, celery-flavoured leaves may be chopped and added *sparingly* to salads.

Oregano — stronger than sweet marjoram, to which it is related; used extensively in Mediterranean cooking.

Vinaigrettes

Vinaigrette

> 90-120ml (6-8 tbs) olive oil
> 30ml (2 tbs) wine vinegar
> salt and freshly ground pepper
> optional
> 1 ice cube

Place the vinegar in a small bowl and season to taste with salt and pepper. Stir well and gradually add the olive oil, beating with a fork or whisk until the mixture thickens. An ice cube added to the mixing bowl will produce a creamier dressing, but be sure to remove it once the desired consistency is achieved.

Vinaigrette à la moutarde

Add 1.25ml (¼ tsp) dry mustard or 5ml (1 scant tsp) French mustard to the salt and vinegar. Stir well before blending with olive oil.

Vinaigrette aux fines herbes

Add 30ml (2 tbs) chopped fresh herbs to the basic dressing. Choose from tarragon, parsley, basil, marjoram, chives, thyme or mint.

Vinaigrette au citron

Crush a peeled clove of garlic with a pinch of salt and pound to a pulp. Place in a small bowl and stir in 15ml (1 tbs) lemon juice, 15ml (1 tbs) white wine vinegar and 1.25ml (¼ tsp) dry mustard. Blend until smooth. Gradually add the olive oil, beating with a fork or whisk until the mixture thickens. Season with salt, freshly ground pepper and a sprinkling of freshly chopped herbs.

Caper dressing

To the basic vinaigrette, add 5ml (1 tsp) chopped capers plus 1 peeled clove of garlic, finely minced. Prepare well in advance so that the oil has time to absorb the flavours.

Curry dressing

Add 2.5ml (½ tsp) curry powder and 5ml (1 tsp) finely chopped shallots to the vinegar and salt, then proceed as for basic vinaigrette.

Chopped vegetable vinaigrette

A delicious dressing for seafood salads, cold artichokes and crudités.

> *2 small firm tomatoes, peeled (p 246) and finely chopped*
> *1 small green pepper, deseeded and finely chopped*
> *1 clove garlic, peeled and minced*
> *2 small shallots, peeled and finely chopped*
> *15ml (1 tbs) capers, chopped*
> *90-120ml (8-9 tbs) olive oil*
> *30-45ml (2-3 tbs) lemon juice, freshly squeezed and strained*
> *5ml (1 tsp) chopped fresh tarragon leaves*
> *salt and freshly ground pepper*

Place all the ingredients in a jar with a tight-fitting lid. Shake well and chill for at least an hour. Before serving, correct the seasoning with more salt or pepper.

Vinaigrette with walnut oil

Walnut oil, a product of the Perigord and Burgundy regions of France, adds a unique, aromatic flavour to salads. As it may be difficult and expensive to obtain many cooks prefer to mix it in equal proportions with arachide or ground-nut oil.

Salade Quercynoise (p 13), a traditional recipe from the Dordogne, uses a walnut dressing. Walnut oil can also be substituted for olive oil in mayonnaise, making a distinctive céleri rémoulade, Waldorf salad, or dressing for any chicken salad.

Low calorie vinaigrette

Home-made stock is substituted here for the usual quantity of olive oil, the calorie demon in salad dressings.

> *15ml (1 tbs) olive oil*
> *75ml (5 tbs) vegetable stock*
> *1 clove garlic, peeled*
> *2.5ml (½ tsp) fresh tarragon, finely chopped*
> *5ml (1 tsp) fresh parsley, finely chopped*
> *2.5ml (½ tsp) fresh basil, finely chopped*
> *15ml (1 tbs) white wine vinegar*
> *10ml (2 tsp) lemon juice*
> *salt and freshly ground pepper*

Pour the stock into a small bowl and gradually whisk in the olive oil. Add the garlic and herbs and allow to marinate for several hours. Remove the garlic and add the vinegar and lemon juice, beating with a fork to blend thoroughly. Season to taste with salt and pepper and whisk again before serving.

Vinaigrette à l'oeuf

Dressing made with a raw egg yolk has a glossy adhering quality that combines nicely with cooked vegetable salads if added while the vegetables are still lukewarm.

Break the egg yolk into a small bowl and combine with a pinch of salt and 5ml (1 tsp) French mustard. Gradually stir in the vinegar to form a smooth paste. Then proceed as for basic vinaigrette.

Eliza Acton's Salad Sauce

Many traditional English dressings use hard-boiled eggs, pounded to a paste. Cream and sugar are also commonly included, as in this recipe from Eliza Acton's 1845 *Modern Cookery*:

To a couple of yolks (hard-boiled and cooled) broken up and mashed to a paste with the back of a wooden spoon, add a small saltspoon of salt, a large one of pounded sugar, a few grains of cayenne, and a teaspoonful of cold water; mix and add as much common or French vinegar as will acidulate the mixture agreeably. A tablespoon of either will be sufficient for many tastes, but it is easy to increase the proportion when more is liked. Six tablespoons full of olive oil, of the purest quality, may be substituted for the cream: it should be added in very small portions to the other ingredients, and stirred briskly as each is added until the sauce resembles custard. When this is used, the water should be omitted. The piquancy of this preparation — which is very delicate, made by the directions just given — may be heightened by the addition of a little eschalot vinegar, Harvey's sauce, essence of anchovies, French mustard, or tarragon vinegar; or by bruising with the eggs a morsel of garlic, half the size of a hazelnut: it should always, however, be tendered as appropriate as may be to the dish with which it is to be served.

Sydney Smith's Salad Sauce

The nineteenth century bon vivant Sydney Smith made his contribution to the literature of salads with an amusing verse describing the preparation of a dressing and the way to use it. Such was his confidence in the formula that he wrote, 'As this salad is the result of great experience and reflection, it is hoped young salad-makers will not attempt to make any improvement on it.'

To make this condiment, your poet begs
The pounded yellow of two hard-boiled eggs;
Two boiled potatoes, passed through kitchen sieve,
Smoothness and softness to the salad give.
Let onion atoms lurk within the bowl,
And, half-suspected, animate the whole.
Of mordant mustard add a single spoon,
Distrust the condiment that bites so soon;
But deem it not, thou man of herbs, a fault,
To add a double quantity of salt.
Four times the spoon with oil from Lucca brown,
And twice with vinegar procured from town;
And, lastly, o'er the flavoured compound toss
A magic soupçon of anchovy sauce.
Oh, green and glorious! Oh, herbaceous treat!
'Twould tempt the dying anchovite to eat.
Back to the world he'd turn his fleeting soul,
And plunge his fingers in the salad bowl.
Serenely full, the epicure would say,
'Fate cannot harm me, I have dined today'.

Bacon Dressing

This recipe must be prepared *immediately* before serving. Have the choice of greens washed, dried and arranged in the salad bowl, ready for tossing once the dressing is added.

> 4 rashers streaky bacon, cut into small pieces
> 15ml (1 tbs) lemon juice
> salt and freshly ground pepper

Sauté the bacon in a small frying pan. When the pieces are cooked but still tender (*al dente*), pour the entire contents of the pan onto the lettuce. Return the pan to a low heat and add the lemon juice, stirring for several seconds until warm. Add this to the salad and toss well with salt and freshly ground pepper to taste.

Cream Dressing I

> 90ml (6 tbs) double cream
> 20ml (4 tsp) white wine vinegar
> 2.5ml (½ tsp) salt
> 2.5ml (½ tsp) finely ground white pepper
> 30ml (2 tbs) light vegetable oil

Combine the salt, pepper, vinegar and cream in a small bowl and beat with a fork or wire whisk for 20-30 seconds, or until the mixture achieves

28

a foamy consistency. Gradually add the oil and continue mixing. Correct the seasoning and chill until ready to serve.

Cream Dressing II

> *1 hard-boiled egg yolk, mashed*
> *10ml (2 tsp) tarragon vinegar*
> *½ clove garlic, crushed (optional)*
> *2.5ml (½ tsp) Dijon mustard*
> *5ml (1 tsp) sugar (or less, to taste)*
> *120ml (4 fl oz) single cream*
> *15-30ml (1-2 tbs) freshly chopped tarragon and chives*

In a small bowl, combine the mustard, sugar, vinegar, garlic (if desired) and the mashed egg yolk. Beat with a fork until creamy smooth, then gradually add the cream, stirring constantly, until all the ingredients are well blended. Chill, and just before serving, stir in the fresh herbs.

Note If the vinegar curdles the cream, add a few drops of milk or water to the dressing.

Low Calorie Buttermilk Dressing

These quantities make approximately 300ml (½ pt) of dressing which, if kept refrigerated in a tightly sealed jar, will last for at least a week. Each 15ml (1 tbs) contains about 10 calories.

> *240ml (8 fl oz) buttermilk*
> *60ml (4 tbs) cider vinegar*
> *15ml (1 tbs) light salad oil*
> *5ml (1 tsp) salt*
> *2.5ml (½ tsp) ground white pepper*

Place all ingredients in a jar with a tight fitting lid. Shake well and chill until ready to serve.

Mayonnaise

Together with vinaigrette, mayonnaise is probably the most popular dressing for salads. It goes wonderfully well with cold meats and seafood; it makes a perfect 'dip' for vegetable crudités — either plain or blended with an infinite variety of herbs, spices or chopped vegetables; it is the basis for dishes like cole slaw, potato salad and egg salads; and it can be mixed effectively with sour cream, crème fraiche, double cream or liquid gelatine to achieve different consistencies.

Although mayonnaise certainly has a French pedigree, there is no common agreement on exactly where and when this combination of egg and oil was first created. The word may derive from the old French *moyeu* (middle), referring to the centre of the egg or egg yolk; or from the verb *manier* (to stir); or, as one theory goes, from Port Mahon, where in 1628 the chef of the Duc de Richelieu discovered a local sauce made with raw egg yolk, garlic, salt and olive oil. *Mahonnaise*, without the garlic, becomes mayonnaise.

The basic method for making mayonnaise is quite simple, as long as certain essential rules are strictly followed:

1. All ingredients must be at room temperature. Eggs, if they have been refrigerated, should be allowed to stand; the bowl in which the mayonnaise is to be prepared should be rinsed in hot water and thoroughly dried. The lemon juice or vinegar and oil should also be at room temperature.

2. The eggs should be fresh and any gelatinous threads should be removed from the yolks before they are beaten. *Always* beat the eggs before any oil is added.

3. If the mayonnaise is to be mixed by hand, have a damp cloth available to place under the mixing bowl to hold it steady.

4. Measure the oil into a spouted jug so that it can be dripped slowly into the egg yolks. *Note* The maximum oil an egg yolk can absorb is about 150ml (¼ pt).

Master recipe (for hand or electric beater)   *Yield: 300ml (½ pt) +*

> *2 egg yolks*
> *2.5ml (½ tsp) salt*
> *freshly ground pepper*
> *300ml (½ pt) olive oil*
> *2.5ml (½ tsp) dry mustard*
> *lemon juice and/or wine vinegar*
> *15ml (1 tbs) boiling water*

With a wire whisk or fork, beat the egg yolks for 2 minutes, or until smooth and paste-like in consistency. (If using an electric beater, set it to the speed used for whipping cream.) Add the dry mustard, salt, 5ml (1 tsp) lemon juice (or wine vinegar). Beat for a further minute.

Begin adding the oil slowly, *drop by drop*, while beating continuously. When approximately 150ml (¼ pt) of the oil has been added and thoroughly absorbed, the beating can stop. When resumed, the beating should alternate with additions of oil (less caution is necessary at this stage and larger quantities of oil can be added each time) and more lemon juice or vinegar (5ml (1 tsp) at a time) if the mixture becomes too thick.

When all the oil has been added, adjust the seasoning with a pinch or two of salt, if desired, and a few grinds of pepper. If the mayonnaise is not to be used immediately, add 15ml (1 tbs) boiling water as a protection against curdling. If the correct texture has been achieved, the sauce should be thick enough to cut with a knife!

Ways to deal with curdled mayonnaise

Here are five remedies for mayonnaise which has separated. As you become more expert, your eye will be the best judge as to which cure is appropriate each time.
1. While beating with a fork or wire whisk, add 5-10ml (1-2 tsp) boiling or very hot water.
2. In a clean bowl, break an egg yolk and beat lightly with a few drops of hot water or lemon juice. Gradually add spoonfuls of the curdled mayonnaise, beating after each addition.
3. In a clean bowl, beat 1 egg yolk with a few drops of oil until very thick. Gradually add the curdled mayonnaise, beating continuously.
4. In a clean bowl, put 15ml (1 tbs) Dijon (or a similar prepared mustard), plus 5ml (1 tsp) of the curdled mayonnaise. Beat until well blended; then slowly, one teaspoon at a time, add more of the mayonnaise until it again emulsifies. The remaining curdled mayonnaise can then be added to the fresh mixture in larger quantities.
5. Stir the curdled mixture with an electric beater (or in a blender) at very high speed for several seconds.

Storage

Mayonnaise will store well in the refrigerator, in a tightly covered jar, for up to one week. Before stirring or serving, allow it to stand at room temperature for at least two hours.

Speedy Whole-egg Mayonnaise   *Yield: 300ml (½ pt) +*

The use of a whole egg in this quick blender method, prevents the mixture from becoming too thick before all the oil is added. If a larger quantity is required, only extra egg yolks are necessary. Increase the oil and other ingredients in proportion (see general notes above).

> *1 whole egg*
> *2.5ml (½ tsp) salt*
> *1.25ml (¼ tsp) dry mustard*
> *15ml (1 tbs) (or more, if required) lemon juice or wine vinegar*
> *300ml (½ pt) olive or salad oil*

Place the egg, mustard and salt in the blender jar. Cover and blend at high speed for 30 seconds. Add 15ml (1 tbs) of lemon juice or vinegar, cover, and blend for a further 15 seconds. Uncover the jar, continue to blend at high speed, and gradually add the oil, drop by drop. When half the quantity has been added, the mixture will begin to thicken. Continue adding oil until the mixture is thick enough to almost stop the action of the blades. Stop the machine and, with a rubber scraper, push all the mayonnaise from the sides into the centre of the jar. Cover and blend for a few seconds at high speed. Turn the mayonnaise in a serving bowl, or storage jar, and correct the seasoning with additional salt and freshly ground pepper.

Aïöli

This famous French garlic mayonnaise from Provence is traditionally served with cold fish and boiled potatoes. It is excellent with crudités and, as with ordinary mayonnaise, can be stored for a week in the refrigerator in a tightly sealed jar.

> *3-4 cloves garlic*
> *2 egg yolks*
> *300ml (½ pt) olive oil*
> *15ml (1 tbs) lemon juice*
> *2.5ml (½ tsp) salt*
> *freshly ground pepper*

Peel the garlic and mash with the salt. Add the egg yolks and beat with a wire whisk until smooth. Add the lemon juice and beat for a few seconds more. Gradually add the oil, drop by drop, until the mixture becomes smooth and thickens. When approximately half the oil has been added, the rest can be incorporated at a faster rate; if the mixture becomes too thick, add a few extra drops of lemon juice or warm water.

Pour into a serving dish and adjust seasoning with freshly ground pepper, and extra salt if desired.

Green Mayonnaise

> *300ml (½ pt) mayonnaise (see p 30)*
> *45ml (3 tbs) fresh spinach (or*   *or approximately 120ml (8 tbs)*
> *   watercress), chopped*   *chopped fresh mixed herbs*
> *45ml (3 tbs) fresh parsley, chopped*   *in any pleasing*
> *30ml (2 tbs) chives, basil or chervil, etc*   *combination*
> optional
> *a pinch of nutmeg*

Blanch the herbs in a small quantity of boiling water for 1-2 minutes. Drain, rinse with cold water and pat dry with a cloth. Press through a sieve*, remove any remaining excess liquid, and blend into the mayonnaise.

32

Serve with eggs, fish, cooked or raw vegetables.

*The herbs may also be puréed in an electric blender.

Sauce Rémoulade

> *300ml (½ pt) mayonnaise (see p 30)*
> *15ml (1 tbs) chopped capers*
> *10ml (2 tsp) gherkins, chopped*
> *10ml (2 tsp) parsley, chopped*
> optional
> *5ml (1 tsp) anchovy paste*

Prepare the mayonnaise as described above and blend in the other ingredients. The addition of anchovy paste will give the rémoulade a flavour similar to that of sauce tartare.

Serve with seafood or cold vegetables.

Other Suggested Variations

Curry mayonnaise

Use approximately 5ml (1 tsp) curry powder to each 300ml (½ pt) mayonnaise. Blend the powder into the egg yolk mixture *before* the oil is added. If a stronger curry flavour is desired, add additional powder to a little mayonnaise in a separate dish. When well blended, add this to the main mixture. Excellent with hard-boiled eggs and raw or par-boiled cauliflower.

Lemon mayonnaise

This is best made by the quick blender method. Use 30ml (2 tbs) grated lemon rind to each 300ml (½ pt) of mayonnaise. Add to the egg yolk mixture *before* the oil is added.

Anchovy mayonnaise

To 300ml (½ pt) mayonnaise, add 4-5 finely chopped anchovy fillets, 15ml (1 tbs) of finely chopped chives and 5-10ml (1-2 tsp) of fresh lemon juice, to taste. Blend thoroughly and serve with egg dishes and cold vegetables.

Horseradish mayonnaise

Another excellent variation for eggs and seafood. Add 15-30ml (1-2 tbs) of lemon juice to 300ml (½ pt) of mayonnaise, then blend in 30ml (2 tbs) freshly grated horseradish. Serve at once.

Russian mayonnaise

To 300ml (½ pt) mayonnaise, add 45ml (3 tbs) tomato ketchup (or, for spicier taste, 30ml (2 tbs) ketchup and 15ml (1 tbs) chilli sauce); 45ml (3 tbs) red caviar (or red lumpfish roe); 15ml (1 tbs) finely grated onion; 40ml (2 heaped tbs) sour cream and some freshly cut dill, if available. Blend thoroughly.

Pimento mayonnaise

Chop 2 tinned pimento, which have been thoroughly drained, and pass through a sieve to purée. Add to 300ml (½ pt) mayonnaise, along with 1 clove garlic, crushed, and a few drops of lemon juice, to taste. Grind in some fresh pepper and serve with poached fish and cold egg dishes.

Creamy mayonnaise

To 300ml (½ pt) slightly chilled blender mayonnaise (made with a whole egg), add approximately 100ml (3 fl oz) of whipped double cream. Gently fold the cream into the mayonnaise, add salt and pepper to taste, and serve.

Sour Cream Dressings

Commercially bought sour cream can be used as a base for dressings. Sweetened with sugar or honey, fruit juices or fruit purées, and served well chilled, it makes a refreshing accompaniment to a variety of fruit salads. It also combines well with mayonnaise, herbs, spices, crumbled cheeses and crunchy chopped vegetables. If a more liquid consistency is preferred, thin the sour cream with single cream, lemon juice or cider vinegar.

Basic Sour Cream Dressing

240ml (8 fl oz) sour cream
45ml (3 tbs) cider vinegar
15-30ml (1-2 tbs) caster sugar, to taste
2.5ml (½ tsp) salt
freshly ground pepper
a selection of freshly chopped seasonal herbs (e.g. for fruit salads, use
*   chopped mint; eggs, tomatoes and peppers are delicious with basil and*
*   oregano)*

Beat the vinegar, sugar, salt and pepper until well blended. Fold in the sour cream, stir and add chopped herbs to taste.

Roquefort Sour Cream Dressing

240ml (8 fl oz) sour cream
5ml (1 tsp) shallots, finely chopped
2.5ml (½ tsp) dry mustard
30ml (2 tbs) cider vinegar

50g (2 oz) Roquefort (or blue) cheese, crumbled
salt and freshly ground pepper

Combine the vinegar, mustard and shallots and add to the sour cream, stirring to blend well. Crumble the cheese into this mixture, stir again and season to taste with salt and pepper. Chill before serving.

Cooked Sour Cream Dressing

> *240ml (8 fl oz) sour cream*
> *2 egg yolks, well beaten*
> *45ml (3 tbs) tarragon vinegar*
> *10-15ml (2-3 tsp) powdered sugar, to taste*
> *5ml (1 tsp) salt (or to taste)*
> *5ml (1 tsp) dry mustard*
> *2.5ml (½ tsp) celery salt*
> *2.5ml (½ tsp) paprika*

In the top of a double boiler, away from the heat, beat the cream with the egg yolks. Gradually add the vinegar. Stir in the sugar, salt and spices. Place over simmering water (the upper section should not touch the water) and whip until creamy smooth. Turn into a serving dish and chill until ready to serve.

Sour Cream and Honey Dressing for Fruit Salads

30ml (2 tbs) of honey (Hymettus, or other dark golden pouring honeys mix best) to 240ml (8 fl oz) sour cream is a useful ratio to start; adjust the balance to taste and according to the other ingredients to be added.

Orange Rind Dressing

To the sour cream and honey (above), add 5ml (1 tsp) grated orange rind, plus 30-45ml (2-3 tbs) fresh orange juice.

Coconut Dressing

An excellent accompaniment to tropical fruit salads. Soften 75ml (5 tbs) freshly grated coconut with 10-15ml (2-3 tsp) of lemon juice, and fold into honeyed sour cream.

Minted Sour Cream

Wonderful with summer berries, melons and sliced peaches. Use slightly less honey — 15-25ml (1-1½ tbs) — plus 15ml (1 tbs) Crème de menthe liqueur and 15ml (1 tbs) finely chopped fresh mint. Mix well and chill before serving.

Fruity Sour Cream

A purée of fresh fruit pulp — approximately 150ml (¼ pt) fruit to 240ml (8 fl oz) sour cream — makes a delicious dressing for fresh fruit salads. Add sugar according to taste and the natural sweetness of puréed fruit.

Sour Cream Verte

A simple mixture of chopped herbs and finely chopped green vegetables to garnish a salad of hearty greens (cabbage, spinach, cos, watercress). Sprinkle the leaves with some well-cooked crumbled bacon for a crisp complement to this fresh and fragrant dressing.

300ml (½ pt) sour cream
3 spring onions, finely chopped (including 5cm (2 in) of green tops)
45ml (3 tbs) green pepper, finely chopped
salt
pinch of white pepper
10ml (2 tsp) freshly squeezed lime juice
5ml (1 tsp) fresh parsley, finely chopped
15-30ml (1-2 tbs) fresh dill, finely chopped

Mix the lime juice with the sour cream and season to taste with salt and white pepper. Add the herbs and then the chopped vegetables. Mix well and chill for several hours to allow the flavours to penetrate the sour cream.

Irish Sour Cream Dressing

2 hard-boiled eggs
5-10ml (1-2 tsp) sugar, to taste
10-15ml (2-3 tsp) malt vinegar
5ml (1 tsp) dry mustard
225ml (7½ fl oz) sour cream
75ml (2½ fl oz) single cream
salt and freshly ground pepper

'Rice' the eggs by passing through a sieve and pound them together with the mustard and 5ml (1 tsp) sugar until well blended. Gradually add the vinegar while stirring with a wooden spoon. Continue stirring and slowly add the creams, which have been mixed together. Blend well and season with salt and pepper. Add additional sugar, if desired. Chill until ready to serve.

Thousand Island Dressing

240ml (8 fl oz) mayonnaise (p 30)
60ml (4 tbs) ketchup or chilli sauce

30ml (2 tbs) pimento-stuffed olives, finely chopped
30ml (2 tbs) green pepper, finely chopped
15ml (1 tbs) fresh chives or spring onions, finely chopped
1 hard-boiled egg, finely chopped
15ml (1 tbs) fresh parsley, finely chopped

Put the mayonnaise into a mixing bowl and add all the remaining ingredients, folding in gently with a wooden spoon. When well blended, cover carefully and chill for at least an hour before using. If stored in a tightly sealed jar in the refrigerator, this dressing will keep well for up to one week.

Low Calorie Russian Dressing

225ml (7½ fl oz) cottage cheese
15ml (1 tbs) lemon juice
60ml (4 tbs) tomato juice
a dash of Worcestershire sauce
salt and freshly ground pepper
1 hard-boiled egg, finely chopped
1 small gherkin, finely chopped

Place the cottage cheese and lemon juice in an electric blender and mix at high speed for 10 seconds. Add the tomato juice and blend at a low speed until the mixture is creamy smooth. Season to taste with salt, pepper and Worcestershire sauce. Chill for a couple of hours, and just before serving, stir in the chopped gherkin and egg.

Green Goddess Dressing

A popular favourite for serving with seafood and vegetable salads, this famous dressing was created at the Palace Hotel, San Francisco in honour of the actor George Arliss for his performance in a play called *The Green Goddess*.

240ml (8 fl oz) mayonnaise (p 30)
150ml (5 fl oz) sour cream
1 clove garlic, peeled and minced
75ml (5 tbs) fresh parsley, finely chopped
30ml (2 tbs) fresh chives, finely chopped (or 15ml (1 tbs) dried chives)
15ml (1 tbs) spring onions, finely chopped
5-6 anchovy fillets, rinsed, drained and chopped
45ml (3 tbs) tarragon vinegar
15ml (1 tbs) lemon juice
salt and freshly ground pepper

Place the chives, garlic, parsley, spring onions and chopped anchovy

37

fillets in a mixing bowl. Add the sour cream and mayonnaise, and gently stir. Season with lemon juice and vinegar. Stir and add salt and pepper, to taste. Cover and chill for at least 2 hours. Just before serving, stir again.

Roquefort Dressing

Note As Roquefort is such an expensive cheese, you may wish to substitute blue cheese in this recipe.

> *50g (2 oz) Roquefort cheese*
> *5ml (1 tsp) Worcestershire sauce*
> *30ml (2 tbs) double cream (more, if desired)*
> *60ml (4 tbs) olive oil*
> *15ml (1 tbs) white wine vinegar*
> *2.5ml (½ tsp) onion, finely grated*

Mash the cheese until smooth and pasty by gradually adding the cream and Worcestershire sauce, stirring with a wooden spoon. In a separate bowl, blend the oil and vinegar. Add this vinaigrette, along with the grated onion, to the cheese mixture. Blend well, add additional cream if desired and chill until ready to serve.

Oriental Salad Dressing

This and the following recipe both make delicious dressings for salads composed of fresh Chinese cabbage, bean sprouts, chopped water chestnuts and bamboo shoots. They are also delicious with white or red cabbage and with Webb (iceberg) lettuce.

> *60ml (4 tbs) light soy sauce*
> *30ml (2 tbs) oriental sesame oil*
> *30ml (2 tbs) rice wine vinegar*
> *5ml (1 tsp) Chinese mustard, dissolved in 5ml (1 tsp) water*
> *15ml (1 tbs) toasted sesame seeds (p 245)*

Place all the liquid ingredients in a small jar with a tight-fitting lid. Shake well and chill. Just before serving, add the sesame seeds to the mixture, shake again and pour over the salad.

Oriental Dressing with Chopped Peanuts

> *75ml (5 tbs) peanut oil*
> *50ml (3 tbs) + 5ml (1 tsp) rice vinegar*
> *45ml (3 tbs) roasted peanuts, shelled and chopped*
> *15ml (1 tbs) caster sugar*
> *3 spring onions, thinly sliced (including 7.5cm (3 in) green stem)*
> *30ml (2 tbs) toasted sesame seeds (p 245)*

Place all the liquid ingredients along with the sugar and spring onions into a jar with a tight-fitting lid. Shake well and chill. Just before serving, add the chopped peanuts and sesame seeds, cover, shake again and pour over the salad.

Kuah Lada

Spicy Malaysian dressing

> *2 red chilli peppers*
> *1 clove garlic, crushed*
> *2.5ml (½ tsp) salt*
> *15ml (1 tbs) vinegar*
> *30ml (2 tbs) water*
> *pinch sugar*

Red chilli peppers are a favourite spicing agent in Malaysia. Traditionally, this dressing is prepared by pounding the peppers with the garlic and salt to a pasty consistency. It is much quicker to deseed and chop the peppers (p 243) and blend them with the other ingredients in a liquidiser until a purée-like mixture is achieved.

This should be used sparingly, more as a condiment than a dressing. Serve it with crudités or fresh prawns.

Bagna Cauda

Italian garlic and anchovy dressing

Not strictly a salad dressing, this sauce is served as a 'hot bath' for a variety of raw vegetables in the Piedmont region of Italy. The white truffle is the essential ingredient to make an authentic Piedmontese sauce. It is brought to the table in the pot in which it has been cooked and kept warm on top of a spirit stove.

> *150ml (¼ pt) olive oil*
> *100g (4 oz) butter*
> *2-3 cloves garlic, finely chopped*
> *6-7 anchovy fillets, chopped*
> *a few leaves of fresh basil, chopped*
> *pinch of salt*
> optional
> *1 small white truffle, thinly sliced*

Place 15ml (1 tbs) each of oil and butter in a small frying pan over a low heat. While it melts, put the remaining oil and butter in a small pot (preferably earthenware) over simmering water. Add the basil and garlic to the frying pan and cook until the garlic softens. Add the anchovy fillets

39

and cook, stirring regularly, until they dissolve to a paste. Add salt, stir, and transfer these ingredients to the pot of oil and butter. Add the white truffle (if available) to the sauce just before it is brought to the table.

Poppy Seed Dressing

Excellent with fruit salads and delicate greens, such as bibb lettuce.

90ml (6 tbs) sunflower oil
30ml (2 tbs) lemon juice
5ml (1 tsp) poppy seeds
1.25ml (¼ tsp) dry mustard
15ml (1 tbs) caster sugar
2.5ml (½ tsp) grated onion (use more with vegetable salads)
salt

In a small bowl, blend the mustard with the lemon juice and sugar. Add the onion, if desired, and gradually stir in oil. Season to taste with salt and toss in the poppy seeds. Pour immediately onto fruit salads and allow to macerate and chill before serving. For lettuce salads, dress and toss just before serving.

Orange juice for fruit salads may be used in place of lemon juice, or try a mixture of the two.

Party Poppy Seed Dressing

A 'spiked' dressing ideal for buffet fruit salads. Use nearly twice as much fruit as dressing, since the fruit will give off plenty of its own liquid. Try an assortment of tropical fruits — melons, mangoes, citrus, pineapple, etc.

30ml (2 tbs) white wine vinegar
30ml (2 tbs) lime juice, freshly squeezed
2.5ml (½ tsp) dry mustard
2.5ml (½ tsp) grated onion
30ml (2 tbs) caster sugar
30ml (2 tbs) hymettus honey
120ml (4 fl oz) sunflower oil
salt to taste
30ml (2 tbs) bourbon whisky
30ml (2 tbs) poppy seeds

Place the vinegar, lime juice and dry mustard in a small saucepan and stir with a fork or wire whisk until smooth. Add the grated onion, sugar, honey, sunflower oil and salt. Stir this mixture over moderate heat until it begins to boil; reduce the heat and simmer, while stirring, to dissolve the sugar and salt.

Remove from the heat and add the bourbon and poppy seeds. Stir and cool to room temperature before serving. Spoon some of the dressing onto the fruit and serve the rest in a sauceboat.

Honey Cream Dressing for Fruits

> *2 eggs*
> *120ml (4 fl oz) honey*
> *120ml (2 fl oz) lemon juice*
> *60ml (2 fl oz) orange juice*
> *pinch of salt*
> *120ml (4 fl oz) double cream, whipped*
> *10ml (2 tsp) grated orange rind*

Beat the eggs in a small saucepan and stir in the honey, lemon juice, orange juice and salt. Place the saucepan over a low heat and cook, stirring constantly, until the mixture coats the back of a spoon. Remove from the heat and cool to room temperature. Fold in the whipped cream and orange rind. Chill for a couple of hours and serve in a sauceboat with fresh fruit salads.

For additional tips on dressing fruit salads, see chapter on Fruit and Nut Salads.

A–Z Single Vegetable Salads

The salads in this section are composed primarily of one main ingredient, providing an opportunity to indulge temptations for seasonal impulse buying.

A wide range of recipes is included for most of the vegetables which can be obtained fresh in European and North American markets. The brief introductions provide snippets of historical information, folklore, and useful tips for preparation; however, for a truly comprehensive and delightful survey of the vegetable kingdom, I highly recommend Jane Grigson's *Vegetable Book*.

Artichokes (Globe)

These beautiful, flower-like vegetables are now available most of the year, with supplies coming generally from the Mediterranean, where the artichoke originated.

The ancient Romans considered them a delicacy and devised tasty ways for preserving the hearts in vinegar and brine. Catherine de Medici is said to have brought the artichoke with her to France, where its popularity derived not only from its distinctive flavour, but also, if the Parisian street vendors were right, from its power to 'heat the body, the spirit and the genitals'.

The most delicate of the varieties available today is the small Florence artichoke (rarely seen in Britain) which can be boiled and eaten whole. The ubiquitous variety in British and American markets usually weighs between 250-325g (10-12 oz), with smooth, closely clinging leaves, a roundish head and a green or purplish-green colour.

Cold boiled artichokes, served with vinaigrette or stuffed, make an excellent first course. To prepare for cooking, break off the stem and remove the small leaves at the base of the artichoke. With a sharp knife, slice off 2.5cm (1 in) from the top of the centre cone of leaves and trim the base so that the artichoke will stand upright. Trim the outer pointed leaves with scissors and immerse the artichoke in acidulated water (water with 15ml (1 tbs) of lemon juice or vinegar added) to avoid discolouration until ready to use.

The prepared artichokes should be dropped into a large pan of lightly salted boiling water. Bring the water quickly back to the boil, reduce the heat, cover leaving a small aperture for steam to escape, and boil gently for approximately 30-40 minutes. The artichokes are ready if the bottoms feel tender when pierced with a fork. Remove from the water and drain, upside down, in a colander.

If you wish to remove the choke before serving — unnecessary, but an attractive way of presenting the artichoke — gently spread the outer leaves so you can reach into the centre. Pull out the tender, pale-leaved cone in one piece, scrape off the hairy growth which covers the top of the heart, and remove the choke gently with a spoon. Sprinkle the exposed heart with a few drops of lemon juice, and salt and pepper, if desired. Replace the cone of leaves upside down in the hollow now formed.

Tip The *fond d'artichaut* is the delicate bottom with the innermost leaves still adhering to it but the choke removed. Artichoke bottoms can be purchased in tins from gourmet grocers and used as a beautiful, tasty base for chopped vegetables or mixtures of seafood dressed with mayonnaise or vinaigrette.

Artichauts à la Provence

Serves 6

> *6 small young artichokes*
> *2 lemons, halved*
> *salt and freshly ground pepper*
> *2 medium onions, sliced into rings*
> *200ml (7 fl oz) best light olive oil*
> *90-150ml (6-10 tbs) water, as required*
> *3 cloves garlic, crushed*
> *1 sprig fresh thyme, or 2.5ml (½ tsp) dried thyme*
> *1 bay leaf*
> *30ml (2 tbs) fresh parsley, finely chopped*
> *15ml (1 tbs) lemon juice*
> garnish
> *a few sprigs of fresh parsley*

Prepare the artichokes for cooking as described above. Fill a large saucepan with salted water, add the lemons and bring to the boil. Add the artichokes and simmer gently for 20-25 minutes. Remove and drain, upside down, in a colander.

Place the artichokes in a heavy enamel or cast iron saucepan and add the onions, parsley, thyme and bayleaf. Sprinkle liberally with oil, add the water and cook, partially covered, over a medium heat for 10 minutes, or until the artichokes are very tender. Remove the artichokes with a slotted spoon and arrange them in a deep serving dish. Add some of the cooked onion rings. Strain the cooking oil and combine with 15ml (1 tbs) lemon juice, freshly ground pepper and salt, to taste. Pour over the artichokes and garnish with parsley.

Insalata di Carciofi

Serves 4

Raw artichoke salad

Elizabeth David, in *Italian Food*, describes the following method for preparing an unusual salad of raw artichokes:

'As a component of an hors d'oeuvre for four people you need 2 medium sized artichokes; if the dish is to be served as a salad, have twice as many. The other essential elements are a sharp knife, a lemon, and olive oil. Draw your knife through the lemon and at the same time squeeze lemon juice all over the artichoke in order that it may not turn black. Cut off the stalk close to the head, remove all the tough outer leaves, then cut off the top half of the artichoke, which is discarded. Now cut the half which is left in half again, lengthways, exposing the choke, or 'hay' as the French call it. This is now easily removed with the knife. Squeeze more lemon over the artichoke, and cut each half, downwards, into the thinnest possible slices, so that they emerge fan-like and delicate. When all the artichokes are sliced, season them with oil, salt and possibly a little more lemon. Treated in this way, artichokes have an unexpected, slightly nutty flavour. The combination of this salad of raw artichokes with a few fine slices of salt beef or raw ham is a very good one.'

Jerusalem Artichokes

Jerusalem artichoke is actually a misnomer for a kind of sunflower; it is certainly no real relation of the French globe artichoke. How this native American root vegetable acquired its strange name (in early colonial records it is sometimes referred to as 'the Canadian Potato') is still something of a mystery, though there does appear to be some agreement that Jerusalem was a corruption of the Spanish word for sunflower, *girasol*, and artichoke was appended for the slight resemblance in flavour.

A nourishing winter vegetable — more popular in Great Britain than America — the Jerusalem artichoke is sometimes forsaken by the less adventurous because its knobby surface makes it awkward to clean. Persevere — the taste is worth the extra preparation time.

Jerusalem Artichoke Salad   *Serves 2-3*

> *450g (1 lb) Jerusalem artichokes*
> *60ml (4 tbs) olive oil*
> *juice of 1 small lemon*
> *30ml (2 tbs) fresh parsley, chopped*
> optional
> *2 rashers well-fried streaky bacon, finely chopped*

Scrub the artichokes and peel as you would a small potato. Immerse in acidulated water (water to which a few drops of lemon juice or vinegar has been added) to prevent discolouration. Once peeled, cut each artichoke into walnut-sized pieces and place in gently boiling, lightly salted water, along with half the lemon juice. Simmer for 7-8 minutes, or until just tender but not soft. Drain.

While the vegetable cools, blend the remaining lemon juice with the oil; add salt and pepper to taste. Place the artichokes in a glass bowl, pour on dressing and add the chopped parsley and bacon bits, if desired.

For a delicious variation, add one firm avocado, which has been peeled and cubed, along with 30ml (2 tbs) chopped spring onion.

Asparagus

The asparagus is a member of the lily-of-the-valley family, originating in the eastern Mediterranean where it still grows wild today.

The Romans considered this vegetable a great delicacy. It was also highly regarded as a cure for heart trouble, dropsy and toothache and, by the time it was brought to England, it was vested with aphrodisiac properties. Nicholas Culpeper wrote in his *Compleat Herball* (1652): 'The decoction of the roots boiled in wine and being taken fasting several mornings together, stirreth up bodily lust in man or woman, whatever some have written to the contrary'.

The green varieties are those most commonly available today in Great Britain and North America, although many consider the less common, white-stalked asparagus more delicate in taste.

When choosing asparagus, look for firm, straight stalks with well-formed and tightly-closed tips. They should be used as soon as possible after purchase, but if they must be kept for several days, wrap the butt ends in a damp cloth or paper towel and store in the refrigerator. Before cooking, rinse the stalks in cold running water and snap off the woody ends.

Asparagus Vinaigrette   *Serves 3-4*

One of the simplest and loveliest ways to serve cold asparagus.

> *a large bunch of asparagus*
> *90-120ml (6-8 tbs) olive oil*
> *juice of 1 lemon or 30ml (2 tbs) white wine vinegar*
> *salt, freshly ground pepper and a pinch of sugar*
> *a pinch of grated nutmeg*

Trim the lower ends of the stalks and tie the asparagus into loose bundles. Stand them upright in a deep pan and pour over boiling water, leaving the tips uncovered. Salt well and cover the pan. Boil gently for 15-20 minutes, or until the asparagus are tender. Drain and then refresh by rinsing them with cold water. Drain again and arrange the stalks on a serving platter.

Mix the ingredients for the vinaigrette and pour over the asparagus.

Salata de Sparanghel   *Serves 3-4*

Rumanian asparagus salad

> *1 large bunch of asparagus (prepared as for asparagus vinaigrette)*
> or *1 392g (14 oz) tin of whole asparagus, drained*

46

15ml (1 tbs) capers
45ml (3 tbs) olive oil
15ml (1 tbs) white wine vinegar
fresh parsley, finely chopped
salt and freshly ground pepper
3 hard-boiled eggs

Arrange the asparagus stalks on a shallow serving platter. Mash the hard-boiled egg yolks and add salt and pepper. Gradually stir in the oil until the mixture is well-blended, then add the vinegar and finally, the capers. Pour the sauce over the asparagus, sprinkle with chopped parsley and egg whites, finely chopped or cut into slivers. Chill and serve.

Note If the sauce is not quite thin enough, add either more vinegar or a little fresh sour cream.

Asparagus and Hard-boiled Egg Salad   *Serves 3-4*

1 large bunch of asparagus (prepared as for asparagus vinaigrette)
1 head of Boston (round) lettuce
4 hard-boiled eggs
4 firm tomatoes
2 pieces of pimento
parsley
vinegar, oil, salt and freshly ground pepper

Remove damaged leaves from the outside of the lettuce. Wash and drain the remaining head. Place the largest leaves all around a large, flat platter. Separate the tender, light-coloured leaves from the heart and place them in the middle of the dish. Dress lightly with oil and vinegar and toss to cover.

Place the cooked asparagus, separated into 4 equal bunches, in a circular fashion around the platter. In the quarter sections created, place the hard-boiled eggs and tomatoes, sliced into halves.

Cut the pimento into thin strips and wrap one strip around each bunch of asparagus. Place additional pimento strips in criss-cross fashion on top of the eggs. Season with salt and pepper and garnish generously with parsley.

This very attractive salad, with its colourful contrasts, should be served with a bowl of mayonnaise or vinaigrette.

Aubergine (Eggplant)

Aubergines, an international favourite — as demonstrated by the variety of recipes here — were originally cultivated in India and China.

They were brought to the West by Arab traders, and later, to the New World, by Spanish explorers. Although introduced to England in the late 1500s, the present popularity of aubergines is part of the post-World War II vogue for Mediterranean cooking.

The ubiquitous purple variety is generally available throughout the year, but there are other less common varieties, including white — which may have given rise to the American name 'eggplant'.

When selecting aubergines, look for firm, unwrinkled skin and a shiny purple colour.

Tip Aubergines contain a large quantity of bitter juice, which should be partially removed. They can be sliced, salted and left standing to drain while still in a raw state or, if the aubergine is to be made into a paté, the cooked pulp can be squeezed or the juices drained through a sieve. With either method, a quick rinse under a cold running tap is the final step.

Caponata alla Siciliana
Serves 4-6

Italian sweet and sour aubergine salad

Note the addition of chocolate — an authentic but unexpected taste to the uninitiated.

> *3 (2½ lb/1kg approx) medium-sized aubergines*
> *1 small head of celery*
> *vegetable oil, for frying*
> *salt and freshly ground pepper*
> *30ml (2 tbs) sugar*
> *15ml (1 tbs) capers*
> *12 green olives, pitted and chopped*
> *75ml (2½ fl oz) white wine vinegar*
> *45ml (3 tbs) grated bitter chocolate*

Peel the aubergines and cut into 2.5cm (1 in) cubes. Sprinkle with salt and leave in a sieve to drain for 1 hour, tossing occasionally during this time. Drain and pat dry.

Using enough oil to cover the bottom of a large frying pan, fry the aubergines, stirring constantly until golden brown and soft. Add additional oil during cooking, if required. Drain.

Dice the celery and fry in the same oil until translucent. Drain and mix with the aubergines. Put the vegetables in a large bowl, add the remaining ingredients and season with salt and pepper to taste.

Caponata will store well in the refrigerator for several days.

Lebanese Aubergines
Serves 4

> *2 large aubergines*

48

360ml (12 fl oz) natural yoghurt
2 cloves garlic
vegetable oil for frying
salt
30ml (2 tbs) fresh mint, chopped or 15ml (1 tbs) dried mint
paprika

Peel the aubergines and slice into 1cm (½ in) pieces. Sprinkle with salt and leave in a sieve to drain for 1 hour, tossing occasionally. Rinse and pat dry. Heat the oil in a large saucepan and fry the aubergines until lightly cooked. Remove from the pan and drain off the excess oil which has been absorbed during cooking.

To the yoghurt, add the 2 cloves of garlic, crushed, and salt to taste.

When the aubergines are completely cool, place them in a shallow serving dish, pour on the yoghurt and garnish with mint and a sprinkling of paprika.

Chinese Spiced Aubergines   Serves 4

775g (1¾ lb) fresh young aubergines
45ml (3 tbs) light soy sauce
30ml (2 tbs) red wine vinegar
30ml (2 tbs) caster sugar
1.25ml (¼ tsp) salt
7.5ml (1½ tsp) dry sherry
15ml (1 tbs) sesame oil
5ml (1 tsp) peanut, corn or vegetable oil
15ml (1 tbs) chopped fresh garlic
15ml (1 tbs) chopped fresh ginger
15ml (1 tbs) white sesame seeds

Place the aubergines in the top of a steamer, cover, and cook over boiling water for 30-45 minutes, until they are very soft. Cool.

While the aubergines are steaming, mix together the soy sauce, vinegar, sugar, salt, wine and sesame oil. Set aside. In a small saucepan, heat the vegetable oil over a high flame, add the chopped ginger and garlic and cook for no more than 30 seconds. Stir in the vinegar and soy sauce mixture, bring to the boil, then immediately remove from the heat. Set aside to cool.

Toast the sesame seeds in a dry frying pan over a medium low heat, or under the grill, shaking the pan constantly to avoid burning. When the seeds are golden brown, remove from the heat, shake the pan for a few more seconds and then set aside to cool.

Break the aubergine into pieces, discarding seeds or skin that falls away. Place in a serving dish, pour over the cooked sauce and garnish with toasted sesame seeds.

(If this is prepared in advance, keep chilled and add the seeds just before serving.)

Aubergines à la Provençale I   *Serves 4-5*

Both versions of this salad make a delicious appetiser, or accompaniment to cold chicken, veal and omelettes.

> *3 large young aubergines*
> *coarse salt*
> *900g (2 lb) ripe tomatoes, skinned (p 246)*
> *0.75ml (⅛ tsp) caster sugar*
> *olive oil*
> *3 cloves garlic*
> *30ml (2 tbs) fresh parsley, finely chopped*
> *15ml (1 tbs) lemon juice*
> *salt and freshly ground pepper*

Cut the unpeeled aubergines into long slices about 1cm (½ in) thick. Place on a cutting board, sprinkle lightly with salt, and put a plate on top to help press out excess liquid. Allow to drain for about 30 minutes, then wipe with a damp paper towel.

Heat enough oil to cover the bottom of a large enamel frying pan. Add the aubergines and fry gently over medium heat, turning often, until they are tender. Remove from the pan and drain.

Skin and de-seed the tomatoes. Sauté the remaining pulp in a little olive oil until just soft. Add the garlic, finely chopped, the caster sugar, and the parsley. Cover and leave to reduce over a medium heat for approximately 30-40 minutes. Remove from the heat, cool, and add 15ml (1 tbs) lemon juice.

Place the aubergines in a shallow serving dish or glass bowl and pour over the tomato mixture. Correct seasoning with salt and freshly ground pepper and chill until ready to serve. Garnish with a sprig of fresh parsley.

Aubergines à la Provençale II   *Serves 5-6*

> *3-4 medium-sized aubergines*
> *1 large red pepper*
> *1 large green pepper*
> *60ml (4 tbs) freshly made mayonnaise (see p 30)*
> *45ml (3 tbs) finely chopped onion*
> *1 clove garlic*
> *1.25ml (¼ tsp) cayenne pepper*

Left: Yam Koong; *bottom:* Thakkali Sambol; *right:* Celery Salad with
Coconut Dressing

Top: Gobi ki Sabzi; *right:* Maiwa Kachumar; *bottom:* Phool ka Achar

salt and freshly ground black pepper
15ml (1 tbs) lemon juice
garnish
black olives and 30ml (2 tbs) fresh chopped parsley

Place the aubergines and peppers under the grill and cook, turning frequently, until both vegetables are well charred — approximately 15-20 minutes. When cool enough to handle, remove skin, stems and seeds from the peppers and cut into fairly small pieces. Place in a bowl with mayonnaise, chopped onion, cayenne and garlic.

Slice the aubergines in half and remove the skin, seeds and soft centres. Cut the remainder into smallish cubes and place in a sieve to drain for 10-15 minutes. Add to the pepper and onion mixture and season with salt and pepper. Mix well and turn into a glass serving bowl. Add the lemon juice, stir, and garnish with olives and chopped parsley.

Simpoog Aghtzan   *Serves 4*

Armenian aubergines

2 medium-sized aubergines (approx 450g (1 lb) each)
2 large tomatoes, deseeded and cut into small wedges
2-3 spring onions (scallions), finely chopped
70g (3 oz) green pepper, deseeded and diced
100g (¼ lb) cucumber, peeled and diced
25g (1 oz) fresh parsley, chopped
1 clove garlic
60ml (2 fl oz) olive oil
45ml (3 tbs) wine vinegar
salt and freshly ground pepper

Remove the stems from the aubergines and bake in a preheated (180°C/350°F, Gas 4) oven for 45 minutes — 1 hour, or until they are quite soft. When cool enough to handle, peel off the skin, halve and remove the seeds. Cut the remaining pulp into small pieces, place in a sieve to drain for 10-15 minutes, and turn into a large salad bowl. Add the tomato wedges, onions, green pepper, cucumber and parsley.

In a separate small bowl, crush the garlic with the oil, whisk several times and then discard any remaining garlic pieces. Add the vinegar and whisk until well blended. Season with salt and pepper and pour over the salad. Toss well and chill for at least 1 hour. Toss again gently before serving and garnish with a sprinkling of chopped parsley.

Avocado

The avocado pear is actually a fruit, but it is generally prepared and eaten as an hors d'oeuvre or vegetable salad.

Its origins are probably in tropical America. There is a story that Spanish conquistadors in Mexico noticed that the Aztecs enjoyed a strange green fruit which they called *ahuacatl*. The natives explained that this meant 'testicle', and that the fruit was so named because it was capable of exciting intense sexual passion.

Even without this somewhat dubious aphrodisiac property, the avocado — with its smooth, creamy texture, distinctive nutty flavour and high protein content — surely deserves its popularity.

The main British supply of avocados comes today from South Africa and Israel. In America, however, they have been cultivated indigenously since the agriculturalist Henry Perrine planted them in southern Florida in 1833.

When buying avocados for immediate use, choose those that feel slightly soft when light pressure is applied and appear free of bruises or black marks. Ready-to-eat avocados can be stored uncut in the refrigerator for 4-7 days. Avocados can also be bought hard and ripened on a sunny windowsill. Once cut in half and destoned, the flesh should be sprinkled with lemon juice to avoid discolouration, especially if it is not to be consumed immediately.

Stuffed Avocados

A delicious way of serving the avocado as an hors d'oeuvre is to stuff the cavity left by the stone with a specially-prepared filling, a fragrant herbal vinaigrette, or a rich, creamy dressing such as Thousand Islands, Green Goddess or Roquefort (see p 36-38). The following recipes illustrate a few of the many fillings that may be used. Experiment with your own combinations.

Avocado with Shellfish   *Serves 4*

> *2 large ripe avocado pears*
> *150g (6 oz) crabmeat, lobster or peeled prawns*
> *4 sprigs fresh parsley*
> *4 large lettuce leaves*
> sauce
> *5 sprigs parsley*
> *4 sprigs tarragon*
> *50g (2 oz) spinach*
> *300ml (½ pt) mayonnaise (see p 30)*
> *30ml (2 tbs) double cream*
> *salt and freshly ground pepper*

To prepare the sauce cook the parsley, tarragon and spinach in a small quantity of boiling salted water until just tender (5-8 minutes). Drain well and purée in a sieve or electric blender. Gently fold the greens into the mayonnaise, add the cream and season with salt and pepper to taste. All this should be done very close to serving time.

Cut the avocados in half, destone, and lightly sprinkle with lemon juice. Scoop out some of the pulp to increase the cavity. Mix the shellfish with the mayonnaise and pile in the centres of the halved pears. Garnish with parsley and serve on individual plates lined with a lettuce leaf.

Avocado with Ham and Cheese filling

Serves 4

> *2 large ripe avocado pears*
> *100g (4 oz) cottage cheese*
> *50g (2 oz) cooked ham, cut into small dice*
> *10ml (2 tsp) lemon juice*
> *5ml (1 tsp) fresh chives, finely chopped or 2/3 tsp dried chives*
> *15ml (1 tbs) sour cream*
> *salt and freshly ground pepper*
> *25g (1 oz) flaked toasted almonds*

Mix the cottage cheese with the ham, chives, lemon juice and sour cream. Season with salt and pepper and chill for at least 1 hour. Cut the avocado pears in half, destone and sprinkle lightly with lemon juice. Scoop out some of the pulp to increase the cavity. Fill the centres with the mixture, sprinkle with the almonds and serve immediately.

See *Salade aux Avocats et Poulet* (p 124)

Stuffed and Sliced Avocados

Serves 4

> *2 large ripe but firm avocados*
> *90ml (6 tbs) cream cheese*
> *10ml (2 tsp) mayonnaise*
> *45ml (3 tbs) single cream*
> *salt and freshly ground pepper*
> *large lettuce leaves*
> *5ml (1 tsp) fresh chives, finely chopped*
> *23ml (1½ tbs) walnuts, chopped*
> *15ml (1 tbs) black olives, destoned and chopped*
> *a few drops of lemon juice*
> optional
> *fresh grapefruit sections to garnish*

Cut the avocados in half, destone and peel. Scoop out approximately 15ml (1 tbs) of flesh from each half to enlarge the cavity. Sprinkle lightly with lemon juice and set aside. To prepare the filling, mix the cream cheese, single cream, mayonnaise, chives, chopped nuts and olives. Blend

53

thoroughly and season with salt and pepper to taste.

Fill the centres with this mixture and replace the halves together. Enclose carefully in aluminium foil or cling film wrap and chill for several hours. When ready to serve, unwrap the avocados and cut into thick crosswise slices. Place the slices on a large platter lined with lettuce leaves and garnish with grapefruit sections if desired.

Aquacate con Coliflor   *Serves 4*

Mexican avocado and cauliflower salad

> *1 medium-sized cauliflower*
> *30ml (2 tbs) wine vinegar*
> *4 small very ripe avocados*
> *50g (2 oz) ground almonds*
> *6 red radishes, thinly sliced*
> *salt and freshly ground pepper*
> *2.5-5ml (½-1 tsp) nutmeg*

Wash and trim the cauliflower, removing outer leaves and the hard stalk. Cut into florets and cook in boiling salted water for just 5 minutes. Drain and cool. Sprinkle with vinegar and a dash of salt and pepper, and set aside in a large bowl.

Cut the avocado pears in half, destone and remove flesh. Mix the flesh with the ground almonds and nutmeg, salt and pepper to taste. Add this mixture to the cauliflower and blend gently. Chill and serve on a round plate garnished with radish slices.

Beans

Beans are more than beans, good for food and pleasant to the taste: they are a moral lesson. The priests of Egypt held it a crime even to look at beans — the very sight of them unclean. Lucian introduces a philosopher in Hell declaring that it would be difficult to say which were the greater crime — to eat beans or to eat one's father's head. Pythagoras forbade his disciples to eat beans, because they are formed of the rotten ooze out of which man is created. The Romans ate beans at funerals with awe, from the idea that the souls of the dead were in them. Two thousand years pass by, and here are we now eating beans with the most thorough enjoyment and the most perfect unconcern. Moral — Get rid of prejudice and call nothing unclean.

Kettner's Book of the Table (1877)

Fresh beans — stringbeans (French), runner beans or broad beans — make exquisite salads.

54

Broad beans originated in the East but have been grown in Britain for hundreds of years. In America they are sometimes called 'horsebeans' because some varieties can grow as long as 18 inches. However, broad beans are best eaten small and young, when both the pod and bean are tender and tasty — serve them raw with a bowl of salt as part of a selection of crudités.

Runner beans are probably the most popular variety grown in Britain. When picked young they are a passable but not really desirable substitute for French beans.

Stringbeans are my favourite, but the French variety, much superior to the homegrown kind, are often expensive and therefore, a delicacy. In France, haricots verts vinaigrette — the simplest and most delicious way of serving beans — is a popular first course.

Beans for salads should be cooked *al dente*, anywhere from 5-10 minutes in boiling, salted water, depending on age.

Green Bean Salad
Serves 3-4

> *450g (1 lb) French beans (or runner beans)*
> *1 small onion, finely chopped*
> *1 clove garlic*
> *10ml (2 tsp) salt*
> *60-75ml (4-5 tbs) good olive oil*
> *15ml (1 tbs) lemon juice*
> optional
> *2 rashers streaky bacon, well cooked and drained*

Wash and top and tail the beans. Cook in boiling, salted water until just tender (5-8 minutes). Drain and place in a serving bowl.

Crush the garlic with the salt. Add lemon juice, chopped onion and oil. Mix well and pour over the beans while still warm. If desired, the chopped bacon makes a delicious garnish.

Bohnensalat, a favourite German recipe, requires vinegar rather than lemon juice in approximately the same proportions as above. A sprinkling of herbs — dill, tarragon, oregano — can also be added.

Insalata di Fagiolini
Serves 4-5

Italian string bean salad

> *750g (1½ lb) stringbeans*
> *60ml (4 tbs) olive oil*
> *1 onion, thinly sliced*
> *50g (2 oz) freshly grated Parmesan cheese*
> *lettuce leaves*

30ml (2 tbs) white wine vinegar
1 clove garlic, finely chopped
5ml (1 tsp) fresh parsley, finely chopped
salt and freshly ground pepper
1 hard-boiled egg, chopped

Wash, trim and slice the beans in half. Cook in boiling, salted water for 5-8 minutes. Drain and set aside. While the beans are cooling, prepare the salad bowl by lining it with a few crisp lettuce leaves. Combine the olive oil, vinegar, chopped garlic, salt and freshly ground pepper. Pour over the beans and add sliced onion. Mix lightly and chill. Just before serving, arrange the beans on the lettuce base and sprinkle with the egg and grated cheese.

Insalata alla Macedone I   *Serves 6-8*

Italian mixed vegetable salad

An ideal first course all year round.

900g (2 lb) French beans
450g (1 lb) cooked fresh or frozen peas
225g (½ lb) haricot beans
2-3 pieces of tinned pimento, or 2 small fresh red peppers, finely chopped
90-120ml (6-8 tbs) olive oil
30ml (2 tbs) lemon juice
salt and freshly ground pepper
garnish
fresh chopped parsley and chives (when available)

Soak the haricot beans for about 2 hours. Drain and cook in enough gently boiling water to cover for 45 minutes, or until tender but not mushy. Add 5-10ml (1-2 tsp) salt to beans during last 10 minutes of cooking.

Both peas and beans should be cooked separately in boiling salted water for 5-8 minutes.

Drain the vegetables well and place in a large glass or ceramic bowl. Add the chopped pimentos or peppers.

Combine olive oil, lemon juice, salt, freshly ground pepper and chopped fresh herbs. Mix well and pour over the salad. Stir ingredients until thoroughly coated with dressing.

Insalata alla Macedone II

Following the same basic procedures as above, substitute 75g (3 oz) pine nuts (which have been gently sautéed in oil until golden brown, and then drained) for the haricot beans; one chopped medium Spanish onion for

56

the green peas; and 30ml (2 tbs) vinegar in place of the lemon juice. This blend of ingredients has the same colourful appeal as the first recipe.

Broad Bean Salad   *Serves 4*

900g (2 lb) fresh broad beans
1 large clove garlic
4 rashers streaky bacon, well-cooked, drained and finely chopped
45ml (3 tbs) olive oil
15ml (1 tbs) lemon juice
15ml (1 tbs) fresh basil, chopped
salt and freshly ground pepper

Shell the beans and cook in gently boiling, salted water until just tender (*al dente*), 8-10 minutes. Drain and set aside to cool. Cut the clove of garlic in half and rub it all over the inside of a salad bowl. Add the beans and bacon. Combine oil, lemon juice, fresh herbs and seasoning. Mix well and pour over the beans. Chill, and just before serving, sprinkle a little chopped basil over the top.

Fave alla Romano   *Serves 4*

Italian Broad Bean Salad

1½kg (3 lb) broad beans
1 large onion, finely chopped
75ml (5 tbs) olive oil
1 sprig of fresh sage, chopped or 5ml (1 tsp) dried sage
10ml (2 tsp) tomato purée
parsley, chopped, to garnish

Shell the beans. In a medium-sized saucepan heat 45ml (3 tbs) of the olive oil and cook the chopped onion on low heat until nearly tender, but still crisp. Add the chopped sage, tomato purée and the beans. Pour on boiling water to cover and continue cooking at a fast boil until the liquid has reduced by half.

Serve cold with a sprinkling of fresh chopped parsley and an extra 15-30ml (1-2 tbs) of best olive oil.

Beetroot

The edible root of *beta vulgaris* was virtually unknown to the Ancients. The Greeks cultivated the vegetable only for its leaves and the Romans, for many centuries, used the root strictly for medicinal purposes. Today, we do the opposite: the vitamin-rich tops are often discarded, when they could be cooked as a tasty dish on their own. Beetroot plays an important part in the cuisine of Slavic peoples and for the Scandinavians, pickled beetroot is as popular a standard accompaniment as lettuce and tomatoes are for the English.

Tip Never cut into beets before cooking or the lovely red pigment will end up in the cooking liquid. Cook in boiling water until tender when pierced with a fork.

Syltede Rødbeder

Serves 4-6

Danish Pickled Beets

> *120ml (4 fl oz) cider or wine vinegar*
> *120ml (4 fl oz) water*
> *25-50g (2 oz) sugar (or, to taste)*
> *5ml (1 tsp) salt*
> *1.25ml (¼ tsp) freshly ground pepper*
> *900g (2 lb) beetroot, cooked, peeled and thinly sliced*
> optional
> *10ml (2 tsp) caraway seeds*

In a large saucepan, combine the vinegar, sugar, salt and pepper. Bring to a fast boil, stirring occasionally, then remove from the heat and cool. Place the beets in a deep bowl and pour the dressing over them. Sprinkle with caraway seeds (optional) and chill for 12 hours, occasionally turning the beets in the dressing. Drain off some of the liquid before serving.

Russian-Style Pickled Beets with Walnut Sauce

Serves 4-6

> *900g (2 lb) beetroot*
> *250ml (8 fl oz) wine vinegar*
> *5ml (1 tsp) salt*
> *45ml (3 tbs) sugar (or, to taste)*
> *6 peppercorns*
> *5 whole cloves*
> *1 bayleaf*
> *large round lettuce leaves*
> Sauce
> *75g (3 oz) shelled walnuts*
> *2-3 cloves of garlic*
> *5ml (1 tsp) ground coriander*
> *salt and cayenne pepper*
> *45-60ml (3-4 tbs) liquid from the pickled beets*

If the beetroot is purchased with the tops still on, cut them off leaving 2.5cm (1 in) of stem. (Save the tops to cook as a green vegetable.) Wash the beets but do not peel them. Place in a large saucepan and pour on boiling water to half cover. Cook with the lid on over medium heat for 45 minutes, or until tender but still firm (adding more water if necessary).

When cooked, drain the beets, reserving 250ml (8 fl oz) of the liquid. Plunge the beets immediately into cold water. When cool enough to handle, peel and cut into thick slices. Place in a glass storage jar. In a saucepan, combine the reserved liquid and remaining ingredients. Bring to the boil. Pour the liquid over the beets to cover completely. Seal the jar and store in the refrigerator for at least 24 hours before serving.

To make walnut sauce, combine the nuts with the garlic, coriander, salt and cayenne and pound with a mortar and pestle to a smooth paste. Adding 5ml (1 tsp) of beet liquid at a time, stir the paste until it attains the consistency of a thick sauce. Adjust the seasoning. Take about half the prepared quantity of pickled beetroot and chop into thick dice. Mix with the sauce and toss gently. Serve on a bed of crisp lettuce leaves. The remaining quantity of beetroot will keep well in a tightly sealed jar for several weeks.

Remolacha   *Serves 6-8*

Spanish beetroot salad

> *675g (1½ lb) beetroot*
> *450g (1 lb) cold boiled potatoes*
> *4 large spring onions*
> *45ml (3 tbs) olive oil*
> *15ml (1 tbs) wine vinegar*
> *salt and freshly ground pepper*

Wash and scrub the beetroot. Trim the tops to 25cm (1 in). Cook in boiling water for 45 minutes, or until tender but still firm. Drain and plunge immediately into cold water. When cool enough to handle, peel and slice thinly. Slice potatoes into pieces of a similar size.

Chop the spring onion coarsely and place all three ingredients in a salad bowl. Combine oil, vinegar, salt and freshly ground pepper to taste. Pour this dressing over the vegetables and toss gently.

Another variation is made with mayonnaise rather than vinaigrette. Prepare the beetroot and potato as in the above recipe, but instead of spring onion, use 4-5 shallots which have been boiled for 3-5 minutes, and coarsely chopped. Add 4-5 finely chopped anchovy fillets, a dash of cayenne pepper, and enough mayonnaise to bind the ingredients.

Keundae Namul   *Serves 6*

Korean beetroot salad with soy sauce

4 large, uncooked beetroots (if possible, with tops still on)
15ml (1 tbs) soy sauce
15ml (1 tbs) vinegar
a little sesame or peanut oil
5ml (1 tsp) salt
5ml (1 tsp) caster sugar
10ml (2 tsp) white sesame seeds

Wash beetroots. Cut off tops leaving 2.5cm (1 in) stem and set aside. Cook beetroots in boiling water until tender (about 45 minutes).

Meanwhile, chop the green tops and add to the boiling beetroots during the last 15 minutes of cooking. Drain and reserve a little liquid for the dressing. When cool enough to handle, peel and cut the beetroot into thin pieces, approximately 2.5cm (1 in) long. Mix these with the beetroot tops.

Combine the vinegar, salt, sugar and about 15ml (1 tsp) each of oil and beet juice plus the soy sauce. Blend and pour over the vegetables.

Toast the sesame seeds under the grill or in a dry frying pan, shaking the pan occasionally to avoid burning. Crush with a mortar and pestle and add to the salad.

Mix lightly and serve chilled.

Broccoli

Broccoli is actually a type of cauliflower, cultivated originally from a wild cabbage. It was eaten by the Greeks and Romans over 2,000 years ago, but was virtually unknown in America until about the 1920s, when the enterprising D'Arrigo brothers of Northern California began a nationwide promotion for the vegetable.

There are many varieties of broccoli, but the green sprouting kind, often known by its Italian name, *calabrese,* is the best kind for salads. The cooking time should be very carefully monitored so that the flowery heads do not become mushy.

Broccoli makes an attractive addition to a bowl of green salad, its dark green leaves providing an aesthetically pleasing contrast to the paler green lettuce leaves.

Broccoli Vinaigrette   *Serves 4-6*

2 bunches of young, crisp broccoli
100ml (3½ fl oz) olive oil
45ml (3 tbs) lemon juice
15ml (1 tbs) parsley, chopped
15ml (1 tbs) fresh chives, chopped (or 5ml (1 tsp) dried chives)

7ml (½ tbs) fresh tarragon, chopped (or 5ml (1 tsp) dried tarragon)
5ml (1 tsp) grated lemon rind

Wash and trim the broccoli and separate the florets from the stalks. Divide the stalks into quarters and cook gently in a small amount of boiling salted water for 4-5 minutes. Add the florets and cook for a further 5-6 minutes until just tender (*al dente*). Drain and place in a shallow bowl. Mix oil, lemon juice, parsley, chives and tarragon. Pour this dressing over the broccoli while still warm, cover and leave to marinate for at least 4 hours, turning frequently. Chill, and sprinkle with the lemon rind just before serving.

Broccoli with Mayonnaise Dressing   *Serves 4-6*

> *900g (2 lb) fresh broccoli*
> *lemon juice*
> *salt and freshly ground pepper*
> *150ml (¼ pt) white wine*
> *450ml (¾ pt) mayonnaise (see p 30)*
> *3 shallots, finely chopped*
> *15ml (1 tbs) chives, finely chopped*
> Garnish
> *1 hard-boiled egg*

Wash the broccoli in cold water and trim the stems to a maximum length of 8cm (3 in). Boil in a little lightly-salted water for 8-10 minutes, or until just tender. Drain and place in a shallow serving dish. Grind fresh pepper over the broccoli and sprinkle with a few drops of lemon juice.

Put the shallots and wine into a saucepan and cook until the liquid has completely evaporated. Add the shallots and the chopped chives to the mayonnaise and pour over the broccoli.

Chill for 2-3 hours before serving, garnished with sieved hard-boiled egg.

Brussels Sprouts

The Brussels sprout is a member of the cabbage family, producing numerous small heads, instead of one. It was discovered in Belgium by a seventeenth century botanist who described a plant that 'bears fifty heads the size of an egg'.

The sprout was introduced to England in the nineteenth century and is today a favourite accompaniment to the traditional Sunday roast. Though sprouts are not generally considered in the preparation of salads, a little experimentation will bring pleasing rewards: they are delicious when dressed simply with vinaigrette and add unusual variety to a winter mixed salad. When buying sprouts, look for those with firm, compact heads and a bright green colour. Avoid wilted or yellow leaves and heads that have grown puffy.

Brussels Sprout Salad   *Serves 2-3*

> *450g (1 lb) young sprouts*
> *salt and freshly ground pepper*
> *150ml (¼ pt) olive oil*
> *30-45ml (2-3 tbs) wine vinegar*
> *scant 1.25ml (¼ tsp) dry mustard*
> *pinch of sugar*
> *60ml (4 tbs) fresh parsley, finely chopped*
> *30ml (2 tbs) finely chopped onion*

Wash the sprouts thoroughly in cold water, remove any yellow or overblown leaves and trim the butt ends. Cut an 'x' into each stem to ensure quick and even cooking. Place the sprouts in a saucepan of lightly salted, boiling water — just enough to cover the vegetables. Simmer for 5-7 minutes, or until just tender.

While the sprouts are cooking, combine the olive oil, vinegar, sugar and mustard. Beat with a fork and add salt and pepper to taste. Set aside. Drain the sprouts, making sure to remove all excess moisture. While still warm, place in a glass bowl and pour over the dressing. Add the chopped parsley and onion and stir well to blend all ingredients. Allow to marinate for at least 2 hours before serving.

Mixed Sprout Salad   *Serves 4-5*

This is a colourful and crunchy mixture for the winter dinner table.

> *450g (1 lb) small sprouts*
> *1 large leek*
> *4 stalks celery, chopped*
> *1 small red pepper, deseeded and chopped*
> *30ml (2 tbs) fresh parsley, chopped*
> *75-90ml (5-6 tbs) olive oil*
> *20ml (2 tbs) lemon juice*
> *15ml (1 tbs) grated lemon rind*
> *salt and freshly ground pepper*
> optional
> *5-6 water chestnuts, cut into slivers*

Wash and trim the sprouts as described above. Cut the base off the leek, remove any bruised leaves and about 5cm (2 in) of the dark green top

62

leaves. Slice into 5mm (¼ in) rounds and wash thoroughly in a sieve. Drain both vegetables and place in a saucepan of gently boiling, salted water for about 5-7 minutes. Plunge into cold water and drain again.

Place in a large wooden salad bowl with the chopped celery, red pepper and water chestnuts, if desired. Prepare the dressing from the remaining ingredients, mix well and pour over the vegetables. Toss gently and chill before serving.

Cabbage

Cabbage may be one of the most ancient vegetables still grown today; it is certainly one of the most versatile and inexpensive. Both the Celts and the Romans introduced varieties of the plant to the areas they conquered. Some form, possibly kale or collards, was known to the Greeks, who believed that eating cabbage before a banquet would inhibit the inebriating effects of wine.

Cabbage was probably introduced to the New World by the French explorer Jacques Cartier who, in 1541, brought it to Canada where it was cultivated by colonists and Indians alike.

The name cabbage covers a large family of plants, including cauliflower, broccoli and brussels sprouts — all treated separately in this chapter — but the most popular varieties for salad are the white, red and chinese cabbage. White cabbage is generally shredded and eaten raw; likewise for red cabbage, though this is sometimes parboiled to make it more digestible; and chinese cabbage can be shredded raw or broken into larger pieces in the way one would treat a cos lettuce.

Lebanese Cabbage Salad   *Serves 6*

> *450g (1 lb) shredded cabbage*
> *1 large clove garlic*
> *10ml (2 tsp) salt*
> *75ml (2½ fl oz) lemon juice*
> *30-90ml (2-6 tbs) olive oil (to taste)*
> Garnish
> *fresh parsley, finely chopped*

Crush the garlic with the salt and add the lemon juice* and olive oil to taste. Pour over the shredded cabbage, toss thoroughly to cover, chill and serve. Garnish with the chopped parsley.

*Middle Eastern dressings tend to use more lemon juice than the Western palate is accustomed to. Use a little less if you like, but be sure not to completely lose the distinctively Middle Eastern flavour.

Káposzta Saláta *Serves 6-8*

Hungarian cabbage salad

> *900g (2 lb) shredded white cabbage*
> *15ml (1 tbs) salt*
> *75ml (5 tbs) white wine vinegar*
> *45ml (3 tbs) salad oil*
> *10ml (2 tsp) sugar*
> *dash of freshly ground pepper*
> *1 small onion, finely chopped*
> *1 green pepper, chopped*
> *2 medium-sized firm tomatoes*

Remove the outer bruised leaves of the cabbage; rinse, cut into quarters, discarding the core, and shred finely. Place in a large bowl and toss with salt. Allow to stand for one hour, turning occasionally.

Meanwhile, combine the vinegar, oil, sugar and pepper in a small jar. Skin the tomatoes by immersing them in boiling water for a few seconds. Peel and cut each one into eighths. Set aside with the dressing.

After the cabbage has stood, it must be squeezed to remove excess juices. This should be done with the hands, taking a small amount at a time. Place the cabbage in a salad bowl and add the chopped onion and pepper. Shake the dressing until well blended and pour over salad. Using a large spoon and fork, turn and toss the cabbage mixture until it is thoroughly coated with dressing. Garnish with tomato wedges and chill until ready to serve.

Gaghamp Aghstan *Serves 4*

Armenian cabbage salad

> *½ a white cabbage approx 450g (1 lb) shredded*
> *½ a small green pepper, deseeded and thinly sliced*
> *1 small onion, thinly sliced*
> *salt and freshly ground pepper*
> *1 small tomato, seeded and finely chopped*
> *75ml (5 tbs) fresh mint, finely chopped*
> *60ml (4 tbs) olive oil*
> *30ml (2 tbs) freshly squeezed and strained lemon juice*

Combine the cabbage, sliced green pepper, sliced onion, tomato and chopped mint in a salad bowl. Whisk the olive oil and lemon juice until well blended and season with salt and freshly ground pepper. Pour the dressing over the vegetables and toss gently but thoroughly. Chill, toss again, and serve.

Festival Cabbage Salad   *Serves 6-8*

A seventeenth century Scottish recipe

900g (2 lb) white cabbage, coarsely grated
1 medium onion, finely chopped
15ml (1 tbs) chives, finely chopped
1 sprig thyme, finely chopped or 2.5ml (½ tsp) dried thyme
150ml (¼ pt) mayonnaise (see p 30) flavoured with 5ml (1 tsp) of pre-
pared mustard
15-30ml (1-2 tbs) fresh parsley, finely chopped
3 hard-boiled eggs, sliced
1 small tin anchovy fillets, drained and chopped

Mix together the cabbage, onion, chives, thyme and half the parsley. Add
the mustard mayonnaise and blend gently until all ingredients are covered.
Put a generous portion of salad onto individual salad plates and garnish
with anchovy fillets, sliced eggs and a sprinkling of parsley.

Szechwan Cabbage Salad   *Serves 4*

This is actually a pickle, but the Chinese eat it as we would eat a salad.
Szechwan peppercorns are tiny and reddish-brown in colour, with a
strong, pungent aroma. Look for the seeded variety which are sold by
weight in small packages at most Chinese grocery stores. Once opened,
the peppercorns should be transferred to an airtight container to retain
their pungency.

960ml (32 fl oz) water
salt
5ml (1 tsp) Szechwan peppercorns
450g (1 lb) white cabbage
4 dried red chilli peppers
4 cloves garlic, peeled and crushed

Boil the water in a saucepan, adding salt to taste. Remove from heat and
pour into a clean 2l (4 pt) heat-proof jar. Allow to cool. Place the
peppercorns in a frying pan and cook over low heat for about 5 minutes,
shaking them occasionally until they are aromatic. Add to the water.
   Cut the cabbage into pieces approximately 5cm (2 in) square. Rinse
well, drain and shake to remove excess water. Add the cabbage to the
water, followed by the chillies and the crushed garlic. Cover tightly and
store in a cool place for 24 hours before eating. If stored in the refrigerator,
this will keep well for up to 2 weeks.

American Cole Slaw

There are many recipes for this classic American dish. The Dutch settlers of old New York mixed finely shredded cabbage with vinegar for *koolslaa*. The following is a recipe from the settlements of old New England.

> 1 large white cabbage
> 225g (½ lb) grated carrots
> 60ml (4 tbs) grated onion
> 5ml (1 tsp) caraway seeds
>
> Dressing
> 45ml (3 tbs) flour
> 10ml (2 tsp) dry mustard
> 5ml (1 tsp) salt
> 15ml (1 tbs) sugar
> 2 eggs, lightly beaten
> 90ml (6 tbs) vinegar
> 180ml (6 fl oz/3/4c) milk
> 45ml (3 tbs) butter
> 60ml (4 tbs) sour cream

Shred the cabbage into a large bowl. Add cold water to cover and place in the refrigerator for at least 2 hours. Drain and dry well between tea towels. Return the cabbage to a clean bowl and add the carrots, onion and caraway seeds. Set aside, and prepare the dressing as follows. Place the dry ingredients in a saucepan and slowly add the eggs, then milk, blending constantly with a sturdy wire whisk. When the mixture is smooth, add the vinegar and cook over a medium heat, stirring constantly. When the mixture begins to warm through, add the butter and continue to stir until the mixture has thickened. Remove from the heat, add the sour cream and allow to cool. Pour over the vegetables, mix well and serve.

This dressing can be prepared in advance and stored in a refrigerator for several days.

Sauerkraut or Pickled Cabbage

Sauerkraut is finely-shredded white cabbage which has been pickled in brine. It is part of the staple diet in many central and eastern European countries, where most families prepare their own versions in large barrels each year, to be consumed during the winter months.

Nowadays, there are so many excellent prepared varieties available in delicatessens and specialist grocers that I would hardly recommend the effort of making your own, but for the very ambitious, here is an authentic Ukranian recipe from a Russian family cookbook:

Choose sound, mature heads of cabbage with thin leaves. Remove outside leaves, cut out cores. Wash thoroughly with cold water. Cut the cabbage into 0.5cm shreds, or into pieces not longer or wider than 1cm. Place the shredded cabbage into a tub. Combine with the seasoning, spices and salt. Pack.

Spread a layer of clean cabbage leaves (1-2cm thick) on bottom of the barrel. Pack the shredded cabbage firmly into the barrel until it draws juice. Cover the cabbage with a layer of clean cabbage leaves (2-3cm thick). Cover with a clean cloth or cheesecloth. Adjust the wooden lid scalded with boiling water and weight it down. During pickling the level of the liquid must be kept above the wooden lid. Do not use iron items, bricks or rocks for weights. Use a lump of granite washed and scalded beforehand.

Permit the cabbage to stand for 5-6 days in a warm place until the main period of fermentation has ceased. The beginning of the fermentation process is signalled by the appearance of scum on top of the cabbage, and by a change in the brine (it becomes misty). Remove the scum carefully with a skimmer or clean cloth.

After 5-6 days remove the cabbage to a cool place and store. The cabbage will be cured in 40-50 days.

Should a mould appear on the surface of the brine and weight, remove it carefully. Remove the wooden lid and cloth. Wash in water. Cover the barrel again.

Make certain the brine covers the wooden lid.

Use fine salt when preparing sauerkraut. Use 1.5-2 percent of salt per weight of cabbage, ie 150-200g per 10kg of cabbage.

To obtain delicious pickled cabbage add seasoning and spices during the pickling process. By varying the seasoning we get many varieties of sauerkraut or pickled cabbage. To 10kg of cabbage add — 300g carrots or add — 200g carrots, 800g apples; or add — 250g carrots, 500g quince, etc.

Sauerkraut and Cranberry Salad   *Serves 4*

This is a delicious accompaniment to cold duck or cold roast pork.

> *450g (1 lb) sauerkraut*
> *15ml (1 tbs) olive oil*
> *15ml (1 tbs) sugar*
> *1 eating apple, peeled and chopped*
> *2 stalks of celery, diced*
> *100g (4 oz) cranberries, softened in boiling water*

Pour cold water over the sauerkraut, drain, and squeeze out excess liquid.

Place in a large glass bowl and mix with the oil and sugar. Add the diced celery, chopped apple and cranberries. Toss all ingredients until well mixed and serve.

Red Cabbage Salad

Serves 6-8

1 medium-sized, approx 900g (2 lb), red cabbage, coarsely shredded
50g (2 oz) dripping or 90ml (6 tbs) vegetable oil
225g (½ lb) onions, sliced
100g (4 oz) raisins
2 small cooking apples, chopped
30-60ml (2-4 tbs) cider or wine vinegar
sea salt and freshly ground pepper

Heat the dripping or vegetable oil in a large frying pan and cook the onions until just tender and translucent in appearance. Add the shredded cabbage and cover the pan. Cook over a low heat for approximately 10 minutes, then add a little water, the cider, the raisins, apple, sea salt and pepper. Cook for a further 10-15 minutes, then drain off excess liquid. Add additional salt and pepper if necessary, mix well and allow to cool before serving.

Rot Koh Isalat

Serves 8

Bavarian cabbage salad

> *900g (2 lb) red cabbage, shredded*
> *salt*
> *3 rashers bacon, cooked and chopped*
> *5-10ml (1-2 tsp) caraway seeds*
> *10-20ml (2-4 tsp) sugar*
> *45ml (3 tbs) vinegar*
> *45ml (3 tbs) oil*
> optional
> *sour cream*

In a large bowl, mix the shredded cabbage with salt and allow to stand for at least 1 hour. Squeeze to remove excess water. Sprinkle caraway seeds and sugar to taste over the cabbage, then add the vinegar, oil and chopped bacon. Toss well and leave to stand for an hour or so before serving. If desired, a few tablespoons of sour cream may be added to the salad.

Red and Green Cabbage Salad

Serves 4

A lovely decorative salad for a buffet table.

25g (1 oz) seedless raisins

225g (½ lb) green cabbage, coarsely shredded
225g (½ lb) red cabbage, coarsely shredded
75g (3 oz) white rice
vinaigrette (see p 25), made with 120ml (8 tbs) olive oil and 30ml (2 tbs)
vinegar
Garnish
parsley

Soak raisins in cold water for 1 hour to soften. Drain. Boil rice in a large saucepan of lightly salted water for 12-15 minutes, or until just tender. Drain, rinse in cold water, and drain again. When cool, mix with the raisins in a small bowl and pour over one third of the vinaigrette. In a separate bowl, mix the red and green cabbage and dress with the remaining vinaigrette, tossing well. Place the rice in the centre of a large serving dish, surrounded by the cabbage. Garnish with a few sprigs of fresh parsley and serve.

Tricolour Slaw
Serves 8-10

450g (1 lb) white cabbage, finely shredded
225g (½ lb) red cabbage, finely shredded
2-3 large carrots, peeled and finely grated
½ a large white onion, thinly sliced
142ml (5 fl oz) pot of plain yoghurt
45ml (3 tbs) olive oil
30ml (2 tbs) vinegar
salt and freshly ground pepper
30ml (2 tbs) fresh chives, chopped

In a large bowl, mix together the red and white shredded cabbage, the grated carrots and the sliced onion. Blend the oil and vinegar in a bowl, adding salt and pepper to taste. Slowly add the yoghurt, beating continuously until a smooth, creamy consistency is achieved. Pour over the vegetables, add the chives and mix well to ensure all ingredients are evenly moistened. Chill for several hours before serving.

Chinese Cabbage Salad
Serves 4

This unusual member of the cabbage (*brassica*) family is more like a lettuce. It is native to Asia, having been introduced to Europe by eighteenth century missionaries who brought back seeds from the Far East.

Nowadays, chinese cabbage can readily be found at greengrocers and in some supermarkets. It makes an excellent salad on its own or in combination with other greens.

1 head chinese cabbage, thinly sliced or shredded
1 cucumber, peeled and diced
1 large green pepper, diced
30ml (2 tbs) onion, finely chopped
30ml (2 tbs) sesame seeds, toasted
salt and freshly ground pepper
vinaigrette, made with 120ml (8 tbs) olive oil and 30ml (2 tbs) wine
   vinegar, flavoured with 15ml (1 tbs) soy sauce

Place the diced cucumber, lightly salted, in a sieve to drain for 30-45 minutes. In a large bowl, combine the cabbage, cucumber, green pepper and onion. Add the toasted sesame seeds, vinaigrette, pepper and salt (not too much, as the soy sauce is very salty). Mix well and chill. Before serving, garnish with a further sprinkling of toasted sesame seeds. Sesame seeds can be toasted under the grill or in a dry frying pan, shaken at intervals to ensure that the seeds are evenly cooked. They are done when golden brown and beginning to pop.

Carrots

The orange carrot that we eat today is a relative newcomer to the vegetable scene. If you look at Dutch paintings of the sixteenth century, you will see purple and even white carrots. The Dutch also developed the orange variety and about a hundred years later this carrot was introduced to England. The English fondness for the vegetable went well beyond an appreciation of the tasty root; the feathery, fernlike leaves became quite the thing as decoration for female coiffures!

A medicinal value was early attributed to the carrot by the second century Roman physician Galen, who recorded that they helped break wind and scoured the digestive tract. Modern doctors prescribe carrots in the diet as a cure for nightblindness, as it is a vegetable rich in vitamin A, as well as vitamins B, C and calcium.

Grated carrots make wonderfully decorative and nourishing salads in combination with raisins, nuts or cheese. Carrots, peeled and cut into small sticks, make an ideal crudité to serve with dips.

An attractive decoration are carrot curls made with fresh young carrots which have been washed and scraped clean. Using a sharp-edged potato peeler, take a thick scraping along the length of the carrot. Immerse immediately in a bowl of iced water. Repeat the process and chill the curls for several hours before using as a garnish.

Carpetas Elixatas   *Serves 6*

Roman Carrot Salad

900g (2 lb) carrots

75ml (5 tbs) dry white wine
45ml (3 tbs) olive oil
2.5ml (½ tsp) cumin powder
2.5ml (½ tsp) coriander
2.5ml (½ tsp) salt
1.25ml (¼ tsp) freshly ground pepper
1 large Spanish onion, finely chopped

Wash, peel and dice the carrots. Cook in just enough boiling salted water to cover until tender (10-12 minutes). Drain and set aside.

In a small saucepan, gently boil the wine until it is reduced by half. Cool and blend with the olive oil and seasonings. Pour this dressing over the carrots and add the chopped onion. Chill until ready to serve.

Herbed Carrot Salad
Serves 3-4

450g (1 lb) carrots
1 large clove garlic, peeled
0.75-1.25ml (⅛-¼ tsp) ground cinnamon
1.25ml (¼ tsp) ground cumin
2.5ml (½ tsp) paprika
pinch cayenne pepper
juice of 1 lemon
0.75ml (⅛ tsp) granulated sugar
olive oil, to taste
salt
freshly chopped parsley, to garnish

Wash, peel and dice the carrots. Cook in boiling water, to which the peeled garlic has been added, for 10-12 minutes or until barely tender. Drain and set aside.

Combine the spices with the lemon juice, sugar and salt. Mix until thoroughly blended, add to the carrots, and chill.

Just before serving, sprinkle with oil and chopped parsley.

Minted Carrot Salad
Serves 4

450g (1 lb) baby carrots
30ml (2 tbs) vegetable oil
30ml (2 tbs) long grain rice
45-75ml (3-5 tbs) freshly chopped mint
15ml (1 tbs) lemon juice
salt and freshly ground pepper

Wash, lightly scrape the carrots and trim the ends. Slice in half lengthways. Heat the oil in an enamel frying pan, add the carrots and cook gently over

71

low heat for 3 minutes. Stir in the rice and add sufficient water to cover the ingredients. Season with a dash of salt and a few grinds of black pepper.

Cook covered over low heat for about 20 minutes, or until the liquid has evaporated and the carrots are tender.

Remove from the heat and place in a serving dish. Add the fresh mint and lemon juice. Stir and chill before serving.

Moroccan Carrot Salad   *Serves 4*

> *450g (1 lb) carrots*
> *1 large navel orange*
> *30-45ml (2-3 tbs) lemon juice*
> *5ml (1 tsp) orange flower water*
> *5ml (1 tsp) cinammon*
> *10ml (2 tsp) caster sugar*
> *pinch of salt*
> optional
> *50g (2 oz) raisins, soaked for an hour, to soften*

Wash, peel and finely grate the carrots. Peel the orange and carefully remove all the white pith. Divide the orange into segments, removing the flesh from the membranes. Add the segments to the carrots. Into a separate bowl, squeeze the juice from the remainder of the orange. Add the other ingredients and stir thoroughly. Pour over the orange and carrot mixture and chill for an hour before serving. Plumped-up raisins can be added just before the salad is brought to the table.

Cauliflower

Cauliflower is another member of the cabbage family, or, as Mark Twain called it, 'a cabbage with a college education'. Native to the Mediterranean and the Near East, it was introduced to London markets in the early seventeenth century. The British called it 'cyprus coleworts' as most cauliflower then came from Cyprus.   For salads, cauliflower can be used raw or just slightly cooked (*al dente*). The raw florets, containing large quantities of vitamins A, B and C and mineral salts, make a nutritious addition to any selection of crudités.

When choosing cauliflower in the shops, look for compact, white heads with fresh, green leaves. Heads that are loose and spread out are a sure sign of overmaturity.

Insalata di Carolfiore   *Serves 3-4*

Italian cauliflower salad

> *1 large cauliflower with green leaves removed*

5 anchovy fillets, chopped
6 black olives, pitted and chopped
2 red pimentos, chopped
90ml (6 tbs) best olive oil
30ml (2 tbs) freshly squeezed and strained lemon juice
30ml (2 tbs) fresh parsley, finely chopped
30ml (2 tbs) capers
salt and freshly ground pepper

Cook the cauliflower in boiling salted water, until just tender, about 5-8 minutes. Drain and leave until it is cool enough to handle. Separate the florets and arrange in a shallow salad bowl. Add the chopped anchovies, olives and pimentos. Make the dressing from the oil, lemon juice, salt and pepper. Pour over the cauliflower while still warm and toss gently but thoroughly to moisten all ingredients. Allow to stand for 1 hour, toss again, and garnish with chopped parsley and capers.

Gobi ki Sabzi   *Serves 4*

Indian spicy cauliflower

1 large cauliflower, separated into florets
75ml (5 tbs) vegetable oil
5ml (1 tsp) mustard seeds
2.5cm (1 in) piece of green ginger, peeled and finely chopped
1 medium onion, thinly sliced
5ml (1 tsp) turmeric
2.5ml (½ tsp) coriander powder
1 green chilli pepper, finely chopped (see p 243)
freshly squeezed juice of ½ a lemon
salt, to taste
15ml (1 tbs) fresh coriander leaves, chopped (Italian parsley makes an acceptable substitute)

Heat the oil in a large frying pan, add the mustard seeds and cook covered for 2 minutes (the seeds will pop in response to the heat). Add the chopped ginger, chilli pepper, onion, coriander powder and turmeric and cook for a further 3 minutes. Add the cauliflower and salt, stir all ingredients for about a minute, then sprinkle over the lemon juice. Cover the pan and simmer gently for 15 minutes.

Turn into a serving dish and cool. Just before serving, garnish with chopped coriander leaves.

Salade de Choufleurs au Roquefort et Anchois   *Serves 4*

Cauliflower with Roquefort dressing

73

1 whole large cauliflower
French Roquefort dressing (see p 38)
2 hard-boiled eggs, quartered
4 anchovy fillets, a few large lettuce leaves

Trim the cauliflower by removing all the leaves and the tough base. Cook or steam it whole until the stems are tender when pressed with a finger. Drain, cool thoroughly, and place in a deep bowl.

Prepare the Roquefort dressing and pour it over the cauliflower. Leave to stand for 30 minutes, basting frequently.

To serve, place the cauliflower on a serving dish lined with lettuce leaves. Pour over the dressing and surround with hard-boiled eggs and anchovy fillets.

Admiral's Cauliflower *Serves 4-5*

This Norwegian salad makes a particularly nice Spring hors d'oeuvre

1 large cauliflower
75g (3 oz) peeled shrimps or small prawns
150ml (¼ pt) mayonnaise (see p 30)
15ml (1 tbs) olive oil
small bunch of mixed herbs (parsley, chives, basil, tarragon)
2 hard-boiled eggs, sliced
2 medium tomatoes, quartered
sprig of parsley, for garnish

Trim the cauliflower by removing all the leaves and the tough base. Cook in boiling salted water for about 8 minutes, until just tender. Drain and cool.

In the meantime, prepare green mayonnaise sauce. Immerse the mixed herbs in boiling water for about 2 minutes, drain and dry thoroughly between paper towels. Purée them in an electric blender with the olive oil and gradually beat this purée into the mayonnaise.

Place the cauliflower on a round platter, cover with the mayonnaise and sprinkle with shrimps.

Decorate the platter with hard-boiled eggs and tomato wedges. The admiral's hat gets a large parsley feather at the top.

Celery

The original strong, bitter flavour of the wild plant harvested by the Romans mainly for medicinal purposes has been tempered through centuries of cultivation. It was certainly a culinary delicacy by the seventeenth century as John Evelyn tells us: 'This herb celery is for its high and grateful taste ever placed in the middle of the grand sallet at our great men's tables, and at our proctor's feasts, as the grace of the whole board'.

Celery is a popular crudité: it can be served plain, cut into small stalks, or stuffed with a variety of savoury spreads and pastes. It is generally available throughout the year but should be examined closely before purchase. If the stalks are woody and the leaves wilted or yellow, the celery has probably lost its crispness. Celery should be stored in the refrigerator.

Sedano alla Greca   *Serves 4-6*

Celery à la Grecque

> *2 heads celery*
> *150ml (½ pt) court boullion (see p 244)*
> *freshly squeezed and strained juice of 1 lemon*
> *60ml (4 tbs) olive oil*
> *3 bay leaves*
> *15ml (1 tbs) coriander seeds*
> *salt and freshly ground pepper*

Remove any bruised outer stalks from the celery and trim the leaves and base. Cut into 5cm (2 in) lengths and wash well in cold water. Parboil in salted water for 5 minutes. In the meantime, place all other ingredients in a deep frying pan and bring to a gentle boil. Add the celery and cook over low heat until tender, about 10-15 minutes. Remove the celery and place in a shallow dish. Continue cooking the stock until it has reduced by one third. Cool and pour over the celery.

Celery Salad with Coconut Dressing   *Serves 4*

Coconut cream (see p 243) is commonly used to dress salads in many south-east Asian countries. This salad, from Sri Lanka, is served as an accompaniment to meat dishes.

> *1 large head celery*
> *1 small green pepper, finely chopped*
> *2.5ml (½ tsp) salt*
> *15ml (1 tbs) green ginger, finely chopped*
> *15ml (1 tbs) freshly squeezed lemon juice*
> *15ml (1 tbs) onion juice*
> *2.5ml (½ tsp) paprika*
> *coconut cream from 1 coconut (see p 243)*

Trim the leaves and base from the celery and wash thoroughly. Drain, dry and chop into small dice. Place in a bowl and add the chopped green pepper. In a separate small dish, blend together the lemon juice, salt, paprika, onion juice and chopped ginger. Pour over the celery and leave to stand for 1 hour, tossing occasionally to re-moisten all ingredients. Just before serving, pour on the coconut cream and toss again.

Salade de Céléri à l'Ancienne
Serves 4-6

> *2 heads of celery*
> *3 hard-boiled eggs*
> *75ml (¼ pt) mayonnaise (see p 30), strongly flavoured with Dijon*
>   *mustard*
> *3 small tomatoes, quartered*
> *6 each of green and black stoned olives*
> *35g (1½ oz) shelled walnuts*

Trim leaves and base from celery and wash thoroughly. Drain, dry and cut into strips approximately 2.5cm (1 in) long.

Mash the hard-boiled egg yolks with a fork and slowly add the mustard mayonnaise to achieve a smooth paste. Cut the whites into strips the same size as the celery. In a large bowl, blend together the celery, egg white and mayonnaise. Leave to stand in the refrigerator for several hours. Before serving, stir in the walnuts and turn out the mixture onto a shallow platter. Decorate with tomato wedges and olives.

Celery Leaf Salad

The young green leaves from the heads of celery can also be used to make delicious salads. They are especially tasty in combination with fennel and watercress. Dress with a simple French vinaigrette.

Celery Knob or Celeriac

Long popular on the Continent, celeriac has recently gained wider favour in Britain. Its extremely high iron content makes it a wonderfully nourishing winter vegetable which can be eaten raw or cooked. *Céléri remoulade* is the famous French hors d'oeuvre made from raw shredded celeriac mixed with a well-seasoned sauce remoulade, but try one of these less familiar recipes.

Sellerisalat
Serves 8-10

Danish celeriac salad

> *3 medium-sized celeriac*
> *juice of ½ freshly squeezed lemon*
> *120ml (4 fl oz) double cream, whipped*
> *120ml (4 fl oz) mayonnaise (see p 30)*

5ml (1 tsp) prepared mustard
salt and freshly ground pepper
30ml (2 tbs) fresh parsley, chopped

Peel the celeriac to remove the knobbly outer skin. Cut into slivers as thin as possible, about 1mm (1/16 in). Discard the woody core. Immerse the pieces immediately in water with the lemon juice added, to prevent discolouration. Combine the whipped cream, mayonnaise and mustard, and season to taste with salt and freshly ground pepper. Drain the celeriac and fold into this dressing. Chill for at least 2 hours. Before serving, garnish with freshly chopped parsley.

Celeriac Salad with Cubed Ham   *Serves 6*

900g (2 lb) celeriac, peeled
15ml (1 tbs) Dijon mustard
5ml (1 tsp) finely grated horseradish
2 small dill pickles, finely chopped
15ml (1 tbs) white wine vinegar
225ml (7½ fl oz) mayonnaise (see p 30)
30ml (2 tbs) fresh parsley, finely chopped
15ml (1 tbs) fresh chives, finely chopped
100g (4 oz) ham, finely cubed
1.25ml (¼ tsp) ground white pepper
salt

To prevent discolouration, immerse the peeled celeriac in water to which lemon juice or vinegar has been added. In a large pan, bring to a rapid boil enough salted water to cover the vegetable by at least 5cm (2 in). Add the celeriac and cook until tender when pierced with a fork, approximately 20-30 minutes. Drain, and when cool enough to handle, cut into small cubes, place in a serving bowl and sprinkle with lemon juice.

Combine the mustard, horseradish, pickles and vinegar and blend with the mayonnaise. Add to the celeriac. Season with salt and pepper, then add the parsley, chives and cubed ham.

Toss gently and chill for at least 2 hours before serving.

Salata De Telina   *Serves 4-6*

Romanian celeriac salad

1 large celeriac
75ml (5 tbs) olive oil
15ml (1 tbs) wine vinegar
salt and freshly ground pepper
30ml (2 tbs) fresh parsley, finely chopped

Garnish

4 small sour pickles, a few black olives

Wash and peel the celeriac. Cook as in previous recipe. Remove from the water, drain and cool. Cut crosswise into round slices about 2mm (⅛ in) thick. Mix the oil and vinegar with salt and freshly ground pepper to taste. Pour over the celeriac, add the chopped parsley and toss. Allow to stand for at least an hour, tossing again from time to time.

To serve, arrange on a shallow platter and garnish with pickles and olives.

Corn

Every American schoolchild knows the story of the friendly Indian named Squanto who showed the pilgrim settlers how to plant corn with a fish head under each mound for fertiliser. Corn was certainly the most important staple crop in the early colonies, but its historical importance goes back to the pre-Columbian civilisations of South and Central America. The mythology of these early cultures has a plethora of legends about gods, goddesses and sacred animals bringing corn as a gift to man.

Corn has become increasingly popular in Britain, but as it needs a lot of sun to ripen, can only be grown successfully in southern England and in warm summers.

To prepare corn off the cob for salads, hold the cobs downwards and run a sharp knife down the length of the ears, as close to the cob as possible. The kernels will need only a brief cooking period in a little lightly salted boiling water.

Succotash   *Serves 4*

Corn with broad beans

A classic North American Indian dish.

> *5-6 ears of corn*
> *450g (1 lb) broad beans*
> *salt and freshly ground pepper*
> *60ml (4 tbs) vegetable oil*
> *15ml (1 tbs) cider or wine vinegar*
> optional
> *30ml (2 tbs) chives, chopped*

Shell the beans and cook in boiling salted water for about 5 minutes. Drain and set aside. Prepare the corn as described above and cook in a little lightly salted boiling water for a few minutes. Drain and place in a

78

salad bowl with the beans. Mix the oil, vinegar, salt and fres
pepper with the chives, if desired, and blend well. Pour over th
and toss. Serve while still slightly warm.

Crunchy Corn Salad

> *8 ears of corn*
> *225g (½ lb) fresh bean sprouts*
> *3 stalks celery, finely chopped*
> *1 large red pepper, diced*
> *4 large spring onions, sliced*
> *90ml (6 tbs) olive oil*
> *30ml (2 tbs) white wine vinegar*
> *75g (3 oz) shelled roasted peanuts*
> *salt and freshly ground pepper*
> optional
> *1 clove garlic, crushed*

Prepare and cook corn as described above. Drain and cool. In a large bowl, mix the corn, bean sprouts, chopped celery, red pepper and spring onions. Mix together the oil, vinegar, salt, pepper and garlic, if desired, and pour over the vegetables. Toss and chill for at least an hour. Just before serving, add the roasted peanuts and toss again.

This is a colourful and filling dish to accompany cold meats and poultry. A richer variation can be made by substituting a dressing of mayonnaise and sour cream (in a 2:1 ratio) for the vinaigrette.

Courgettes (Zucchini)

These small cultivated vegetable marrows are members of the squash family. In the United States, the Italian name, zucchini, is more commonly used.

Courgettes are best eaten when young, and should not be stored too long after purchase. They are delicious either cooked or raw.

Courgettes à la Grecque   *Serves 4-6*

> *900g (2 lb) small courgettes*
> *1 large onion, finely chopped*
> *1 large clove garlic, finely chopped*
> *150ml (¼ pt) dry white wine*
> *150ml (¼ pt) water*
> *salt*
> *90ml (6 tbs) olive oil*
> *12 coriander seeds*

79

12 black peppercorns
freshly squeezed and strained juice of 1 lemon
bouquet garni
45ml (3 tbs) fresh parsley, finely chopped

Wipe the courgettes with a damp cloth. Trim the ends and slice thickly crosswise. Set aside.

In a large pan or casserole, heat 45ml (3 tbs) of olive oil and add the finely chopped onion and garlic. Sauté until transparent. Add the wine, water, bouquet garni, coriander seeds, peppercorns, lemon juice, and salt to taste. Bring to the boil and simmer gently for 5 minutes. Add the courgettes to this stock and continue cooking over a low heat for a further 10-12 minutes, or until just tender.

With a large slotted spoon, remove the courgettes and place in a deep serving dish. Discard the bouquet garni and continue boiling until the liquid is reduced by half. Pour over the vegetables and chill for at least an hour. Just before serving, add the remaining olive oil. Check the seasoning, adding more salt and pepper if required, and garnish with chopped parsley and a sprinkling of lemon juice.

Kolokythia Yiachni   *Serves 6-8*

Greek stewed courgettes

A delicious hors d'oeuvre for summer, when fresh mint and dill are available.

900g (2 lb) small courgettes
150ml (¼ pt) olive oil
2 large onions, coarsely chopped
450g (1 lb) ripe tomatoes
5ml (1 tsp) sugar
150ml (¼ pt) water
15ml (1 tbs) fresh dill, finely chopped
10ml (2 tsp) fresh mint, finely chopped
salt and freshly ground pepper

Trim the ends of the courgettes but leave them whole if they are small; otherwise, cut them in half. Heat the oil in a large pan or casserole and gently fry the onions for 5 minutes, until translucent. Skin the tomatoes by immersing in boiling water for several seconds, and either sieve them or put them in a blender to make a smooth purée. Add to the onions, along with the sugar and cook for 10 minutes. Stir in the water, bring to a gentle boil and add the courgettes, herbs and seasonings. Cover and simmer gently for about 20-30 minutes, until the courgettes are quite tender.

Cool, adjust the seasoning, and chill until ready to serve.

Ensalada de Calabacita   *Serves 4-6*

Mexican courgette salad

In Mexico, this recipe is often prepared using *chayote*, a vegetable pear, instead of courgettes. The *cebollas encurtidas*, a kind of Mexican relish, is well worth the extra effort to make this salad an authentically spicy Mexican dish.

> *675g (1½ lb) courgettes*
> *1 firm avocado, peeled and cut into strips*
> *1 small packet, approx 85g (3½ oz), cream cheese*
> *90ml (6 tbs) olive oil*
> *5ml (1 tsp) oregano*
> *8 green olives*
> *30ml (2 tbs) wine vinegar*
> *salt and freshly ground pepper*
> *cebollas encurtidas (see below)*

Trim the ends of the courgettes and slice thickly crosswise. Cook in lightly salted boiling water for 5-8 minutes, or until just tender. Drain, cool and place in a large bowl. Add the strips of avocado. Blend together the oil, vinegar, salt, pepper and oregano. Pour over the vegetables and toss gently. Garnish with *cebollas,* olives and strips of cream cheese.

Cebollas Encurtidas: In a 480ml (16 oz) glass jar, place 1 large thinly sliced onion, 10 peppercorns, 2.5ml (½ tsp) oregano, 2 cloves garlic (peeled and sliced), and 2.5ml (½ tsp) salt. Pour over this mixture approximately 210ml (7 fl oz) of wine vinegar and water mixture, in 1:2 ratio. Cover tightly and store in a cool place for at least 48 hours.
    If kept in a tightly sealed jar, *cebollas encurtidas* will last indefinitely.

Cucumber

The cucumber is grown throughout the world and plays a versatile role in almost every national cuisine. It is said to have originated in the valleys of India between the Bay of Bengal and the Himalayan mountains – and some of the most interesting recipes I have included here come from Asia and the Far East. In fact, the cucumber was cultivated by most of the ancient civilisations. A Roman naturalist described a highly sophisticated method for growing it out of season for the Emperor Tiberius, who demanded that cucumber be available every day of the year. The Emperor Charlemagne included it in his imperial vegetable garden and Columbus brought cucumber seeds to Haiti in 1494. Cucumbers were not, however, introduced to England until the late sixteenth century.

There are two varieties of cucumber generally cultivated today in Britain and the United States — the slightly irregular-shaped and thick-skinned ridge cucumber, easily grown at home, and the long smooth-skinned variety, greenhouse-grown and the type most commonly found in shops. Cucumbers are rich in vitamins B and C and because of their high water content, lack of carbohydrates and fats, are an excellent low-calorie addition to slimming diets.

Tip Cucumbers can be bitter at the blossom end. To avoid spreading the bitter taste, remember to cut a cucumber in half first and peel it from the cut edge to within 1.75cm (½ in) of the ends. To remove some of the water from cucumbers, which is essential when mixing with mayonnaise, yoghurt or other creamy dressings — put the peeled, sliced cucumbers in a sieve or colander, sprinkle with salt and leave to drain for at least half an hour, shaking occasionally. Rinse to remove salt, but make sure the cucumbers are quite dry before dressing.

Aqurkesalat   *Serves 6-8*

Danish pickled cucumbers

> *2-3 cucumbers*
> *10ml (2 tsp) salt*
> *180ml (6 fl oz) cider or wine vinegar*
> *10-20ml (2-4 tsp) sugar, to taste*
> *1.25ml (¼ tsp) ground white pepper*
> *10ml (2 tsp) fresh dill, finely chopped, or 10ml (2 tsp) dried dill*
> optional
> *10ml (2 tsp) fresh parsley, chopped*

Wash and peel the cucumbers. Slice into paperthin rounds (a vegetable slice is best for this, if you have one). Place the slices in a deep bowl, sprinkle with salt, and cover with a plate directly on top of the cucumbers. Weight this down with something heavy and leave to stand at room temperature for approximately 2 hours. Turn the cucumbers into a sieve or colander and drain thoroughly, squeezing out any remaining juice.

Combine the vinegar, sugar, salt and pepper and pour over the cucumbers. Add the chopped dill, correct the seasoning and chill for several hours before serving. If desired, sprinkle chopped parsley over the cucumber just before bringing to the table.

Kyurimomi   *Serves 3-4*

Japanese cucumber salad

Top: Rot Koh Isalat; *left:* Raw Mushroom and Orange Salad; *bottom:* Herring Salad; *right:* Aqurkesalat

Top: Tropical Fruit Salad; *left:* Hearts of Palm Salad; *bottom left:* Cebollas Encurtidas; *bottom:* Ensalada de Calabacita; *right:* Hawaiian Stuffed Pawpaws

The Western distinction between cooked vegetables and fresh salads is largely ignored by the Japanese. When cooked at all, vegetables are only cooked briefly and even then, often served cold.

Many vegetables are marinated in vinegar and dressed with shoyu sauce. This recipe is topped with toasted sesame seeds and makes an excellent accompaniment to grilled fish or as a side dish with the Japanese *sashimi*, sliced raw fish.

> 1 large cucumber
> 5ml (1 tsp) salt
> 150ml (¼ pt) vinegar
> 30ml (2 tbs) sugar
> 30ml (2 tbs) light shoyu sauce★
> 15ml (1 tbs) white sesame seeds

★Soy sauce can be used as a substitute for *shóyu* sauce, which is the same thing. However, soy sauces produced in the West are much thicker and stronger than the Japanese varieties. *Usukuchi*, a light and delicately flavoured *shóyu*, is best for this recipe. Supermarket soy sauce can be substituted, but it should be used more sparingly.

Wash the cucumber and slice, unpeeled, into paperthin rounds. Sprinkle lightly with salt and place in a colander or sieve to drain for 30 minutes. If a plate is placed on top of the cucumber and occasionally pressed down hard, even more liquid can be removed. Place cucumber in a clean tea towel and pat dry. Transfer to a bowl or dish. Mix together the vinegar, sugar, *shóyu* (or soy) sauce. Pour over the cucumber and toss gently.

Toast the sesame seeds in a dry frying pan, shaking constantly until they begin to jump (they can also be tosated under the grill). Remove from the heat and crush with a mortar and pestle. Sprinkle over the cucumber and serve.

Khira Ka Raita   *Serves 6-8*

Indian cucumber and curd

> 2 very large cucumbers
> 600ml (1 pt) curd or strained yoghurt (see p 246)
> salt
> 3 green chillies, seeded and finely chopped (see p 243)
> 2.5ml (½ tsp) chilli powder
> 5ml (1 tsp) fresh coriander leaves, finely chopped (parsley is an acceptable
>   substitute)
> 5ml (1 tsp) cumin seeds, roasted and crushed

Peel and grate the cucumber, salt lightly and leave to drain in a sieve or colander for at least half an hour. Meanwhile, mix together the powdered chilli and pounded cumin seeds. Add the chopped green chillies and coriander and blend all the seasonings with the curd or strained yoghurt. When the cucumber is ready, rinse off the salt, pat dry in a tea towel and add to the other ingredients.

Serve with curries or tandoori dishes.

Michoteta   *Serves 4-6*

Middle-Eastern cucumber and cream cheese

Feta can be used on its own for this salad, or combined with a small quantity of yoghurt or cottage cheese for those who find it too strong.

> *225g (8 oz) Feta (or Feta/cottage cheese or yoghurt mixture)*
> *juice of 1 lemon*
> *30ml (2 tbs) olive oil*
> *a large cucumber, peeled and diced*
> *freshly ground black pepper*
> *1 medium-sized onion, finely chopped*

Place the peeled and diced cucumber, lightly salted, in a sieve or colander to drain for 15-20 minutes.

Crumble the feta with 15ml (1 tbs) water and using a fork, blend in the lemon juice, olive oil and other cheese, if desired. Add the chopped onion and cucumber and season to taste with freshly ground pepper.

Cacik (see p 152)

Thanthat   *Serves 8*

Burmese cucumber salad

This unusual method of preparing cucumbers can also be used for other crunchy vegetables, such as cabbage, green beans and bean sprouts. It makes a decorative addition to a buffet table of oriental dishes.

> *2-3 cucumbers*
> *45-60ml (3-4 tbs) wine vinegar*
> *salt*
> *150ml (¼ pt) sesame oil*
> *1 large onion, finely chopped*
> *6-7 cloves garlic, thinly sliced*
> *5ml (1 tsp) ground turmeric*
> *30ml (2 tbs) mixed roasted black and white sesame seeds*

Peel the cucumbers, remove the seeds and cut into matchstick strips about 2.5cm (1 in) long. Place these in boiling water to which 15ml (1 tbs of wine vinegar has been added. Bring back to the boil and cook for a few minutes until the cucumber appears transparent. Drain in a sieve or colander, sprinkle lightly with salt and set aside. Heat the oil in a large frying pan. When very hot, fry the onion until golden brown. Remove onion and repeat the process with the garlic slivers. Next add the turmeric to the oil (it will turn bright yellow) and then the salt and half the sesame seeds. Fry for a few minutes. Remove this dressing from the pan and leave to cool.

Just before serving, add the vinegar to the dressing, a little at a time and tasting after each addition. Add the cucumbers, stir, and turn the mixture, pyramid fashion, on to a serving plate. Surround with the fried garlic and onion and sprinkle with the remaining sesame seeds.

Spicy Tropical Cucumbers

Serves 4-5

> *2 medium-sized cucumbers*
> *5ml (1 tsp) salt*
> *1 large clove garlic, crushed*
> *45-60ml (3-4 tbs) lime juice, freshly squeezed*
> *15ml (1 tbs) green chilli peppers, finely chopped*
> Garnish
> *zest of lime, a few sprigs of parsley*

Peel the cucumbers, remove the seeds, and chop coarsely. Place in a sieve or colander, sprinkle with salt and leave to drain for 20 minutes. To make the dressing, mix together the crushed garlic, lime juice and chopped chillies. Turn the cucumbers into a bowl, add the dressing and toss. Chill and serve garnished with lime zest and parsley.

Fennel

Not to be confused with bitter fennel — a tall, wild herb — Florence fennel or *finocchio*, the type available in supermarkets, has large white bulbous roots and short round stalks topped with soft, feathery leaves. It has the same crunchy texture as celery, but its own distinctly sweet, aniseed flavour.

Choose bulbs that are solid, crisp and pale green; avoid those which have turned dark green.

Fennel makes an unusual addition to winter salads. It tastes delicious with fruits as well as vegetables.

Fennel with Orange Salad

Serves 4-6

An excellent salad to serve with duck or game.

85

2 large bulbs of fennel
3 large oranges
60ml (4 tbs) sunflower (or corn) oil
30ml (2 tbs) lemon juice
15ml (1 tbs) white wine vinegar
1 large pinch caster sugar
freshly ground pepper

Cut the fennel into 5mm (¼ in) slices and set aside. Remove the peel and pith from 2 of the oranges and divide into segments; grate approximately 10ml (2 tsp) of rind from the third and squeeze out the juice. Put the fennel and orange segments into a salad bowl, arranging them decoratively in layers.

In a separate bowl, mix the orange juice and rind with the remaining ingredients. Blend with a wire whisk and pour over the salad. Season with freshly ground pepper.

Fennel with Anchovies   *Serves 4-6*

2 large bulbs of fennel
1 small bunch of watercress
1 hard-boiled egg, quartered
1 tomato, cut into small wedges
4 anchovy fillets, cut into small pieces
90ml (6 tbs) olive oil
30ml (2 tbs) lemon juice
salt and freshly ground pepper

Cut the fennel into 5mm (¼ in) slices and place in a large salad bowl. Wash, drain and remove the damaged stalks from the watercress. Mix with the fennel. Add the anchovies and garnish with the egg and tomato wedges. Mix the oil, lemon juice, salt and pepper and pour over the salad just before serving.

Fennel à la Grecque

The two *à la grecque* recipes given in the mushroom section (pp 93-94) can be adapted for fennel. Trim the feathery leaves from the bulbs before preparing them for cooking, and use as a garnish when serving.

Hearts of Palm

These tender young shoots from a variety of palm tree are a great delicacy. In their native tropical climates they are widely consumed fresh in salads and as a vegetable. In most of Europe and North America they are bought pre-cooked in tins, preserved in lightly salted water.

Hearts of palm make a beautiful hors d'oeuvre, dressed with a herby vinaigrette and garnished with chopped pimento or tomato. Green mayonnaise (p 32) and sauce rémoulade (p 33) also go well with hearts of palm.

For something extra special, place two thick slices of avocado pear on each individual salad plate. On top of these, put one (or two, if the budget allows) palm heart. Garnish with a tablespoon of sieved hard-boiled egg, and sprinkle over the top a heaped teaspoonful of red lumpfish roe. Decorate with a sprig of parsley and a wedge of tomato and serve with a sauceboat of mayonnaise or vinaigrette.

Kohlrabi

Although similar in appearance and flavour to the turnip, kohlrabi is not a root: it is a swollen stem. It is native to Northern Europe and has been known since the sixteenth century — yet it remains something of a novelty to most British and American cooks.

Choose only very young vegetables, approximately 5cm (2 in) in diameter, with thin skins.

Kohlrabi, like turnip, can be grated raw for salads, sliced and marinated in French dressing, or cut into sticks, lightly steamed, cooled, and served with *bagna cauda* sauce (see p 39).

Oriental Kohlrabi Salad   *Serves 4*

225g (8 oz) kohlrabi, washed and peeled
3 stalks celery, washed and sliced into 1cm (½ in) pieces
3 large spring onions, washed and trimmed (with at least 5cm (3 in) of
   stem preserved) and thinly sliced
45ml (3 tbs) oriental sesame oil
30ml (2 tbs) light soy sauce
2.5ml (½ tsp) caster sugar
5ml (1 tsp) Tabasco sauce
salt

Coarsely grate the kohlrabi and place in a deep glass bowl. Sprinkle lightly with salt and allow to stand for half an hour. Rinse several times in cold water and turn into a sieve or colander to drain.

In a separate small bowl, blend the soy sauce, sugar and Tabasco. Gradually add the oil while whisking constantly with a fork.

Dry the glass bowl and return the kohlrabi. Add the celery, spring onion and the dressing. Toss well to thoroughly coat all ingredients. Chill for about an hour, toss again and serve.

Leeks

If leekes you like, but do their smelle dis-leeke
Eat onyons, and you shall not smelle the leeke;
If you of onyons would the scente expelle,
Eat garlicke, that shall drown the onyon's smelle.

The Philosopher's Banquet, (1633)

The advice in this verse is somewhat misleading. Leeks are actually the mildest and most delicately flavoured members of the onion family. Their ancestry dates back to ancient times, when they were cultivated by most of the early Mediterranean civilisations. The Romans were especially fond of leeks and the vain Emperor Nero is said to have eaten them to improve his singing voice.

The leek figures most importantly in Welsh history. In 640 A.D. the Welsh defeated the Saxons, a victory partly attributed to the leeks pinned to their hats — which prevented them from attacking one another by mistake. Ever since, the leek has been the Welsh national emblem.

When choosing leeks, look for smallish tender ones with several inches of blanched or white skin at the root end, and fresh, green tops.

Leeks must be washed thoroughly under cold running water to remove all the grit. If a recipe calls for whole leeks, it is a good idea to first stand them, green ends down, in cold water for half an hour. Then rinse under a running tap.

Prassa Me Domata *Serves 4-5*

Greek-style leeks

> *900g (2 lb) leeks*
> *225g (8 oz) canned tomatoes*
> *240ml (8 fl oz) stock or broth*
> *1 medium-sized onion, coarsely chopped*
> *1 stalk celery, chopped*
> *30ml (2 tbs) fresh parsley, chopped*
> *5ml (1 tsp) oregano*
> *45ml (3 tbs) vegetable oil*
> *30ml (2 tbs) lemon juice*
> *salt and freshly ground pepper*

Trim the stem ends of the leeks and remove the tough green tops. Wash thoroughly and cut into 2.5cm (1 in) slices. Soak in hot water for 5-10 minutes then drain. In a large enamel saucepan, combine the tomatoes, stock, onion, celery, parsley, oregano and oil. Add the leeks, season with salt and pepper and cook over a low heat for 12-15 minutes, or until the

88

leeks are tender, adding the lemon juice during the last 5 minutes of cooking.

Remove the vegetables from the pan and bring the liquid to a rapid boil, cooking until the quantity has been reduced by one-third. Add to the leeks and chill for several hours before serving.

Porros in Baca   *Serves 4-5*

Leeks and olives

This is a recipe reputedly to have graced the banquet tables of Imperial Rome.

> *8 young crisp leeks*
> *180ml (6 fl oz) white wine*
> *45ml (3 tbs) olive oil*
> *1.25-2.5ml (¼-½ tsp) cumin*
> *1.25-2.5ml (¼-½ tsp) coriander*
> *1.25ml (¼ tsp) caraway seeds*
> *0.75ml (⅛ tsp) freshly ground black pepper*
> *16 green olives, pitted and stuffed*

Rinse the leeks and trim about 7.5cm (3 in) from the root end. Trim the darker green tops to remove any bruised leaves. Cut the leeks into 5mm (¼ in) slices and wash well. Drain.

Put the wine, oil and seasonings to taste into a saucepan and bring to a gentle boil. Add the leeks and simmer until tender (10-12 minutes). In the meantime, chop the olives coarsely. Add these to the leeks as soon as they are removed from the heat. Refrigerate in a covered container until serving.

Persian Leeks with Lemon and Sugar   *Serves 4-5*

In her book *Middle Eastern Food*, Claudia Roden describes the 'similarity between the early philosophy of the Persians and principles of harmony which they apply to their food . . . Both ancient and modern Persian dishes blend opposite flavours and textures, coupling sweet with sour or spicy, strong with mild'.

This is one of her sweet and sour recipes which makes an unusual first course or an excellent accompaniment to spicy meat dishes.

> *900g (2 lb) leeks*
> *2-3 cloves garlic, crushed*
> *15ml (1 tbs) sugar*
> *45-60ml (3-4 tbs) corn or nut oil*
> *juice of 1-2 lemons*

Wash the leeks carefully, removing any grit. Cut off the tough green part of the leaves. Cut the remainder into longish slices. Fry the garlic and sugar in hot oil until the sugar becomes slightly caramelised. Add the leeks and turn them over a moderate heat until they colour lightly. Sprinkle with lemon juice and stew gently, covered, until tender. Cool and chill until ready to serve.

Leeks Vinaigrette   *Serves 4*

> *8 young thin leeks*
> *60ml (4 tbs) olive oil*
> *15ml (1 tbs) lemon juice*
> *salt and freshly ground pepper*
> *pinch of sugar*

Trim roots and coarse green top leaves and remove any damaged outer leaves. Clean as described above by running the leeks under a cold tap and then immersing them in cold water.

Cook the leeks whole in just enough boiling salted water to cover, for 10 minutes, or until just tender. Drain and place on a serving dish to cool.

Mix the oil, lemon juice, salt, pepper and sugar, and pour over the leeks just before serving.

Garnished with a little crumbled hard-boiled egg and chopped parsley, leeks vinaigrette is a veritable 'poor man's asparagus'.

Mushrooms

Few vegetables arrive at the table steeped in such history, legend and myth as the mushroom. 'Food of the gods' to more than one ancient civilisation, the mushroom has been as much feared as enjoyed — and not without cause. Of the 38,000 known varieties, there are sufficient fatally poisonous and hallucinogenic types to arouse suspicion and awe. Some famous victims of mushroom poisoning include the Roman emperors Tiberius and Claudius, Russia's Alexander I, Pope Clement VIII and France's Charles V.

The word mushroom comes from the French *mousseron* by way of the late Latin *mussiriones*, first noted by the sixth century Anthrimus, doctor to the Ostrogoth King Theodoric ('Fungi of all kinds', he told the king, 'are heavy and hard to digest. The better kinds are mushrooms (*mussiriones*) and truffles').* However, the actual cultivation of mushrooms as a proper crop did not begin until the seventeenth century when the French botanist Marchant was able to demonstrate a suitable method.

Agaricus bisporus is the most popular variety grown today throughout Europe and America for market consumption. Alas, the tastier field mushroom perishes too easily to be successful as a commercial crop.

90

Mushrooms are sold in three grades: 'button' mushrooms are the smallest — crisp, white and fresh-tasting; 'cup' are medium-sized but still retain the half-spherical shape of their smaller cousins; and 'flat' or 'open' mushrooms are the large, mature variety, generally strongest in flavour.

Mushrooms should be cleaned with as little water as possible — a quick rinse under the tap will generally remove the loosely clinging dirt, or they can be gently wiped clean with a moistened kitchen towel. They do not need to be peeled, although the woody bottom of the stem should be removed.

A large variety of dried mushrooms play an important role in Oriental cooking. Their colour varies from black to speckled brown or grey and they must be soaked in hot water for at least 30 minutes before being used. The stems are always discarded, but the soaking water can be added to stock for cooking. *Mo-er* or 'cloud ear' mushrooms are a szechuan speciality. They are thin and brittle dry chips which, after soaking, expand into clusters of dark brown petals.

Chinese dried mushrooms are available at oriental grocery stores; the continental variety may be substituted but the flavour is quite different from the Chinese dried mushroom.

The Mushroom Feast, Jane Grigson

Insalata di Funghi   *Serves 4*

Italian raw mushroom salad

A simple and delicious way to eat fresh young mushrooms. Vary by garnishing with different combinations of freshly chopped herbs — parsley, chives, basil, coriander, or serve Genoese-style by garnishing with a few finely-chopped anchovy fillets.

> *450g (1 lb) white button mushrooms*
> *90-120ml (6-8 tbs) best olive oil*
> *juice of 1 small lemon*
> *salt and freshly ground pepper*
> optional
> *1 small garlic clove*
> *3-4 anchovy fillets*

Trim the woody bottoms from the mushroom stems, then wash and dry the caps, but do not peel. Arrange in a salad bowl. Mix the oil, lemon juice, freshly ground pepper and crushed garlic, if desired. Pour over the salad, toss gently and chill before serving. Salt should be sprinkled on the salad at the very last minute along with the optional anchovy fillets.

Raw Mushroom and Orange Salad   *Serves 4-5*

A traditional English salad which makes a splendid accompaniment to poultry and game

> *450g (1 lb) large flat-capped mushrooms*
> *4 medium oranges*
> *1 small round or webb lettuce, washed and dried*
> *90-120ml (6-8 tbs) olive oil*
> *15ml (1 tbs) lemon juice*
> *30ml (2 tbs) white wine vinegar*
> *1 clove garlic, finely chopped*
> *salt and freshly ground pepper*
> Garnish
> *chopped walnuts*

Trim the woody bottoms from the mushroom stems, then wash and dry gently with a tea towel. Slice thinly and place in a bowl. Squeeze the juice from one orange over the mushrooms, sprinkle with salt and pepper and set aside.

Peel the 3 remaining oranges, removing all the pith. With a very sharp knife, slice them thinly crosswise. Line the bottom of a shallow dish or platter with crisp lettuce leaves and sprinkle with a few drops of oil. Follow with a layer of orange slices and then mushrooms. Repeat the orange and mushroom layers then dress with oil and lemon juice, and salt and pepper. Chill for at least an hour. Just before serving, garnish well with chopped walnuts.

Mushroom and Pepper Salad   *Serves 6*

> *450g (1 lb) button mushrooms*
> *2 green and 2 red peppers, approximately 125g (5 oz) each*
> *45ml (3 tbs) fresh parsley, chopped*
> *90-120ml (6-8 tbs) olive oil*
> *15ml (1 tbs) lemon juice*
> *30ml (2 tbs) white wine vinegar*
> *1 clove garlic, finely chopped*
> *salt and freshly ground pepper*

Skin the peppers by placing them under the grill until they begin to turn black and blister. Keep turning to ensure that all sides are done. When cool enough to handle, peel off the skins under a cold running tap. Cut the peppers in half and remove the seeds and membrane. Slice thinly and place in a glass salad bowl.

Wipe the mushrooms with a damp tea towel or wet paper towel. Trim the woody bottoms from the stems, then slice thinly and add to the peppers.

In a separate bowl, mix the oil, lemon juice, vinegar and finely chopped garlic. Season with salt and pepper and add half the chopped parsley. Pour this dressing over the salad, toss well and garnish with the remaining parsley.

Salade de Champignons Quercynoise   *Serves 4*

Choose very fresh, large flat mushrooms or, if you live in the country, pick field mushrooms.

> *12 mushrooms*
> *12 small pickling onions*
> *2 stalks celery, diced*
> *2 small hearts round (Boston) lettuce*
> *2 large tomatoes*
> *300ml (½ pt) olive oil*
> *10ml (2 tsp) tomato purée*
> *juice of 1 small lemon*
> *1 glass dry white wine*
> *1 sprig of fresh thyme or 2.5ml (½ tsp) dried thyme*
> *1 bayleaf*
> *5ml (1 tsp) coriander seeds*
> *salt and freshly ground pepper*

Clean the mushrooms by gently wiping with a damp tea towel or wet paper towel. Leave the caps whole but chop the stems coarsely. Fry both caps and stems in half the oil until soft. Remove the mushrooms and set aside to drain. Discard the oil.

Peel the onions, cut the lettuce hearts into quarters and slice the tomatoes. Put into a pan with the lemon juice, tomato purée, herbs, wine, spices and the remaining oil. Season with salt and pepper and simmer for 20-25 minutes, or until the onions are tender. Add the mushrooms and simmer for a further 5 minutes.

Remove the mushrooms to a shallow serving dish and bring the remaining ingredients to a rapid boil for 4-5 minutes. Pour over the mushrooms and chill until ready to serve.

Mushrooms à la Grecque I   *Serves 3*

> *450g (1 lb) small button mushrooms*
> *45ml (3 tbs) fresh parsley, chopped*
> Broth
> *200ml (7 oz) water*
> *75ml (2½ fl oz) olive oil*
> *75ml (2½ fl oz) lemon juice*
> *2.5ml (½ tsp) coarse sea salt*
> *30ml (2 tbs) chopped spring onions (scallions) or shallots*

1 stalk celery, with leaves
1 sprig fresh fennel or 0.75ml (⅛ tsp) fennel seeds
1 sprig fresh thyme or 2.5ml (½ tsp) dried thyme
5-6 sprigs parsley
10-12 whole black peppercorns
8 coriander seeds

Place all the ingredients for the broth in a covered saucepan and simmer gently for 10 minutes.

Meanwhile, wash the mushrooms under a cold running tap and trim the woody bottoms from the stems. Any large mushrooms should be halved or quartered.

Add the mushrooms to the simmering broth, stir with a wooden spoon to cover with liquid, cover, and continue to simmer for a further 10 minutes.

Remove the mushrooms with a slotted spoon and set aside in a serving dish. Boil the liquid rapidly until it has reduced to about 75ml (2½ fl oz). Add more salt and freshly ground pepper if desired, and strain over the mushrooms. Cover the dish and chill until ready to serve. Garnish with chopped parsley just before serving.

Mushrooms à la Grecque II   *Serves 3-4*

450g (1 lb) small button mushrooms
300ml (½ pt) dry red wine
50g (2 oz) raisins
1 small onion, thinly sliced
12 whole black peppercorns
12 coriander seeds
600ml (1 pt) water
45ml (3 tbs) tomato purée
60ml (5 tbs) olive oil
1.25ml (¼ tsp) dried thyme
15-30ml (1-2 tbs) sugar, to taste

Put the wine, water, raisins, onion, tomato purée, oil, sugar and spices into a large saucepan. Bring to the boil and simmer gently for 5 minutes. Add the mushrooms, stir to cover completely with liquid, and simmer for a further 10-15 minutes. Remove the mushrooms with a slotted spoon and set aside in a serving dish. Continue to boil the liquid until it is reduced by one-third. Adjust the seasoning with salt and freshly ground pepper and pour over the mushrooms. Toss and chill until ready to serve, garnished with freshly chopped parsley.

Okra

Known as 'gombo' in South America, 'lady's fingers' in England and *bamia* in the Middle East, okra probably had its origins in the West Indies.
It is actually related to cotton although its edible pods look more like pale green ridged chillies than cotton. Okra is best eaten when slightly under-ripe, about 7cm (2½ in) in length. The gluey substance in the pods can be removed by soaking the okra in vinegar (approx 120ml (4 fl oz) per 450g (1 lb) before using. Discard the gluey liquid, rinse and drain.

Middle Eastern Bamia with Tomato and Onions   *Serves 4-6*

The addition of *taklia* — garlic crushed with coriander — a favourite Arab combination, gives this dish its distinctive Middle Eastern flavour.

900g (2 lb) fresh young okra (usually available from Greek or Middle Eastern groceries)
325g (12 oz) small pickling onions
75ml (5 tbs) olive oil
juice of 1 small lemon
2 cloves garlic, crushed with 5ml (1 tsp) ground coriander
450g (1 lb) ripe tomatoes
salt and freshly ground pepper

Skin the tomatoes by immersing them in rapidly boiling water for several seconds. Remove and when cool enough to handle, peel off the skins. Slice the tomatoes. Wash, scrub and drain the okra. Remove the hard stems. Peel the onions but leave them whole.

Heat the oil in a large frying pan. Add the onions and crushed garlic with coriander and fry over medium heat until the onions become soft and translucent. Add the okra and continue frying for a further 5 minutes; then add the tomatoes and cook for a few more minutes, stirring constantly. Season with salt and pepper, then add just enough water to cover. Simmer gently for 30-45 minutes, or until the okra are very tender. Add the lemon juice, stir, and cook for a further 5 minutes. Allow to cool, then chill for at least 2 hours before serving. A few chopped coriander leaves make an excellent garnish.

Olives

The simple olives, best allies of wine
Must I pass over in my bill of fare?
I must, although a favourite 'plat' of mine
In Spain, and Lucca, Athens, everywhere:

On them and bread 'twas oft my luck to dine,
The grass my tablecloth, in open air,
On Summer or Hymettus, like Diogenes
Of whom half my philosophy the progeny is.

Don Juan, Lord Byron

Olives in salad-making are most commonly associated with the oil which they produce. The olive tree, such a familiar part of the Mediterranean landscape, produces enormous variety in different colours, shapes, sizes and textures of fruit. Olives are nearly always used as one would use a vegetable, or served on their own as a pre-dinner savoury or appetiser.

Olive Schiacciate

Serves 6

Sicilian olive salad

More a relish than a salad, this dish is a perfect component for an antipasto platter; or serve it with slices of salami and Parma ham.

> *1 large red pepper*
> *450g (1 lb) large green Sicilian olives*
> *4 large fresh stalks of celery*
> *120ml (8 tbs) capers, drained*
> *2 cloves garlic, chopped*
> *2.5ml (½ tsp) fennel seed*
> *1 small onion, thinly sliced*
> *120ml (4 fl oz) best virgin olive oil*
> *5ml (1 tsp) freshly ground black pepper*
> *1 carrot, thinly sliced*
> *15ml (1 tbs) wine vinegar*
> optional
> *salt*

Place the pepper under the grill, turning constantly, until it is well charred on all sides (approximately 10-15 minutes). When cool enough to handle, peel off the skin, drain excess liquid, deseed and cut into strips. Place in a large bowl and set aside.

Pound each olive until broken or until a part of the stone is revealed — but do not remove the stones. Add to the peppers along with all the other ingredients. Toss well and taste; add additional salt only if required. Cover the bowl (or place contents in a tightly sealed jar) and store in the refrigerator for at least 24 hours before serving.

See *Moroccan Orange and Olive salads,* p 199

Onions

Let first the onion flourish there,
Rose among roots, the maiden fair
Wine-scented and poetic soul
Of the capacious salad bowl.

To A Gardener, R.L. Stevenson

Throughout history, onions have been celebrated and maligned, prescribed and prohibited, perhaps more than any other vegetable. First domesticated somewhere in the Fertile Crescent area, and used both for culinary and medicinal purposes, the onion was also regarded as a symbol of the universe and eternity because of its spherical shape. John Evelyn writes in *Acetaria:* 'How this noble *Bulb* was deified in Egypt we are told, and that whilst they were building the *Pyramids*, there was spent in this Root *Ninety Tun of Gold* among the workmen'.

The Greeks and Romans also found the onion an extremely versatile vegetable. If the Roman poet Martial is to be believed, the onion was even prized for its aphrodisiac or rejuvenating powers: 'If your wife is old and your member is exhausted, eat onions in plenty'.

The onion — in its various forms (garlic, leeks, spring onions and shallots are part of the same family) is a mainstay of any cook's kitchen. The five main varieties are:

Pickling onions — about 2.5cm (1 in) diameter and generally available during the summer months and early autumn.

Shallots — an essential to French cooking, this delicately flavoured cousin of the onion was probably introduced to Europe during the Crusades and to the New World in 1543, by the explorer De Soto. Also at its best between July and October.

Globe onion — the most common variety, available all year round, and usually ranging from 5-10cm (2-4 in) in diameter. Its strong flavour makes it mainly a cooking onion.

Spanish onions — larger, milder and sweeter than ordinary onions, and at their best during the summer months.

Spring onions (scallions) — these green onions are almost always used raw. The bulb can be used to replace shallots when out of season and the green stems, snipped small, make a colourful garnish for all sorts of dishes.

The Italian onion, unfortunately rarely available in Britain, has a reddish-purple colour and a mild, sweet flavour. It is the perfect salad onion and a great favourite in American steak houses, where it is usually paired with slices of beefsteak tomato and dressed with oil, vinegar and lots of freshly ground pepper.

All onions should be purchased when firm and dry. Spring onions keep best when stored in the fridge.

Not self righteous like the proletarian potato, nor a siren like the apple. No show-off like the banana. But a modest, self-effacing vegetable, questioning, introspective, peeling itself away, or merely radiating halos like lake ripples. I consider it the eternal outsider, the middle child, the sad analysand of the vegetable kingdom.

Fruits and Vegetables, Erica Jong

Sweet and Sour Onions   *Serves 6*

> *900g (2 lb) small pickling onions*
> *450ml (¾ pt) dry white wine*
> *300-450ml (1/2-2/3 pt) water*
> *37g (1½ oz) caster sugar*
> *0.75ml (⅛ tsp) dried dill*
> *125g (5 oz) plumped-up (pre-soaked) raisins*
> *60ml (4 tbs) tomato purée*
> *75ml (5 tbs) olive oil*
> *30-60ml (2-4 tbs) wine vinegar* or *the juice of 1 small lemon*
> *dash of cayenne pepper*
> *1 bay leaf*
> *30ml (2 tbs) parsley, coarsely chopped*
> *salt and freshly ground pepper*

Place the onions in a bowl, cover with boiling water and leave for 5 minutes. Drain and peel. In a saucepan, combine the water, wine, sugar, raisins, tomato purée, dill and olive oil. Add the vinegar (or lemon juice), salt, freshly ground pepper and a pinch of cayenne. Add the onions and simmer for 30 minutes, or until they are tender but still firm (*al dente*). Remove the onions with a slotted spoon to a glass salad bowl or serving dish. Bring the liquid to a rapid boil and reduce the quantity by half. Pour over the onions and chill for several hours. Just before serving, garnish with chopped parsley.

Variation Instead of raisins, use 8 crushed juniper berries and season with 15ml (1 tbs) chopped fresh basil instead of dill.

Cachoombar   *Serves 4-6*

Indian spiced onion salad

> *2-3 large Spanish onions*
> *3 large firm tomatoes*
> *1 small cucumber, peeled*
> *4 green chillies, seeded (see p 243)*
> *5ml (1 tsp) salt*
> *150ml (¼ pt) white wine vinegar*

60ml (4 tbs) coriander leaves, chopped (substitute parsley if coriander is unavailable)

Peel and chop the cucumber into small dice. Lightly salt and allow to drain in a sieve or colander for half an hour. Remove the skins from the tomatoes by immersing them in boiling water for several seconds. When cool enough to handle, chop coarsely. Peel and chop the onion and finely chop the coriander leaves and chillies.

Mix all the ingredients together in a shallow dish and sprinkle with salt and vinegar. Allow to stand, tossing occasionally, for 30 minutes before serving.

Slaphakskeentjies *Serves 2-3*

Cape cooked onion salad

> *450g (1 lb) pickling onions*
> *2 eggs*
> *30ml (2 tbs) caster sugar*
> *30ml (2 tbs) vinegar or lemon juice*
> *30ml (2 tbs) water*

Cook the onions in simmering salt water until tender but not soft (approximately 20 minutes). Remove to a serving dish and allow to cool.

To make the dressing, whisk the eggs with the sugar. Add the vinegar and water, stirring constantly and cooking slowly over boiling water until it thickens. Pour over the onions, cool, and serve at room temperature.

Persian Onion Salad *Serves 4-6*

This salad is especially tasty with lamb or mutton dishes.

> *2-3 large Spanish onions*
> *salt*
> *60-75ml (4-5 tbs) white wine vinegar*
> *30ml (2 tbs) dried crushed mint*

Slice the onions into thick half-circles. Place in a bowl and sprinkle with salt; add the dried mint and vinegar. Toss and allow to stand for at least 1 hour, tossing again from time to time, before serving.

Ensalada de Cebollitas *Serves 6-8*

Mexican spring onion salad

Although truly a mixed salad, the onion flavour strongly dominates this salad. Like many Mexican salads, it is a cooked dish.

16 young spring onions, with well-formed bulbs
225g (½ lb) courgettes
2 large green peppers
3 small firm but ripe tomatoes
90ml (6 tbs) olive oil
30ml (2 tbs) white wine vinegar
salt and freshly ground pepper

Chop the onion bulbs coarsely. Reserve about 8 unbruised stalks for garnish. Wash and cut the courgettes into slices approximately 2.5cm (1 in) thick. Cook each vegetable separately, in a very small quantity of lightly salted boiling water, until just tender (*al dente*). Drain and place both in a large salad bowl.

Wash, seed and cut the green peppers into very thin, shred-like strips. Peel and cut the avocado into small chunks. Add to the salad bowl with the peppers.

Prepare the oil and vinegar dressing with salt and pepper to taste and pour over the vegetables. Toss gently, chill and toss again just before serving. Garnish with the onion stems, snipped into small circles.

See *Cebollas Encutidas*, p 81.

Peas

The impatience to eat them, the pleasure of having eaten them, and the joy of eating them again are the three points of private gossip . . . it is both a fashion and a madness.

Madame de Maintenon, (1696)

Peas have been around a long time. Excavations of Bronze Age sites in Switzerland, for instance, produced evidence that peas were consumed by our early ancestors, though only as a dried vegetable. The Chinese are the first to have eaten them green.

Peas were probably introduced to England by the Dutch in the sixteenth century, described as 'fit dainties for ladies, they came so far, and cost so dear'. In the privy purse expenses of Henry VIII, there is an entry 'paid to a man in reward for bringing pescodds to the king's grace iiijs. viiid'.

The British climate is ideally suited to the cultivation of peas. They are best during the summer months, though generally available through the early autumn as well. For best flavour, peas should be picked young and eaten soon after.

Nowadays, the quality of frozen peas is of a very high standard and these can be substituted when fresh peas are out of season; but avoid tinned peas to which artificial colouring and preservatives have been added.

Mange-touts — 'eat all' — are another podded variety of pea, popular in Chinese cookery. Like the ordinary green pea, they need only the slightest cooking (4-5 minutes). Mange-touts — dressed simply with oil and lemon juice — or mixed with other vegetables, make a crispy and refreshing salad component.

See *Chinese-style Mixed Salad* p 165.

Araka Me Anginares   *Serves 6-8*

Greek green peas with artichoke

This method of stewing vegetables to be eaten as a cold dish is popular all over Greece. When artichokes are not available, try courgettes*, broad beans, or cauliflower*

> *1Kg (2.2 lb) fresh green peas, (weight when shelled) or the equivalent*
> *   quantity of packaged frozen peas*
> *6-8 fresh young artichokes*
> *juice of 1 lemon*
> *1 small bunch of spring onions (both bulb and stem), chopped*
> *2.5ml (½ tsp) caster sugar*
> *2 cloves garlic, cut into slivers*
> *75-120ml (2½-4 fl oz) olive oil*
> *150ml (5 fl oz) tinned tomato sauce*
> *150ml (5 fl oz) water*
> *60ml (4 tbs) fresh parsley, coarsely chopped*
> *5ml (1 tsp) dried marjoram*
> *salt and freshly ground pepper*

Wash and drain the peas. Remove the outer leaves of the artichokes and cut off the stems. Remove the remaining leaves above the base of the heart. With a teaspoon, remove the choke, then immerse in water with lemon juice or vinegar added, to avoid discolouration while the sauce is prepared.

Heat the oil in a large heavy frying pan. Sauté the spring onions until translucent. Stir in the tomato sauce and water and season with herbs, salt, pepper and sugar.

Drain the artichokes and place in the pan. Add the peas and stir gently to ensure that the vegetables are moistened with sauce. Cover and simmer on a low heat for 30 minutes, until the sauce is thick. Adjust the seasoning. Allow to cool and serve at room temperature, garnished with another sprinkling of chopped parsley.

*When substituting cauliflower or courgettes, do not add these vegetables until half the cooking time has elapsed.

Peppers

The pepper — sweet pepper, bell pepper, capsicum — is a native of South America. Various artifacts of Peruvian civilisations dating back 2,000 years show evidence of their early existence. Today, they are cultivated widely and are a popular feature of many international cuisines.

These irregular pear-shaped plants begin green and turn to yellow/orange, and finally red as they reach maturity. Hence, there is little difference between green and red peppers, except that the red ones tend to be softer and somewhat sweeter.

The chilli is related to the sweet pepper, but it is less frequently used in Western cookery due to its fiery hotness. We are more familiar with it in its dried forms — cayenne, paprika and chilli powder — or as the basis for Tabasco and other chilli sauces. Chilli peppers are smaller than sweet peppers — usually about 7.5cm (3 in) long. They are sold in both their green and red stages of development.

Peppers, cleaned and seeded but left whole, can be stuffed with an infinite variety of fillings — ratatouille, chicken salad, crab salad, spiced and herbed cottage cheese — to make an excellent luncheon salad or light summer supper.

Mixed Pepper Salad
Serves 4

This is a delicious salad to serve with cold meats, especially salami and ham, and crusty French bread.

> *2 large red peppers*
> *2 large green peppers*
> *salt and freshly ground pepper*
> *30-45ml (2-3 tbs) olive oil*
> *15ml (1 tbs) lemon juice or white wine vinegar*
> *30ml (2 tbs) fresh parsley, chopped*

Place the peppers under a hot grill and turn until all sides are well charred (10-15 minutes). Remove from the heat and when cool enough to handle, cut away the stalk, remove the inner pith and seeds, and carefully peel away the skin. Rinse and allow the excess juices to drain through a sieve for several minutes. Cut into thin strips and place in a large glass bowl.

Combine the oil, lemon juice or vinegar, salt and pepper, whisk and pour over the salad. Chill for about an hour, toss and garnish with parsley just before serving.

Herbed Pepper and Egg Salad
Serves 4

> *1 large green pepper*

1 large red pepper
2 ripe but firm tomatoes
salt and freshly ground pepper
40ml (4 tbs) olive oil
15ml (1 tbs) white wine vinegar
15ml (1 tbs) each of finely chopped parsley, tarragon, chervil and chives (if
*   fresh herbs are unavailable, reduce quantity to 5ml (1 tsp) each)*
1 clove garlic, finely chopped
8 green or black olives
2 hard-boiled eggs
4 anchovy fillets

Clean the peppers, removing the core and seeds. Slice crosswise into circles and set aside.

Prepare the dressing by combining the oil, vinegar, herbs, garlic, salt and pepper to taste. Whisk well and set aside.

Slice the tomatoes thinly and place them, overlapped, in the bottom of a glass salad bowl. Sprinkle with dressing.

Next, add a layer of green pepper slices and sprinkle again with dressing. Follow with a layer of red pepper slices and more dressing. Finally, slice the eggs and place in a circle around the rim of the bowl. Pour on the remaining dressing and decorate with the olives and anchovy fillets. Chill for an hour before serving.

Schlada L'filfil   *Serves 8-10*

Moroccan green pepper salad

Delicious with cous-cous.

6 large green peppers
6 large firm tomatoes (or 10-12 smaller English hothouse tomatoes)
1 large clove garlic, finely minced
5ml (1 tsp) ground cumin seed
1 red chilli pepper, seeded and finely chopped (see p 243)
5ml (1 tsp) salt
45ml (3 tbs) olive oil
30-45ml (2-3 tbs) freshly squeezed lemon juice (according to taste)

Place the peppers under a hot grill, turning frequently until they are well charred all over. When cool enough to handle, remove the stalks, pith and seeds; peel off the skin and rinse the peppers under a cold tap. Allow to drain.

Skin the tomatoes by immersing them in boiling water for several seconds. Remove, cool and peel. Cut them into 1.2cm (½ in) dice. Slice the peppers into thickish lengthwise strips. Place both in a salad bowl.

Combine the remaining ingredients and whisk well. Pour over the vegetables and marinate for at least 2 hours before serving.

Potatoes

If any vegetable deserves a place in the history of western civilisation, it is surely the potato.

In Ireland, cultivation began near Cork when Thomas Herriott planted a crop in 1565. Sir Walter Raleigh also for a time grew potatoes on his estates at Youghal, but he neither cared for nor understood this plant and ordered the vegetables to be rooted out.

The Presbyterian clergy in Scotland claimed that potatoes were not fit to eat because they were not mentioned in the Bible. The potato was also misunderstood by the sixteenth century French, who, naming it the 'pomme de terre' (apple of the earth) regarded its use solely as an ornament. Even the Dutch, while accepting the potato for consumption, hardly appreciated its nutritional value. 'Potatoes cannot become a staple diet', wrote a Dutch chemist, 'without the eaters not only dwindling in physical condition but growing more dull and torpid in intellect.'

The Germans were probably the first Europeans to wholly accept the vegetable and recipes for potato dishes appeared as early as 1581 with the publication of *Ein Neu Kochbuch*. By the eighteenth century, Frederick the Great was actually distributing seed potatoes with growing instructions to the peasantry.

Eventually, the adaptability of the potato to all kinds of soil and climate and its high yield, made it the staple diet of the masses. Hence, the failure of the potato crops in the 1840s throughout Europe contributed to the political unrest, and sowed the seeds of revolution and immigration, the results of which are still with us today.

So much for history . . . the potato remains a major source of food throughout the world, playing a featured role in most international cuisines.

For salads, new or early potatoes are the best. They should be cooked preferably in their skins to preserve the vitamins stored just below the surface, and peeled, if required, when cool enough to handle. Be careful not to overcook them: potatoes for salad should retain their crispness or they will turn to mush when dressing is added. New potatoes, which should be started in boiling water, need only a very few minutes cooking.

Basic Potato Salad I   *Serves 4-6*

> *900g (2 lb) new potatoes, scrubbed but not peeled*
> *4 large spring onions (tops included), finely chopped*
> *60-90ml (4-6 tbs) best olive oil*

104

15-30ml (1-2 tbs) lemon juice
30ml (2 tbs) fresh parsley, chopped
salt and freshly ground pepper
optional
1-2 cloves garlic, finely chopped

Cook the potatoes for 8-10 minutes in gently boiling salted water. Drain and peel while still warm. Cut into dice or slice and mix with the spring onions, garlic if desired, and parsley.

In a separate bowl, blend the oil and lemon juice, adjusting quantities to taste. Add salt and freshly ground pepper and pour over the potatoes while still warm. Toss gently and leave to stand at room temperature for at least an hour before serving, so that the potatoes fully absorb all the flavours.

For variety, try adding 15ml (1 tbs) of capers or finely chopped anchovies.

Basic Potato Salad II

Some people prefer a creamy dressing for potato salad. Mayonnaise is the most common, but dressings made with fresh single cream, yoghurt or sour cream are also popular.

To transform a vinaigrette-dressed potato salad to a creamy salad, simply add 60-75ml (4-5 tbs) cream just before serving and toss well. For something a little different — especially lovely with cold poached fish — try this green mayonnaise dressing. (Use the same quantity of potatoes as above.)

60ml (4 tbs) mayonnaise (see p 30)
60ml (4 tbs) single cream
60 ml (4 tbs) olive oil
salt and freshly ground pepper
30ml (2 tbs) wine vinegar
2-3 cloves garlic
100g (4 oz) fresh spinach leaves, coarsely chopped
small bunch spring onions, tops removed and roughly chopped

★To ensure the right consistency use an electric blender or liquidiser.

Stir the mayonnaise and cream together in a bowl. Into the liquidiser put the vinegar, oil, chopped spinach leaves, spring onions, garlic, salt and lots of black pepper. Blend until the consistency of a thick purée is achieved. Add slowly to the mayonnaise mixture until thoroughly blended. If it is too thick, add a little cream; if too thin, add more mayonnaise. Use just enough of this mixture to bind the potatoes; the remainder can be stored in the refrigerator in a tightly sealed jar. Garnish the salad with a few sprigs of fresh parsley.

French Potato Salad   *Serves 4-6*

'A dish as simple as potato salad', wrote Alice B. Toklas, 'must be served surrounded by chicory. To serve it with any other green is inconceivable.'

There are rules and there are rules. Chicory makes an excellent base for French potato salad, but any sturdy green may be substituted. Watercress, cos lettuce, or even spinach leaves, are excellent.

> *900g (2 lb) new potatoes, scrubbed, but not peeled*
> *30ml (2 tbs) dry white vermouth*
> *30ml (2 tbs) stock or bouillon*
> *30ml (2 tbs) wine vinegar*
> *5ml (1 tsp) prepared mustard*
> *75-90ml (5-6 tbs) best olive oil*
> *30ml (2 tbs) spring onions or shallots, chopped*
> *salt and freshly ground pepper*
> *30ml (2 tbs) fresh parsley, chopped*

Cook the potatoes as described in the previous recipe. Drain and peel when cool enough to handle. Cut into rouch dice, place in a large bowl and pour on the vermouth and stock or bouillon. Toss and leave to stand for several minutes.

In a separate bowl, combine the mustard, vinegar, salt, pepper and chopped onions. Add the oil slowly, drop by drop, beating continuously with a wire whisk. Pour this dressing over the potatoes, add the chopped parsley and toss gently. Serve at room temperature.

Potato Salad, American Style   *Serves 5-6*

Each region of the USA has its distinctive way of preparing this popular dish. In the South and Midwest, a variety of boiled dressings are made with whipped cream or mayonnaise, and the garnish usually consists of pimentos and olives. In the East, chopped cucumber, chopped eggs, minced onion and celery seed are blended with sour cream or mayonnaise to form a dressing.

Here is an old New England recipe from the days when salt pork was more commonly used in cooking.

> *900g (2 lb) potatoes, scrubbed but not peeled*
> *100g (4 oz) salt pork, cut into 5mm (¼ in) dice*
> *1 large Spanish onion*
> *5ml (1 tsp) salt*
> *30ml (2 tbs) vinegar*

Boil the potatoes in lightly salted water over a medium heat. Meanwhile, fry the salt pork in a little cooking fat. Set aside.

Chop the onion finely and place in a large bowl. Add the salt and crush

106

into the onion. Next add the vinegar, stir and leave to stand for 5 minutes. When the potatoes are cool enough to handle, peel and cut into small pieces. Add to the onion mixture, toss, and add the pork. Blend well and serve at room temperature.

For best results mix all the ingredients while they are still warm.

Burgonya Salata Tejföllel   *Serves 6-8*

Hungarian potato salad with sour cream dressing

This is a very rich potato salad which makes a filling and tasty companion to sausages, frankfurters, ham and salami.

> *900g (2 lb) medium-sized potatoes*
> *½ a large Spanish onion, chopped*
> *3 stalks crisp celery, diced*
> *150ml (5 fl oz) sour cream*
> *60ml (2 tbs) white wine vinegar*
> *37ml (2½ tbs) butter*
> *0.75ml (⅛ tsp) freshly ground black pepper*
> *5ml (1 tsp) salt*
> *7.5ml (1½ tsp) paprika*
> *30ml (2 tbs) fresh parsley, chopped*

Scrub the potatoes and cook in gently boiling salted water until tender when pierced with a fork (15-20 minutes). Drain and when cool enough to handle, peel and cut into 2.5cm (1 in) cubes. Place in a large bowl and add the chopped onion and celery, together with the vinegar, paprika, salt and pepper. Toss lightly and set aside.

Heat the sour cream and butter in the top of a double boiler, stirring well until the butter has completely melted. Pour over the potatoes, toss gently, and chill before serving. Garnish with freshly chopped parsley and a sprinkling of paprika.

Alu Raita   *Serves 4*

Pakistani potato salad

Raita is a popular Indian relish or accompaniment, made from a base of thick curd or yoghurt.

> *3-4 good-sized potatoes*
> *2-3 medium-sized firm tomatoes*
> *600ml (1 pt) Indian curd or thick plain yoghurt*
> *2.5ml (½ tsp) cumin seeds, roasted*
> *salt and freshly ground pepper*

5ml (1 tsp) green chilli pepper, chopped (see p 243)
30ml (2 tbs) coriander leaves (or parsley), chopped

If using yoghurt instead of curd, it is important to partially strain it, so that the raita does not turn out watery. See page 246 for method.

Meanwhile, cook the potatoes in their skins in gently boiling salted water, for 15 minutes or until tender when pierced with a fork. Peel, slice thinly and set aside.

Peel the tomatoes by immersing in boiling water for a few seconds and then removing the skins. Cool and slice, discarding seeds and core. Add to the potatoes.

Mix the curd or strained yoghurt with the cumin seeds, salt and pepper and pour over the tomatoes. Add the chopped chillies and toss lightly to blend all ingredients. Chill before serving, garnished with chopped coriander or parsley.

Batata Bhaji   *Serves 3-4*

Indian potato salad

> *450g (1 lb) medium-sized potatoes*
> *5ml (1 tsp) turmeric*
> *10ml (2 tsp) ground coriander*
> *5-10ml (1-2 tsp) chilli powder*
> *5ml (1 tsp) cumin seeds*
> *1 small onion, finely chopped*
> *100ml (3 fl oz) ghee (see p 244)*
> *5ml (1 tsp) grated coconut*
> *salt*
> *45ml (3 tbs) coriander leaves, finely chopped*

Peel the potatoes and cut each into 8 pieces. Heat ghee in a frying pan and sauté onion until translucent. Add the chilli powder, turmeric, salt, ground coriander and cumin seeds and fry for 2 minutes, stirring constantly. Add the potatoes and fry gently for 10-15 minutes, until lightly browned. Next add 150ml (¼ pt) of water to the pan and simmer gently until the liquid is absorbed and the potatoes are soft.

Cool, turn into a serving dish and garnish with grated coconut and chopped coriander.

Japanese Potato Salad   *Serves 3-4*

> *450g (1 lb) medium-sized potatoes*
> *a few sprigs of parsley, finely chopped (or mitsuba leaves if available)*
> *15ml (1 tbs) black sesame seeds*
> *150ml (¼ pt) white wine vinegar*

15ml (1 tbs) mirin *or sherry*
15ml (1 tbs) sugar
5ml (1 tsp) salt
5ml (1 tsp) light soy sauce

Wash and peel the potatoes and cut into julienne strips. Cook until tender in boiling salted water, 5-6 minutes maximum. Do not overcook or the potatoes will become mushy. Drain and sprinkle with salt. Mix with the chopped parsley (or *mitsuba* leaves).

Roast the sesame seeds in a dry frying pan, or under the grill, shaking the pan continuously, until they begin to jump. Set aside and cool.

Bring the remaining ingredients to the boil in a small saucepan, stirring until all the sugar is dissolved. Remove from the heat, cool slightly and pour over the potatoes. Toss gently and allow to stand for at least an hour before serving. Place in a glass bowl and garnish with the sesame seeds.

Crunchy Potato Salad   *Serves 4-5*

> *450g (1 lb) new potatoes*
> *100g (4 oz) mung bean sprouts*
> *1 medium onion, finely chopped*
> *2 stalks celery, diced*
> *45ml (3 tbs) fresh parsley, coarsely chopped*
> Dressing
> *90ml (6 tbs) sunflower oil*
> *30ml (2 tbs) cider vinegar*
> *15ml (1 tbs) Worcestershire sauce*
> *2.5ml (½ tsp) salt (if desired)*
> *freshly ground pepper*

Scrub the potatoes and immerse, unpeeled, in a saucepan of gently boiling, lightly salted water. Cook for 8-10 minutes, until just tender. Drain and place in a large salad bowl. Steam (do not boil) the bean sprouts for 2 minutes and add to the potatoes.

Blend the Worcestershire sauce, vinegar and pepper. Stir in the oil slowly and add salt if desired. Pour over the vegetables and add the onion, celery and parsley. Toss thoroughly and chill before serving.

Kednakhintzor Aghtzan   *Serves 6*

Armenian potato salad

> *5 medium-sized potatoes*
> *1 small cucumber, peeled and thinly sliced*
> *1 large tomato, cut into 8 wedges*

4 spring onions (including tops), finely chopped
8 black olives
45ml (3 tbs) fresh dill, chopped (or 15ml (1 tbs) dried dill)
90ml (6 tbs) olive oil
30ml (2 tbs) freshly squeezed and strained lemon juice
salt and freshly ground pepper
paprika
3 sprigs fresh parsley

Scrub the potatoes and cook, unpeeled, in lightly salted boiling water for 10-15 minutes, or until just tender. Drain and peel. Cut into cubes and place in a bowl.

Mix together the oil, lemon juice, salt, pepper and dill (although dried dill may be substituted, it is not nearly as nice). Pour over the potatoes while still warm and add the chopped onions. Toss and leave to stand for 15 minutes.

Turn the mixture onto a large serving dish and surround with the cucumber and tomato. Garnish with olives, a few sprigs of parsley and a sprinkling of paprika.

Radishes

There is a story of a rabbi who was invited by the elders of a neighbouring village to advise them on the appointment of a new leader for their community, as their own rabbi had passed away. The honoured visitor was placed at the head of the table and, as custom decreed, he was the first to be offered the bowl of radish salad.

The rabbi ate the whole bowlful.

A second bowl was brought and again he did not take a mere portion and pass the dish around, but once more ate it all himself!

The astonished elders decided not to consult the rabbi on their problem, since he had been so rude and greedy. But some time later they learned the reason for the strange behaviour of the rabbi: the radish had been so oversalted that it was almost impossible to eat it, and fearing that his hostess might be scoffed at for her culinary failure, the old rabbi determined that no one else at the table should taste the radish salad.

Israeli Cookbook, Molly Lyons Bar-David

This very attractive vegetable has an ancient and much admired pedigree. Eaten in England since the fifteenth century, the red varieties are most usually cultivated here but the variety more commonly encountered in the Far East is the *daikon* or *mooli*, a long white radish. (There are also black radishes grown in the Mediterranean.)

The radish was prized by the Egyptian pyramid builders as a source of energy and physical strength. For the Greeks, it became a part of their ceremonious offerings to the gods: it is said that Athenian artists made replicas of turnips in lead, beets in silver, but radishes were fashioned from gold!

Much later, the radish was celebrated as a love stimulant. The poet Claude Bigothier wrote *Raporum Encomium,* a eulogy on radishes which was published in Lyons in 1540. Rossini was another admirer, who made them the subject of one of his compositions, *Four Hors d'Oeuvres* (the other three being anchovies, pickled gherkins and butter).

Radishes make excellent garnishes and crudités. They are delicious simply dipped in coarse salt. Rich in vitamin C and very low in calories, their peppery taste is a flavourful addition to the salad bowl.

Radish flowers for garnish

The Japanese have turned the skill of cutting radishes into flowers into an art form. For Western beginners, here is a simple way of making a radish rose. Take a large well-formed radish and cut a narrow slice across the top to make a flat surface. Around the circumference, cut out thin strips, running vertically, at even intervals. Immerse in cold water and chill for half an hour. Drain and use to garnish.

Daikon Namasu   *Serves 3-4*

Japanese radish and carrot salad

> *325g (12 oz) daikon (white radish)*
> *125g (5 oz) carrots*
> *2.5ml (½ tsp) salt*
> *150ml (¼ pt) white wine vinegar*
> *30ml (2 tbs) light brown sugar*
> *15ml (1 tbs) light soy sauce (shoyu sauce)*

Wash and peel the carrots and radishes. Cut both into julienne strips about 2.5cm (1 in) long. Place in a sieve and sprinkle lightly with salt. Allow to drain for half an hour then press out excess water with the hands. In a large glass bowl, mix together the vinegar, soy sauce and sugar. Add the vegetables, toss to cover thoroughly with dressing and chill for at least an hour before serving.

As a variation, try adding 50g (2 oz) of plumped-up raisins *or* 15ml (1 tbs) toasted sesame seeds.

Russian Radish Salad   *Serves 4*

> *2 bunches radishes*
> *150ml (5 fl oz) sour cream*

2.5ml (½ tsp) salt
freshly ground pepper
3 spring onions (tops included), chopped
1 hard-boiled egg

Wash the radishes, trim the tops and slice thinly. Cut the egg in half, reserving the white and mash the yolk with a fork. In a bowl, blend the yolk with the sour cream and add the radishes, onion, salt and pepper. Mix well and chill. Garnish with the egg white which has been pressed through a sieve.

Minted Radish Salad   *Serves 4*

325g (12 oz) mooli (white radishes)
1 large firm tomato
1 small onion, finely chopped
30ml (2 tbs) fresh mint, finely chopped
30ml (2 tbs) olive oil
15ml (1 tbs) lemon juice
salt and freshly ground pepper

Wash and peel the radishes and slice into thin rounds. Drop the tomato into boiling water for several seconds to loosen the skin. Drain and when cool enough to handle, peel and chop, discarding the seeds and core.

Place the radishes, tomato, onion and mint in a bowl. In a separate bowl, mix the oil, lemon juice, salt and pepper. When thoroughly blended, pour over the vegetables and toss gently. Chill for several hours before serving.

Salsify

This unusual winter vegetable is often known as the 'oyster plant' or 'vegetable oyster', due to its slightly sealike taste. In appearance, the salsify looks rather like an underdeveloped parsnip with white flesh. Scorzonera, with black skin, is a new variety of salsify popular on the Continent. Both require careful scrubbing before cooking.

Salsify can be served simply boiled *al dente* with vinaigrette or with mayonnaise in combination with other vegetables, as below.

Salsifis à la Mayonnaise   *Serves 6*

900g (2 lb) salsify of scorzonera
150ml (¼ pt) mayonnaise (see p 30)
juice of 1 small lemon, to taste
10 anchovy fillets, chopped
6 black olives

Wash, scrub and peel the salsify. Cook in boiling salted water to which a little lemon juice has been added, for 10-15 minutes, until tender but crisp. Drain, cut into 25cm (1 in) dice and place in a salad bowl and chill.

Prepare the mayonnaise and season with lemon juice, according to taste. Blend with the salsify and add the chopped anchovies. Stir well and garnish with the olives.

Spinach

Long before Popeye the Sailorman promoted spinach power, it was recognised that this vegetable is a rich source of vitamins, minerals and iron, bestowing strength, vitality and even, some say, sexual vigour.

Spinach was introduced to Europe by the Moors in Spain. In fact, as late as the sixteenth century, when spinach was being cultivated throughout most of Europe, it was still often known as 'the Spanish vegetable'.

Spinach can usually be purchased all year round, but the delicately flavoured summer variety is more tender, and therefore better for salads. It needs careful cleaning to remove all the dirt that clings to the leaves, and equally careful handling, as the leaves damage easily.

English Spinach Salad

As evidence that the English were early devotees of spinach salad, here is Gervase Markham's seventeenth century recipe, recorded in *The English Housewife*:

To make an excellent compound boyl'd sallet: take of spinage well washt, two or three handfulls, and put into it fair water, and boyl it till it be exceeding soft, and tender as pap; then put it into a cullander and drain the water from it, which done, with the back side of your chopping knife, chop it, and bruise it as small as may be; then put it into a Pipkin with a good lump of sweet-butter and boyl it over again; then take a good handfull of currants clean washt, and put to it and stir them well together; then put to as much vinegar as will make it reasonable tart, and then with sugar season it according to the taste of the master of the house, and to serve it up on sippets.

Spinach, Bacon and Mushroom Salad   Serves 4-6

450g (1 lb) fresh young spinach leaves
4 rashers streaky bacon, cooked and broken into small pieces
8 sprigs watercress
salt and freshly ground pepper
100g (4 oz) button mushrooms
90ml (6 tbs) olive oil

113

> 30ml (2 tbs) lemon juice or white wine vinegar
> 1.25ml (¼ tsp) dry mustard
> optional
> 1 hard-boiled egg, thinly sliced

Clean the spinach carefully, drain and dry thoroughly. If the leaves are large, break them into smaller pieces. Wipe the mushrooms, clean them with a damp paper towel, trim the bottoms and slice.

Place the spinach, mushrooms and watercress in a large wooden salad bowl and add half the crumbled bacon.

In a separate small dish, mix the oil, vinegar, mustard, salt and pepper. Blend thoroughly and pour over the salad. Toss gently but deeply, so that the mushrooms do not collect at the bottom of the bowl. Sprinkle the remaining bacon on top and garnish, if desired, with the hard-boiled egg.

A delicious variation is Joe Allen's Deluxe Spinach Salad — just add two king prawns (boiled and peeled), a few tomato wedges and one artichoke heart per person to your salad bowl. Arrange decoratively around the top.

Spanaki Salata   *Serves 4*

Greek spinach salad

> 900g (2 lb) spinach leaves
> salt and freshly ground pepper
> 60ml (4 tbs) olive oil
> juice of 1 lemon
> optional
> 2 sprigs fresh mint finely chopped
> a few chives finely chopped

Wash the spinach thoroughly and remove the stalks and damaged leaves. Drain and cook in a large covered saucepan, without any additional water, for about 8 minutes, until the spinach is quite tender. Turn into a sieve and drain off as much liquid as possible (pressing with the back of a spoon helps force out the liquid). Add the chopped herbs, if desired, and arrange in a shallow serving dish; gradually add the oil, salt, pepper and lemon juice. Toss thoroughly to ensure each leaf is well coated with dressing.

Japanese-style Spinach Salad   *Serves 2*

> 450g (1 lb) fresh young spinach
> 45ml (3 tbs) white sesame seeds

45ml (3 tbs) light soy sauce
15ml (1 tbs) caster sugar

Wash the spinach carefully and cook, covered, in a little lightly salted boiling water for a maximum of 4 minutes. Rinse in cold water and drain well. Chop coarsely and place in a bowl with half the soy sauce.

Toast the sesame seeds in a dry frying pan or under the grill until they begin to jump. Shake constantly so that they do not burn. Remove from the heat and crush in a mortar or Japanese *suribachi*.

Mix the seeds with the remaining soy sauce and sugar. Pour over the spinach, toss to blend all ingredients and chill for about an hour before serving.

Crunchy Spinach Salad   *Serves 4-5*

450g (1 lb) young crisp spinach leaves
1 large cucumber, peeled and quartered
12 large black olives, pitted and sliced
½ small sweet onion, thinly sliced
75ml (5 tbs) fresh parsley, coarsely chopped
45ml (3 tbs) salted and roasted pistachio nuts, coarsely chopped
salt and freshly ground pepper
90ml (6 tbs) olive oil
30ml (2 tbs) freshly squeezed and strained lemon juice

Wash the spinach thoroughly and remove stalks. Drain and dry. If the leaves are large, break them into smaller pieces. Combine the spinach, chopped cucumber, olives, onion, parsely and nuts in a large salad bowl.

In a separate dish, whisk together the oil, lemon juice, salt and pepper. When thoroughly blended, pour over the vegetables. Toss carefully but thoroughly and serve immediately.

Salade d'Epinards aux Moules   *Serves 6*

1125g (2½ lbs) fresh spinach leaves
1 large tin of mussels preserved in brine (approx. 550g/20 oz)
3 sprigs tarragon, finely chopped
1 hard-boiled egg
90ml (6 tbs) best olive oil
30ml (2 tbs) white wine vinegar
5ml (1 tsp) prepared mustard
salt and freshly ground pepper

Wash the spinach thoroughly and remove the stems. Cook covered in a small quantity of lightly salted boiling water for approximately 8 minutes, or until tender. Turn into a sieve, rinse with cold water and drain, pressing out the excess liquid with the back of a spoon.

Drain the mussels and place in a large salad bowl. Add the spinach.

Place the oil, vinegar, mustard, hard-boiled egg, salt and pepper in an electric blender. Blend for a few seconds at medium speed until creamy in texture. Pour over the salad, toss carefully and chill for at least an hour before serving.

Spanakh yer Madzoon Aghtsan *Serves 3*

Armenian spinach with yoghurt

> *450g (1 lb) spinach leaves*
> *100ml (3 fl oz) water*
> *1 clove garlic*
> *1.25ml (¼ tsp) salt*
> *15ml (1 tbs) freshly squeezed and strained lemon juice*
> *30ml (2 tbs) fresh mint, finely chopped, (or 10ml (2 tsp) dried mint)*
> *salt and freshly ground pepper*
> *150-240ml (5-8 fl oz) thick plain yoghurt*
>
> optional
> *30ml (2 tbs) chopped walnuts*

Wash the spinach thoroughly, remove the stalks, and drain. Place in a large saucepan with the 100ml (3 fl oz) lightly salted boiling water. Cover and cook over a low heat for about 8 minutes, or until tender. Turn into a sieve, rinse with cold water and drain, pressing out excess water with the back of a large spoon.

Chop the spinach; crush the garlic with the salt and place both in a shallow serving bowl. Add the lemon juice, mint, salt and pepper. Stir, then gradually add the yoghurt, mixing constantly. For a thick creamy salad, use only 150ml (5 fl oz); for a more liquid consistency, add more yoghurt. Correct the seasoning and chill in a covered dish for several hours. If desired, garnish with chopped walnuts just before serving.

Tomatoes

Sixteenth century Spanish explorers found the Indians of the New World growing a strange plant called *tomate*, which bore small yellow fruits. When brought back to Europe, this intriguing fruit became known to the Italians as *pomo d'oro* for its golden colour and to the French as *pomme d'amour* for what were believed to be its aphrodisiac powers. In England, where the tomato was introduced in 1596, its use was limited to ornamentation. It was not without status however — Sir Walter Raleigh

116

vas reputed to have given these little fruits to his Queen as a token of his admiration. Americans, too, were cautious in introducing tomatoes to their diet and it was not until the 1880s that the first commercial crop was grown in the USA. Today, tomatoes are available in many shapes and sizes — thanks, mainly, to the Italians who first developed the large red variety from the little *pomo d'oro*.

Tomatoes are available in British markets throughout the year, in both imported and home-grown varieties. They are a wonderfully versatile salad ingredient — sliced, in simple combinations with other vegetables and dressed with vinaigrette; stuffed, with almost anything; or chopped and mixed in the salad bowl with all sorts of exotic vegetables and spices. The recipes in this section only hint at the splendid possibilities — there have been whole cookbooks devoted to tomatoes, and rightfully so.

Sliced Tomato with Chopped Basil   *Serves 4*

A simple summer starter.

> *675g (1½ lb) firm ripe tomatoes*
> *90ml (6 tbs) best olive oil*
> *30ml (2 tbs) white wine vinegar*
> *1 clove garlic, finely chopped*
> *5ml (1 tsp) prepared Dijon mustard*
> *salt and freshly ground pepper*
> *30ml (2 tbs) fresh basil, coarsely chopped*

Slice the tomatoes into 5mm (¼ in) rounds. Prepare the dressing from the oil, vinegar, garlic and mustard. Blend well and add salt.

Dress the tomatoes just before serving, and garnish with generous turns of the pepper mill and chopped basil.

American Steakhouse Salad   *Serves 4-5*

This simple first course is standard steakhouse fare all across the USA. Large firm beefsteak tomatoes are used but the large Mediterranean tomato, more commonly imported to Britain, is a good substitute

> *3 very large tomatoes*
> *1 large Italian red onion (or mild Spanish onion)*
> *oil*
> *vinegar*
> *salt and pepper*
> *few sprigs parsley*

Simply slice the tomatoes and onion into evenly-sized rounds and arrange on a serving dish in an attractive pattern. Garnish with the parsley sprigs.

117

The salad should be dressed individually by each partaker, according to his or her own palate.

Russian Tomato Salad   *Serves 4-6*

> *675g (1½ lb) firm ripe tomatoes*
> *1 Spanish onion, thinly sliced*
> *salt and freshly ground pepper*
> *5ml (1 tsp) prepared mustard*
> *5ml (1 tsp) caster sugar*
> *75ml (5 tbs) olive oil*
> *15ml (1 tbs) wine vinegar*
> *1 hard-boiled egg yolk, sieved*

Slice the tomatoes thickly and season with salt and pepper. Place in a bowl with the onion rings. To prepare the dressing, blend the sieved egg yolk with the mustard. Slowly add the oil, stirring constantly to achieve a smooth consistency. Add the sugar, blend, and finally, add the vinegar. Pour over the tomatoes, toss well, and allow to stand for half an hour before serving.

Tomato and Mozzarella Cheese   *Serves 4*

> *450g (1 lb) firm ripe tomatoes (preferably the large Mediterranean variety)*
> *225g (8 oz) Italian Mozzarella cheese*
> *90ml (6 tbs) olive oil*
> *15ml (1 tbs) lemon juice*
> *5ml (1 tsp) dried oregano*
> *15ml (1 tbs) fresh parsley, finely chopped*
> *15ml (1 tbs) fresh basil, finely chopped*
> *salt and freshly ground pepper*

Slice the tomato thickly. Cut the Mozzarella into slices approximately 2mm (⅛ in) thick. Arrange the tomatoes and cheese alternately on a large shallow serving dish. Mix the oil and lemon juice and pour over the salad. Sprinkle on the oregano and fresh herbs and season with salt and generous turns of the pepper mill.

Thakkali Sambol   *Serves 3-4*

Sri Lanka tomato salad

> *3 very large firm tomatoes*
> *15ml (1 tbs) lemon or lime juice*
> *5ml (1 tsp) salt*
> *15ml (1 tbs) finely chopped onion*
> *15ml (1 tbs) finely chopped green pepper*

> *2.5ml (½ tsp) paprika*
> *60ml (4 tbs) coconut cream (see p 243)*
> optional
> *1 chilli pepper, finely chopped*
> *15ml (1 tbs) crumbled maldive fish (see Bombay Duck, p 243)*

Peel the tomatoes by immersing them for several seconds in boiling water. Remove, cut into halves and deseed. Chop into almond-sized pieces and place in a glass salad bowl. Add the lemon (or lime) juice, salt, chopped onion, pepper and paprika. Pour the coconut cream over the vegetables, stir and chill until ready to serve. The maldive fish — an exotic garnish — should be sprinkled on top just before serving.

Salade de Tomates Cuites   *Serves 5-6*

Cooked tomato salad

This is an ideal salad to serve with cold sliced beef, pork or lamb.

> *900g (2 lb) tomatoes*
> *1 medium cucumber*
> *1 large stalk celery, cut into large dice*
> *150ml (¼ pt) olive oil*
> *pinch of powdered ginger or sage*
> *salt and pepper*
> *juice of 1 small lemon*

Peel the cucumber and cut into large dice. Place in a sieve and sprinkle with salt; leave for 20 minutes to allow excess liquid to drain off.

Peel the tomatoes by immersing in boiling water for several seconds. Slip off the skins, cut into quarters and deseed.

Heat the oil in a large frying pan and add the vegetables. Sprinkle with salt and pepper and add the ginger or sage. Cook over medium heat until most of the liquid has evaporated. Take off the heat and leave to cool. Just before serving, correct the seasoning and add the lemon juice.

Ensalada de Jitomates   *Serves 4*

Mexican tomato salad

> *4 medium firm tomatoes*
> *1 large ripe avocado*
> *5ml (1 tsp) olive oil*
> *0.75ml (⅛ tsp) wine vinegar*
> *1 slice cooked ham, approx 25g (1 oz)*
> *salt and freshly ground pepper*
> *4-5 large lettuce leaves*
> *few sprigs fresh parsley*

119

Halve the avocado, remove the stone and scoop out the flesh into a small bowl. Season with salt and pepper, oil and vinegar. Mash with a fork until well blended.

Chop the ham into small pieces and blend with the avocado. Cut the tomatoes into fairly thin slices.

Line a serving dish with the lettuce leaves and arrange the tomatoes on top. Cover the slices with the avocado and garnish with parsley.

Stuffed Tomatoes

A large firm tomato, hollowed and filled with any of an infinite variety of mixtures, makes a most attractive appetiser or a pleasant light lunch or supper.

There are three important basic instructions to remember when preparing tomatoes for stuffing: 1. Always choose large, firm tomatoes over-ripe fruits will be too soft to hold the filling. 2. Slice only a small cap from the top with a sharp knife, allowing maximum base for the stuffing 3. Once the pulp has been scooped out and reserved (if required for filling), lightly sprinkle the tomato shell with salt and pepper and turn upside down to drain for 15 minutes.

Suggested stuffings:

> *Michoteta p 84*
> *Crunchy Corn Salad p 79*
> *Napoleon's Bean Salad p 131*
> *Salade de Riz Colorée p 143*
> *Hawaiin Chicken Salad in Tomato Petals p 177*
> *Tuna Fish Salad p 190-1*
> *Dannevang Salad p 181*

Turnips

Writing in 1842, in *A History of the Vegetable Kingdom,* William Rhind described the turnip as 'of very universal culture throughout Europe'. In particular, he went on to say, the Russian nobility hand round on a silver salver, thin slices of raw turnip which are consumed with brandy 'as a provocative to the more substantial meal'.

Because it is so rarely eaten in its uncooked state, it may come as a surprise to know that the turnip is actually quite tasty raw. The best time to eat raw turnips is between April and July, when the skins are white and green, and less coarse than the winter varieties.

Add turnips, peeled and cut into matchstick pieces, to a platter of crudités; grate and dress with vinaigrette or rémoulade or try the following Oriental recipe for something savoury and exotic.

Turnip Salad *Serves 4-6*

450g/1 lb young turnips, peeled
salt
1 small onion, thinly sliced
soy sauce, to taste
1.25ml (¼ tsp) caster sugar
60ml (4 tbs) sesame oil

Slice the turnips thinly. Place in a sieve, sprinkle with salt and rinse well with cold water. Drain and pat dry in a clean kitchen towel.

In a glass bowl, mix the turnip slices with the onion rings, sprinkle with sugar and toss. Add soy sauce to taste — usually several teaspoons — and just before serving, heat the sesame oil and pour over the vegetables. Toss well.

Egg, Cheese and Pasta Salads

Phool Ka Achar   *Serves 6-(*

Nepalese egg salad

Served as a chutney in Nepal, this dish makes an excellent accompanimen
to curries and other spicy meals. The curd, which is usually prepared
from buffalo milk in the East can sometimes be bought ready-made from
Indian grocers here. Thick, unsweetened yoghurt makes a reasonable
substitute.

10-12 hard-boiled eggs, halved
15ml (1 tbs) butter
10-15ml (2-3 tsp) fresh chopped chilli pepper (p 243)
5ml (1 tsp) cumin seeds, pounded and crushed
1.25ml (¼ tsp) cardamom seeds, pounded and crushed
600ml (1 pt) thick curd or plain thick yoghurt
150ml (10 tbs) fresh coriander (or parsley), coarsely chopped
1 small lime, finely chopped with peel (½ small lemon may be substituted)

Heat the butter and gently fry the spices to rid them of their 'raw' odour. Remove from the pan and drain. In a large glass bowl, beat the curd or yoghurt, add the coriander and chopped lime. Add the spices and mix until well blended. Drop in the egg halves gently so they do not break. Chill. *Phool Ka Achar* is often served together with finely chopped tomatoes.

*Draining the whey from shop-bought yoghurt will produce a substance closer in consistency to curd. Line a sieve or colander with a piece of cheese cloth or gauze and place the sieve over a large bowl. Put the yoghurt into the sieve and allow the liquid to drain through, squeezing the cloth occasionally. After 20-30 minutes, turn the yoghurt into a bowl and mix with the other ingredients, as directed.

Pipérade   Serves 6

A Basque speciality, excellent for picnics. Strips of lightly fried ham may be used to garnish the eggs.

4 small fresh red peppers
1 large onion, finely chopped
450g (1 lb) tomatoes
8 eggs
60ml (4 tbs) olive oil
2 cloves garlic, crushed
salt and freshly ground pepper
15ml (1 tbs) fresh parsley, chopped

Skin the tomatoes by immersing in boiling water for several seconds. Remove and when cool enough to handle, peel, deseed and chop into large pieces. Cut the pepper into 1.25cm (½ in) pieces, discarding seeds and core. Heat the oil in a medium-sized frying pan and gently fry the onion, garlic and peppers for about 5 minutes. Add the tomatoes and continue cooking over a low heat for a further 10 minutes, stirring occasionally.

Meanwhile, beat the eggs until frothy. Add the parsley and season well.

Remove any excess oil from the pan (i.e. leave just a coating to prevent sticking) and *slightly* increase the heat. Add the eggs to the vegetable

123

mixture and scramble gently until firm. Cook for several minutes and turn onto a large flat dish. Serve cold, garnished with strips of ham and an extra sprinkling of chopped parsley.

Huevos, Judias Verdes y Guistantes   *Serves 5-6*
Hard-boiled eggs, Spanish-style

A pleasant antipasto, excellent with Spanish sausage (*chorizo*).

> *325g (12 oz) fresh green beans*
> *225g (8 oz) shelled peas*
> *6 hard-boiled eggs, halved*
> *freshly ground black pepper*
> *30ml (2 tbs) olive oil*
> *15ml (1 tbs) wine vinegar*
> *2.5ml (½ tsp) salt*
> *5ml (1 tsp) prepared mustard*
> *mayonnaise (see p 30)*

Trim the green beans, wash and cook in gently boiling salted water for 8 minutes, or until just tender. Drain. Boil the peas in the same manner, drain and add to the beans. Make the dressing from the oil, vinegar, mustard and salt and add to the vegetables while still warm. Place this mixture on a large serving dish and surround with the hard-boiled eggs. Garnish generously with black pepper and serve with a bowl of freshly prepared mayonnaise.

Egg Salad and 'Caviar'   *Serves 12 +*

This recipe is my mother's creation and it is a beautiful dish for a party buffet. Lumpfish roe is hardly caviar but it nevertheless makes a wonderful garnish for eggs (and it doesn't cost over £10 an ounce).

> *24 hard-boiled eggs, shelled*
> *30ml (2 tbs) fresh chives, finely chopped*
> *1 tin whole pimentos, approx 225g (8 oz)*
> *210ml (7 fl oz) mayonnaise (see p 30)*
> *1 large jar 100g (4 oz) black lumpfish roe*
> *5ml (1 tsp) butter or margarine*
> *salt and freshly ground pepper*
> Garnish
> *12 tomato wedges or 12 tiny 'cherry' tomatoes*
> *few sprigs parsley*
> *lettuce leaves*

In a large wooden bowl, chop the hard-boiled eggs, add the chives and season with salt and pepper. Drain the pimentos, set one aside for

124

garnish, and cut the rest into small dice. Add to the eggs with the mayonnaise and stir gently until well blended.

Grease an 20cm (8 in) ring mould with the butter or margarine and spoon the egg salad mixture into the mould, making sure it is firmly packed, with no holes. Cover with a plate or piece of kitchen foil and chill overnight.

When ready to serve, turn onto a large platter lined with lettuce leaves. Fill the centre with lumpfish roe and garnish the top with strips of pimento. Decorate the platter with the tomatoes and parsley.

Havgit Aghtsan   *Serves 3-4*

Armenian egg salad

> *4 hard-boiled eggs, shelled and sliced*
> *½ small onion, thinly sliced*
> *1 medium-sized tomato, sliced*
> *1 small green pepper, deseeded and sliced*
> *8 black olives*
> *45ml (3 tbs) olive oil*
> *30ml (2 tbs) freshly squeezed and strained lemon juice*
> *15ml (1 tbs) fresh mint, finely chopped*
> *15ml (1 tbs) fresh parsley, finely chopped*
> *salt and freshly ground pepper*

On a large platter, arrange the eggs, onion, tomato and green pepper in an attractive pattern. Garnish with black olives.

Blend together the olive oil, lemon juice and fresh herbs. Season to taste with salt and pepper and pour over the eggs and vegetables.

Stuffed Eggs: Basic Recipe

Stuffed eggs, served on a bed of crispy lettuce leaves and imaginatively garnished, make excellent appetisers, buffet salads or snacks.

> *8 hard-boiled eggs*
> *23-30ml (1½-2 tbs) softened butter (optional)*
> *60ml (4 tbs) thick mayonnaise (see p 30)*
> *23ml (1½ tbs) double cream*

Cut the eggs in half lengthwise, remove the yolks and *rice* them through a coarse sieve (this increases the bulk to a far greater quantity than mashing — even after the butter and mayonnaise are added).

If the eggs are to be flavoured with curry powder, anchovy paste, chutney, crushed garlic or any similar ingredient, stir it into the softened butter until smooth, then, using a fork, whisk the butter into the yolks with the mayonnaise.

125

If the stuffing is not going to contain curry powder or some similar ingredient, the butter may be omitted and more mayonnaise added instead.

Use cream to make the yolk mixture lighter and smoother. To make a very light stuffing, substitute whipped cream in a 1:2 ratio with the mayonnaise.

Here are some suggested recipes for stuffings:

Curried eggs:

basic yolk mixture
10ml (2 tsp) curry powder
5ml (1 tsp) minced onion
Garnish
small sprigs of parsley
sprinkling of paprika

Anchovy eggs:

basic yolk mixture
5-10ml (1-2 tsp) anchovy paste, to taste
10ml (2 tsp) minced onion
Garnish
toasted almond slivers

Herb-flavoured eggs:

basic yolk mixture
1 clove garlic, crushed
30ml (2 tbs) fresh herbs, finely chopped
(e.g. parsley, chives, chervil, tarragon)
5ml (1 tsp) lemon juice

Experiment with sour cream, curd cheese and cottage cheese as substitutes for mayonnaise and cream. All sorts of chopped vegetables, nuts, flaked tuna or salmon, grated cheese, chutneys and pickles will make delicius fillings.

Grated cheese and cheese-flavoured dressings are popular salad adornments, but cheese can also be the main ingredient in a salad. Cottage cheese is especially good: a large scoop garnished with chopped vegetables (raw or cooked) or seasonal fruits is not only wholesome and filling, but also very low in calories.

Insalata di Fontina   *Serves 4*

Italian cheese salad

Fontina is a lovely Italian cheese, smooth in texture and mild-tasting, produced in the Aosta Valley of Northern Italy.

225g (8 oz) Fontina cheese, diced
3 large yellow peppers
6 colossal green olives, pitted and chopped
5ml (1 tsp) Dijon mustard
salt and freshly ground pepper
30-45ml (2-3 tbs) olive oil
30-45ml (2-3 tbs) single cream
2-3 sprigs fresh parsley

Wash the peppers and cut them in half. Remove the cores, ribs and seeds and grill for 10-15 minutes, or until the skins blister. Remove from the heat and when cool enough to handle, peel away the thin outer skin. Cut the remaining flesh into strips about 1.2cm (½ in) thick. In a shallow bowl, mix the peppers, diced cheese and chopped olives. Mix the oil and cream with salt and plenty of freshly ground pepper. Pour over the salad, stir gently and allow to chill for at least 2 hours. Stir again just before serving and garnish with parsley.

Bernard Shaw's Cheese Salad   *Serves 3*

1 head round lettuce
½ cucumber, peeled
100g (4 oz) Cheddar cheese
5ml (1 tsp) caraway seeds
45ml (3 tbs) sunflower (or corn) oil
15ml (1 tbs) cider vinegar
salt and freshly ground pepper to taste

Wash and dry the lettuce leaves. Arrange them on a large dish. Slice the cucumber into thin rounds and place on top of the lettuce. Grate the cheese and put in the centre of the dish. Sprinkle with caraway seeds. Mix the oil and vinegar and season to taste with salt and pepper. Pour over the salad and serve immediately.

See: *Tomato and Mozzarella Cheese p 118*
       Cottage Cheese with Chopped Vegetables and Herbs p 158
       Michoteta p 84

Patriotic Pasta Salad   *Serves 10*

225g (8 oz) pasta shapes: pipette, pennerigate, pagliaci, *etc*
23ml (1½ tbs) salt

1 packet dehydrated brown bouillon or onion soup (Knorr is a popular
  British brand; George Washington, an American powder)
60ml (4 tbs) fresh dill, coarsely chopped (or 30ml (2 tbs) dried dill)
60ml (4 tbs) milk
30ml (2 tbs) vegetable oil
225g (8 oz) firm ripe tomatoes
2 small green peppers, deseeded
1 small red pepper, deseeded
1 small Spanish onion, peeled
1 large shallot, peeled
120ml (4 fl oz) sour cream
240ml (8 fl oz) mayonnaise (see p 30)
6 sweet pickles, plus 30ml (2 tbs) pickle juice
5ml (1 tsp) white wine vinegar
freshly ground pepper, to taste

Fill a large (5litre/8 pt) saucepan with water, add 15ml (1 tbs) salt, 30ml
(2 tbs) oil and bring to a boil. Add the pasta and when the water reboils,
cook for approximately 10 minutes, stirring occasionally, until the pasta is
just tender (al dente). Drain in a colander, rinse with cold water and drain
again.

Turn the pasta into a large bowl and add the milk. Stir gently until
thoroughly moistened. Set aside.

Chop the onion, tomatoes, pickles and peppers into small dice, reserving
a tablespoon of each for garnish. Mince the shallot.

In a small bowl, whisk the sour cream and mayonnaise together until
creamy, add the bouillon powder, 7ml (½ tbs) salt and plenty of freshly
ground black pepper (thin with a little milk if necessary). Gently fold this
mixture into the pasta, add the vegetables, vinegar and pickle juice and
stir until well blended.

If fresh dill is available, mix half with the vegetables and blend into the
salad, saving the rest for garnish. Dried dill should be added to the salad
with the dressing.

Garnish with the reserved vegetables (and dill) and chill for at least 2
hours before serving.

Pasta with Minced Clams   *Serves 8-10*

        250g (8 oz) pasta shapes
        1,283g (10 oz) tin minced clams, drained
        juice of 1 small lemon
        150ml (10 tbs) olive oil
        2 large cloves garlic
        37g (1½ oz) fresh parsley

25g (1 oz) fresh mint
37g (1½ oz) grated Parmesan cheese
salt and freshly ground pepper

Prepare the pasta as in the preceding recipe. Place in a large salad bowl, sprinkling it with 15ml (1 tbs) of the oil to prevent sticking. Add the drained clams.

In a liquidiser, blend the oil, lemon juice, garlic, herbs and grated cheese. Season with salt and plenty of freshly ground pepper. Pour over the pasta and clams, stir well and chill for several hours before serving. Stir again before bringing to the table.

Middle Eastern Pasta Salad   *Serves 6*

125g (4 oz) small pasta shapes
*300ml (10 fl oz) thick plain yoghurt (*laban*)*
1 large clove garlic
15ml (1 tbs) fresh mint, finely chopped (or 5ml (1 tsp) dried mint)
15ml (1 tbs) salt
15ml (1 tbs) butter
50g (2 oz) pine nuts

Prepare the pasta as in previous recipes.

With a mortar and pestle, crush the garlic, salt and mint to a rough paste. Add to the *laban* and blend well. Pour this mixture over the cooked pasta.

Fry the pine nuts in hot melted butter until golden brown; drain and add to the salad. Serve at once.

See *Salade Bagration* p 183

Grains, Pulses and Sprouts

For economical nourishment, you can't beat dried beans, or pulses as they are known to nutritionists: there is a wonderful variety from which to choose; they provide a cholesterol-free source of protein; dry, they store well and go a long way — 225g (8 oz) of dried beans should easily serve a family of four; they mix well with all sorts of herbs, spices and seasonings; they combine well with cold meats and fish to make delicious buffet salads and cooked, they will keep for days in the refrigerator, making an excellent party dish that can be prepared in advance.

While dried beans and grains have been a staple in the diets of most

130

Third World nations and handsomely treated as gourmet fare by our continental neighbours, the British — and Americans — have made only limited use of this wonderfully versatile food.

Dried beans must always be soaked and cooked. The larger beans, such as red kidney beans, lima beans and butter beans, need several hours or overnight soaking, whereas lentils, small white haricot beans and flageolets need little more than 2 hours in fresh cold water. After soaking, drain well and simmer in a large pot with plenty of fresh water for at least 45 minutes (some beans need much longer cooking time — the best way to test their readiness is to remove one and bite into it: it should be soft, but not mushy). To enhance the flavour, add a bouquet garni, bay leaf, garlic or a small onion stuck with a few cloves — but do not add salt until the final 15 minutes of cooking time. Drain and dress while the beans are still warm as they readily absorb a flavourful vinaigrette just after cooking.

Here is a selection of beans suitable for salads:

Aduki Beans	Chick Peas (Garbanzos)	Mung Beans
Blackeyed Peas	Fava Beans	Navy Beans
Broad Beans	Flageolets	Red Kidney Beans
Brown and Green Lentils	Ful Medames	
Butter Beans	Haricot Beans (Fagioli)	

Tins of ready-cooked beans can be substituted for last-minute convenience — but they lack the crisp, fresh taste of home-cooked beans and will not absorb the dressing flavour as well as the warm beans you prepare yourself.

Napoleon's Bean Salad   *Serves 4*

In her wonderful cookbook, *Good Things,* Jane Grigson tells us that Napoleon in exile on St. Helena used to eat this bean salad at lunchtime every other day.

225g (8 oz) dried haricot beans
20ml (1 heaped tbs) each of fresh parsley, tarragon and chives, coarsely
   chopped
75ml (5 tbs) best olive oil
30ml (2 tbs) tarragon vinegar
salt and freshly ground pepper
15ml (1 tbs) finely chopped shallot
5ml (1 tsp) French moutarde de maille

Soak the beans for 2-3 hours, drain and cook over a low flame in plenty of fresh water until they are soft but not disintegrating (approximately 1 hour). Add salt to taste just before cooking is completed.

131

While the beans are cooking, prepare a dressing of vinegar, oil, mustard and chopped shallots. Drain the beans, add the chopped herbs and dressing while still warm. Mix well, adding plenty of freshly ground pepper and more salt, if necessary, and allow to stand for several hours before serving.

For a delicious variation add thick slices of spicy salami sausage cut into bite-sized cubes.

Germag Lupia Aghtsan *Serves 4*

Armenian bean salad

150g (6 oz) dried white beans (fagioli)
60ml (4 tbs) olive oil
40ml (2½ tbs) freshly squeezed and strained lemon juice
2 medium tomatoes, skinned (p 246) and chopped
90ml (6 tbs) spring onions (including 5cm (2 in) of green top) chopped
1 small green pepper
15ml (1 tbs) white wine vinegar
salt and freshly ground pepper
1 clove garlic, crushed

Garnish
15ml (1 tbs) fresh parsley, coarsely chopped

Soak the beans for several hours in fresh cold water. Drain and rinse. Place in a large pot, cover with more fresh water and bring to the boil over a high flame. Reduce the heat and simmer, partially covered, until the beans are tender but not mushy. (Add extra boiling water, if necessary, during cooking to keep the beans covered.) Add salt to taste just before cooking is completed. While the beans cook, deseed, core and chop the green pepper. Prepare the dressing by blending the oil, lemon juice, vinegar, garlic, salt and pepper with a wire whisk or fork.

Drain the beans and place in a serving bowl. While still warm, add the dressing and toss. Allow to stand for 2 hours. Just before serving, mix in the onions, tomatoes and green pepper. Adjust the seasoning and garnish with a sprinkling of chopped parsley.

Salade des Haricots Blancs *Serves 4-5*

French haricot bean salad

>*150g (6 oz) dried haricot beans*
>*3 medium tomatoes, coarsely chopped*
>*25g (1 oz) black olives, pitted and coarsely chopped*

132

3 hard-boiled eggs, sliced
1 clove garlic, crushed
90ml (6 tbs) best olive oil
45ml (3 tbs) tarragon vinegar
5ml (1 tsp) moutarde de maille
salt and freshly ground pepper

Prepare the beans as in the preceding recipe.

While the beans cook, prepare the vinaigrette with the oil, vinegar, garlic, mustard, salt and pepper to taste, mixing with a fork until smooth and well blended.

Drain the beans, place in a serving bowl and add the dressing while still warm. Add the olives, eggs and tomatoes. Toss carefully and allow to stand for at least 2 hours before serving.

The chick pea, when parched, has been much esteemed among many nations from the earliest periods of history, and in that state it still continues an article of great consumption. According to Bellonius, this pea was the parched pulse which formed the common provision of the Hebrews when they took the field.

In those warm and arid countries where travellers are constrained to carry their scanty provisions with them across vast desert tracts, they gladly supply themselves with small dried substances which require much mastication and thus stimulate the salivary glands. Under these circumstances parched chick peas, or *leblebby,* are in great demand, and are so common in the shops as biscuits in those of England.

A History of the Vegetable Kingdom, William Rhind

'They are under the dominion of Venus. They are thought to increase sperm.'

Culpeper's Complete Herbal (1652)

Chick pea Salad (Garbanzo Beans)   *Serves 6*

225g (8 oz) chick peas
juice of 1 lemon, freshly squeezed and strained
1 clove garlic, crushed
salt and freshly ground pepper
60ml (4 tbs) olive oil
30ml (2 tbs) fresh parsley, finely chopped

Soak the chick peas overnight in plenty of fresh cold water. Drain and rinse. Place in a large pot and cover generously with cold water. Bring slowly to the boil and simmer for about 2 hours, or until tender but not mushy. Add extra boiling water if necessary during cooking to keep beans covered. Add salt 10-15 minutes before cooking is completed.

Drain the peas, place in a large bowl and season with additional salt and plenty of pepper. Blend together the oil, garlic and lemon juice. Pour over the chick peas while they are still warm and sprinkle with chopped parsley. Toss and allow to stand for at least 2 hours before serving.

Ful Medames   *Serves 4*

This national dish of Egypt, Middle Eastern cookery writer Claudia Roden tells us, has 'since time immemorial been faithfully served in the same manner: seasoned with oil, lemon and garlic, sprinkled with chopped parsley and accompanied by *hamine* (hard-boiled) eggs'.

Ful can be bought in most Greek and Middle Eastern delicatessens.

> *225g (8 oz) dried* ful medames, *soaked for several hours*
> *1-2 large cloves garlic, crushed*
> *4-6 hard-boiled eggs★*
> *45ml (3 tbs) fresh parsley, chopped*
> *decanter of olive oil*
> *2 lemons, quartered*
> *salt and freshly ground black pepper*

Drain the soaked beans and place in a large pan of unsalted water. Bring to the boil and simmer over low heat for 2-2½ hours, or until just soft but not mushy. Drain and add crushed garlic to taste.

To serve, give each person a soup bowl of beans with a hard-boiled egg on top and a sprinkling of chopped parsley. Pass round the oil and lemons and allow each person to season with salt and pepper according to taste.

'Silently, we ate the beans, whole and firm at first; then we squashed them with our forks and combined their floury texture and slightly dull, earthy taste with the acid tang of lemon, mellowed by the olive oil; finally, we crumbled the egg, matching its earthiness with that of the beans, its pale warm yellow with their dull brown.'

Claudia Roden

★The Middle Eastern way of boiling eggs, *harrine*, takes about 6 hours. The eggs are simmered in water to which skins from several onions have been added. A drop of oil poured onto the surface prevents the water from evaporating too quickly.

Wyoming Bean Salad   *Serves 6*

Farmers in the State of Wyoming cultivate many varieties of bean — lima, pinto, kidney, navy, garbanzo, etc, and their bean dishes are often a mixture of 3 or 4 kinds.

50g (2 oz) each of kidney beans, lima beans and chick peas, individually
  soaked
30ml (2 tbs) cucumber, peeled and chopped
30ml (2 tbs) green pepper, chopped
30ml (2 tbs) onion, chopped
90ml (6 tbs) olive oil
30ml (2 tbs) wine vinegar
5ml (1 tsp) Worcestershire sauce
2.5ml (½ tsp) sugar
2.5ml (½ tsp) dry mustard
pinch cayenne pepper
salt and freshly ground pepper
2 hard-boiled eggs, quartered, a few large lettuce leaves, washed and dried

Drain the soaked beans. It is best to cook the different beans separately, as the cooking time will vary slightly. Follow the general method described in the introduction, using plenty of fresh water and adding the salt only at the very end of the cooking time.

While the beans cook, make the dressing with the oil, vinegar, Worcestershire sauce, sugar, dry mustard, cayenne and salt and pepper to taste. Whisk all ingredients with a fork or shake in a jar until creamy smooth.

Drain the cooked beans and place them in a large bowl. Pour over the dressing, add the chopped vegetables and toss until thoroughly blended.

Line a large serving dish with lettuce leaves. Place the beans on top and decorate with the quartered eggs.

Fagioli e Tonno   *Serves 6*

Italian bean salad with tuna fish

The large white Tuscan bean is the ubiquitous antipasto favourite, but any white haricot bean can be used for this salad.

> *225g (8 oz) dried white haricot beans*
> *1 carrot, peeled and sliced*
> *1 stalk celery*
> *1 bayleaf*
> *1 large Spanish onion*
> *150-225g (6-8 oz) tin best tuna fish*
> *90ml (6 tbs) olive oil*
> *30ml (2 tbs) white wine vinegar*
> *30ml (2 tbs) fresh parsley, chopped*
> *salt and freshly ground pepper*

Soak the beans for several hours in cold water. Drain and place in a large pot, covered with plenty of fresh cold water, and with the sliced carrot, celery stalk and half the onion. Bring to the boil, reduce the heat and simmer gently for at least an hour. The beans should be tender but not mushy. Just before the end of the cooking period, season with salt.

Drain and discard the vegetables. Put the beans in a large bowl and sprinkle generously with black pepper and additional salt, if required. Blend the oil and vinegar and pour over the beans while they are still warm.

Slice the remaining half onion into thin rings and add to the beans. Pile onto a large flat dish and garnish on the top with chunks of tuna fish, drained of its oil. Sprinkle with chopped parsley and serve.

Some people prefer to dress this salad with oil only. Crushed or finely chopped garlic can be added as another variation to the dressing, or experiment seasoning with oregano or basil, two favourite Italian herbs.

Here is another version of this salad made with red kidney beans.

225g (8 oz) dried red beans (soaked and cooked as described above)
90-120ml (6-8 tbs) olive oil
30ml (2 tbs) white wine vinegar or lemon juice
1 clove garlic, minced
salt and freshly ground pepper
5ml (1 tsp) fresh marjoram, chopped (or 2.5ml (½ tsp) dried marjoram)
15ml (1 tbs) fresh basil, chopped (or 5ml (1 tsp) dried basil)
30ml (2 tbs) fresh parsley, chopped
2 stalks celery, washed and diced
1 small onion, finely chopped
150-225g (6-8 oz) tin tuna fish
2-3 anchovy fillets, chopped

While the beans are cooking, prepare the dressing with oil, vinegar (or lemon juice), garlic, salt and pepper to taste. Drain the beans and dress while still warm. Add the fresh herbs (dried herbs should be mixed into the dressing before it is poured on the beans) and chopped vegetables. Toss until thoroughly blended and allow to stand for at least 2 hours, stirring occasionally. Pile the beans onto a large flat dish and garnish with chunks of tuna fish and chopped anchovies. Serve with an extra sprinkling of fresh herbs.

Lentil Salad   *Serves 4-6*

Brown lentils are large and robust in flavour. They cook quickly without becoming mushy and are, therefore, ideal for salads.

225g (8 oz) large brown lentils

1 bayleaf
60ml (4 tbs) olive oil
1 clove garlic, crushed
15-30ml (1-2 tbs) wine vinegar
3 rashers streaky bacon
1 small onion, chopped
salt and freshly ground pepper

Soak the lentils for about 2 hours in plenty of fresh cold water. Drain and place in a large pot, covered completely with fresh water. Add the bayleaf for flavouring and bring to the boil. Reduce the heat and simmer gently for about 30 minutes (lentils tend to absorb water quickly so you may have to add additional boiling water during the cooking) or until the lentils are tender but still crunchy.

While the lentils cook, fry the bacon until crisp, drain and crumble into small pieces. Prepare a dressing from the oil, vinegar, garlic, salt and pepper.

About 10 minutes before the cooking is completed, season the lentils with salt to taste and stir. When cooked, remove from the heat and drain, discarding the bay leaf. Place the lentils in a large bowl and add the bacon, chopped onion and dressing. Toss gently until well blended, adjust seasoning and leave to stand, stirring occasionally, for at least 2 hours before serving.

Yemiser Selatla
Serves 6

Ethiopian lentil salad

225g (8 oz) green lentils
2-3 fresh green chilli peppers (approx 7.5cm (3 in) long)
45ml (3 tbs) red wine vinegar
45ml (3 tbs) vegetable or olive oil
approx 5ml (1 tsp) salt
8 small shallots, peeled and halved lengthwise
freshly ground black pepper
15ml (1 tbs) fresh parsley, chopped

Prepare lentils as in the previous recipe. Drain and set aside. Cut the chilli peppers (see p 243) into strips approximately 2.5cm (1 in) by 2mm (⅛ in), discarding cores and seeds.

In a large bowl, combine the vinegar, oil, salt and a few grinds of pepper and whisk to blend smoothly. Add the lentils, shallots and chillies and toss gently to coat with dressing. Adjust the seasoning and leave to stand, stirring occasionally, for at least 2 hours before serving. Garnish with chopped parsley.

Our daily paper would surprise us if it carried an ad: 'Wanted: a vegetable that will grow in any climate, rivals meat in nutritive value, matures in three to five days, may be planted any day of the year, requires neither soil or sunshine, rivals tomatoes in vitamin C, has no waste, can be cooked with as little fuel and as quickly as a pork chop.' The Chinese discovered this vegetable centuries ago in sprouted soybeans.

Dr Clive McCay

Sprouts have been cultivated in the Orient for over 5,000 years. In both Eastern Asia and Europe, sprouts were used first as a medicine, being designated as cures for such widely varied maladies as edema with loss of sensation, muscle cramps, pains at the kneecaps, visceral deficiencies, digestive disorders, weakness of the lungs, roughness and spots on the skin and abnormalities of the hair.

It was not until the nineteenth century that Europeans began to take note of sprouts (especially of the soybean) as a major foodstuff, influenced largely by missionaries' accounts of the traditional oriental dishes in which bean sprouts so frequently appear; but only recently in the West has the use of sprouts as a medicine — either a preventive one, as an alternative protein, or a curative one, as in the treatment of scurvy — been superseded by the use of sprouts as a food.

Mungbean (or Chinese) sprouts are those most commonly found in markets — fresh or tinned; but they can be easily grown indoors at home, requiring no special equipment, no garden soil or sun. Many other varieties of bean and seed can also be sprouted — alfalfa, aduki, soybean, fenugreek, chick peas and lentils, for example. Each of these will yield six times its original weight.

Thompson and Morgan now market a selection of sprouting seeds with simple instructions printed on each packet. The basic method requires a glass jar, a clean muslin cloth or J-cloth and an elastic band. Place about 45ml (3 tbs) seeds or beans* in a jar, cover with the cloth and secure tightly with the elastic band. Fill the covered jar with warm water, shake well and turn upside down to drain. Place the jar on its side away from a radiator or any direct source of heat. Repeat the washing and draining process morning and evening until the sprouts are ready (anywhere from 2-9 days, depending on the variety). They should be approximately 4-5cm (1½-2 in) long and nicely plump. Wash and use as soon as possible.

*Chick peas and mung beans grow better if they have been soaked overnight first.

Alfalfa Salad Bowl   *Serves 4*

225g (8 oz) salad alfalfa

138

100g (4 oz) streaky bacon rashers
3 large hard-boiled eggs
100g (4 oz) button mushrooms, cleaned and sliced
2 stalks celery, diced
4 spring onions
8 radishes, washed and sliced
1 clove garlic, crushed
60ml (4 tbs) vegetable oil
15ml (1 tbs) wine vinegar
salt and freshly ground pepper
5ml (1 tsp) Dijon mustard
15ml (1 tbs) fresh parsley, chopped

Trim the roots, tops and any damaged leaves from the spring onions and cut into ½ in pieces.

Grill the bacon until crisp. Drain and crumble.

Cut 2 of the eggs into quarters; chop the remaining egg very finely, or pass through a sieve, and set aside.

Prepare a dressing with the oil, vinegar, mustard and garlic. Season to taste with salt and pepper.

In a large wooden salad bowl, place the alfalfa, radishes, onions, celery and mushrooms. Pour on the dressing and toss to cover all ingredients. Surround the vegetbles with the quartered eggs and decorate the top with crumbled bacon, the sieved egg and the chopped parsley. Serve immediately.

Sook Choo Na Mool   *Serves 6*

Korean bean sprout salad

225-275g (8-10 oz) mung bean sprouts
4 spring onions, trimmed and chopped
1 small red pepper, cored, deseeded and finely chopped
1 clove garlic, minced
60ml (4 tbs) vegetable oil
30ml (2 tbs) white wine vinegar
30ml (2 tbs) soy sauce
salt and freshly ground pepper
30ml (2 tbs) sesame seeds, toasted golden brown

To make the dressing, mix the oil, vinegar, soy sauce, garlic and fresh pepper. Add salt sparingly as the soy sauce is quite salty in itself. Place the bean sprouts, red pepper and spring onions in a large wooden salad bowl. Pour the dressing over the salad and toss gently. Chill for at least an hour. Just before serving, add the toasted sesame seeds and toss again.

Honey-dressed Sprout Salad   *Serves 4-5*

225-275g (8-10 oz) mung bean sprouts, steamed 2-3 minutes and cooled
3 carrots, peeled and grated
1 large apple, coarsely chopped
juice of ½ lemon, freshly squeezed and strained
30ml (2 tbs) sunflower oil
30ml (2 tbs) honey
salt and freshly ground pepper
optional
25g (1 oz) raisins or sultanas

Place the chopped apple, carrots and sprouts in a large bowl. Season with salt and pepper. In a separate small bowl, blend the honey, lemon juice and oil. Pour over the vegetables and toss gently. Chill for at least an hour before serving.

Tabbouleh Burghul   *Serves 8*

Cracked wheat salad

This Middle Eastern favourite has many variations. The indispensable ingredient, however, is the fine cracked wheat — *burghul* — with its rich earthy flavour. It is soaked first then flavoured with large quantities of parsley, mint and lemon. Sometimes chopped vegetables — tomatoes, green peppers, onions and cucumbers are incorporated or simply used for garnish along with extra sprigs of parsley and black olives.

Burghul can be bought at most Hellenic or Middle Eastern delicatessens.

225g (8 oz) burghul
75-100g (3-4 oz) spring onions, trimmed and finely chopped
100g (4 oz) parsley, finely chopped (use the Italian variety if available)
25g (1 oz) fresh mint, finely chopped (or 12.5g (½ oz) dried mint)
60ml (4 tbs) olive oil
60ml (4 tbs) lemon juice
salt and freshly ground pepper
cooked vine leaves or large lettuce leaves
optional
2-3 medium-sized tomatoes, chopped

Soak the burghul in plenty of cold water for about an hour. It will soften and expand enormously. Drain and squeeze out the excess water with your hands. Spread the burghul on a clean kitchen cloth and leave to dry while you are chopping the herbs and onions.

Place the burghul in a large bowl and add the mint, parsley, onions and tomatoes, if desired. Mix well and gradually add the oil, followed by the lemon juice. Season to taste with salt and pepper and add additional lemon juice, if required, to make the flavour quite tart.

Tabbouleh should be served on individual plates, with large lettuce leaves or vine leaves to use as scoops.

Bazargan

Serves 8

Another Middle Eastern salad made from cracked wheat and highly seasoned with Oriental spices.

> *225g (8 oz) burghul*
> *1 large onion, finely chopped*
> *100g (4 oz) tomato purée*
> *15ml (1 tbs) dried oregano*
> *50g (2 oz) walnuts, coarsely chopped*
> *5ml (1 tsp) powdered cumin*
> *5ml (1 tsp) powdered coriander*
> *75ml (2½ fl oz) sunflower oil*
> *25g (1 oz) fresh parsley, finely chopped*
> *2.5ml (½ tsp) allspice*
> *dash of cayenne pepper*
> *salt and freshly ground pepper*

Wash the burghul in a sieve and soak in plenty of fresh cold water for 30 minutes. Drain and squeeze out excess water. Spread on a clean towel to dry.

In the meantime, soften the onions in a little hot oil. They should be translucent but not brown.

In a large bowl, mix the burghul, onions, parsley, nuts and spices. Add the tomato purée and remaining oil. Blend thoroughly, cover and store in the refrigerator for several hours so that all the flavours are absorbed into the burghul.

This salad is a delicious accompaniment to roast lamb and pork.

Rice Salads

Cooking rice for salads

Always use plenty of boiling water for cooking rice: this helps remove its
floury coating. For approximately 6 servings:

> *325g (12 oz) long grain rice*
> *large saucepan, holding approximately 7litres (12 pts)*

10ml (2 tsp) salt
2.5ml (½ tsp) lemon juice
cold water

Fill the pan nearly to the top with water, add salt and lemon juice. Bring to a rapid boil and sprinkle in the rice gradually, so that the water never stops boiling. Stir once across the bottom of the pan to ensure that none of the grains are sticking.

Boil uncovered and moderately fast for about 12 minutes. Begin testing the grains — they should be barely tender, but not soft (the best way is to bite successive grains until there is no hardness at the centre; rice for salads should be slightly undercooked).

Drain the rice in a colander and fluff up under hot running water for another minute to remove any last traces of starch.

Cold rice mixes well with raw and cooked vegetables, leftover meats, seafood, nuts, dried fruits and fresh herbs. It takes well to both oil and cream dressings. It keeps well in the refrigerator and can be prepared in advance in large quantities for party buffets.

Curried Rice Salad
Serves 10-12

450g (1 lb) long grain rice
75g (3 oz) seedless raisins
45ml (3 tbs) curry powder
150g (6 oz) hazel nuts
1 large tin of petit pois (Le Seur or Culina brand), drained
300ml (½ pt) mayonnaise (see p 30), strongly flavoured with lemon juice or
150ml (¼ pt) lemon/oil dressing (see p 25)
salt and freshly ground pepper

Plump up the raisins by soaking for 1 hour in warm water. Prepare the rice as described above, adding the curry powder to the boiling water just before the rice is sprinkled in. Drain in a colander, rinse with hot and then cold water. Drain again.

In a large serving bowl, combine the rice, hazel nuts and peas. Drain the raisins and add to the salad. Dress with a lemon mayonnaise or a lemon/oil vinaigrette. Season to taste with salt and freshly ground pepper.

Salade de Riz Colorée
Serves 10-12

225g (8 oz) dried prunes
a pot of strong tea
450g (1 lb) long grain rice
1 small tin pimentos (approx 4-5 pieces)
75g (3 oz) slivered almonds
30-45ml (2-3 tbs) fresh parsley, chopped

150ml (¼ pt) vinaigrette (see p 25)

Place the prunes in a large pyrex (or heat proof) bowl and cover with strong hot tea. Soak for 1 hour and drain.

Prepare the rice as described above. While it cooks, drain the pimentos and cut into small dice. Destone the prunes and cut into pieces the same size as the pimento.

In a large salad bowl, mix the rice, pimentos, prunes, parsley and almonds. Add the vinaigrette and stir well to thoroughly blend. Chill and serve with an extra sprinkling of chopped parsley.

Salade du 15 Août   *Serves 10-12*

Assumption Day salad

> *450g (1 lb) long grain rice*
> *75g (3 oz) sultanas*
> *1 large green pepper*
> *1 large red pepper*
> *450g (1 lb) fresh shelled green peas (or 225g (½ lb) frozen peas)*
> *4 medium-sized, firm tomatoes*
> *50g (2 oz) large black olives, pitted and chopped*
> *300ml (½ pt) double cream*
> *juice of 2-3 lemons (to taste), freshly squeezed and strained*
> *salt and freshly ground pepper*
> *a few sprigs of parsley*

Prepare the rice as described above, drain well and chill. Soak the sultanas in warm water for 1 hour. Grill the peppers until the skins blister (turn occasionally to ensure that all sides cook), about 10-15 minutes. When cool enough to handle, remove the skins, core and seeds. Slice into thin strips.

Cook the peas in a little boiling salted water until just tender, *al dente*. Drain and cool.

Cut the tomatoes into thin slices. Drain the sultanas.

In a large mixing bowl, combine the rice, peppers, chopped olives, peas and sultanas. When ready to serve, make a dressing with the cream and lemon juice (use 2 or 3 lemons according to taste) and pour over the rice mixture. Season with salt and pepper and stir thoroughly to blend all ingredients.

Turn onto a large serving dish and surround with tomato slices, saving a few slices to decorate the top. Garnish with parsley.

Chirashizuchi   *Serves 6*

Japanese rice salad

> *225g (8 oz) long grain rice*

15-30ml (1-2 tbs) white wine vinegar
salt to taste
5ml (1 tsp) caster sugar
5ml (1 tsp) fresh ginger, peeled and finely chopped
30ml (2 tbs) shoyu sauce (p 245)
2 eggs
225g (8 oz) fresh shelled peas (or frozen peas)
225g (8 oz) carrots

Prepare the rice as described above. Drain, fluff under hot water and drain again. Sprinkle the rice with 15ml (1 tbs) of vinegar and set aside in a large bowl.

Soak the ginger in a mixture of the remaining vinegar, shoyu sauce and sugar for 1 hour.

Meanwhile, cook the peas in a little boiling water until just tender. Peel the carrots, slice into thin rounds and cook in boiling water until soft but still crunchy.

Scramble the eggs in a little melted butter or margarine. Add the peas, carrots and eggs to the rice, stir in the dressing and mix well. Chill for at least 1 hour before serving to let the rice absorb the flavoured sauce.

Rice Stuffing for Cold Vegetables   *Serves 5-6*

A delicious filling for green peppers, large hollowed-out tomatoes, and artichokes; also excellent for stuffing vine leaves and cooked cabbage leaves. Vary the herbs with what is seasonally available.

225g (8 oz) long grain rice
150ml (¼ pt) olive oil
300ml (½ pt) boiling water
15ml (1 tbs) tomato purée
2 small onions, chopped
30ml (2 tbs) pine nuts, chopped
15ml (1 tbs) caster sugar
salt and freshly ground pepper
15ml (1 tbs) currants
15ml (1 tbs) fresh mint, chopped
15ml (1 tbs) fresh sage, chopped

In a large frying pan, heat the olive oil and lightly fry the onions until translucent, but not brown. Add the rice and cook over low heat for approximately 15 minutes, stirring frequently. Add the boiling water, tomato purée, currants, pine nuts, sage and mint. Season to taste with salt and pepper. Stir well, cover tightly and continue cooking over low heat for a further 15-20 minutes. Remove from the heat and stir in the sugar.

145

All the liquid should by now be absorbed; if not, drain off any surplus and leave the rice to cool before stuffing the vegetables.

Saffron Rice Salad with Seafood   *Serves 6-8*

Any mixture of seafood can be substituted for the ingredients given below: leftover fish, tinned (but well drained) sardines or tuna fish, cooked mussels, crabmeat or calamari.

2.5ml (½ tsp) powdered saffron
90ml (6 tbs) dry white wine
325g (12 oz) long grain rice
750ml (1¼ pts) chicken stock
salt and freshly ground pepper
50g (2 oz) black olives
90ml (6 tbs) olive oil
30ml (2 tbs) white wine vinegar
2 cloves garlic, crushed
60ml (4 tbs) fresh parsley, chopped
5ml (1 tsp) Dijon mustard
225g (8 oz) peeled prawns
325g (12 oz) cooked haddock, cod or other white fish
a few sprigs fresh parsley
1 large tomato, thinly sliced

Dissolve the saffron in the white wine. Place in a good-sized saucepan with the stock. Wash the rice thoroughly and add to the pan. Bring to a rapid boil, stir, reduce to a gentle simmer and cook covered for approximately 15 minutes, or until the rice is tender and has absorbed all the liquid. While the rice cooks, prepare a dressing with the oil, vinegar, crushed garlic, chopped parsley, mustard, salt and pepper.

Place the rice in a colander to drain any excess liquid, then turn into a large mixing bowl. While still warm, add the dressing and stir to blend thoroughly. Add the seafood and olives; toss gently and turn onto a large serving dish. Decorate with sliced tomatoes and sprigs of parsley.

Arroz con Adán   *Serves 6*

Spanish rice mould

This salad, with its multi-coloured layers of rice and vegetables, makes a lovely buffet centrepiece. Use a 25cm/9-10 in ring mould.

225g (8 oz) long grain rice
2-3 green peppers
olive oil
3 hard-boiled eggs, quartered

146

a few sprigs of parsley
1 clove garlic, crushed
5-6 medium-sized tomatoes
1 bunch spring onions
mayonnaise (or aioli p 32)
lettuce leaves

Prepare the rice as described above in plenty of boiling salted water. While it cooks, grill the peppers until all sides blister — approximately 10-15 minutes — and when cool enough to handle, remove skins, core and seeds. Cut into strips. To remove tomato skins, immerse in boiling water for several seconds. Peel, chop and set aside. Clean the spring onions, removing damaged outer leaves and all but 5cm (2 in) of green stem. Chop and set aside.

When the rice is tender, drain, rinse with hot water and drain again. Place the colander in a very low oven for a few minutes to dry the rice.

Heat enough oil to just cover the bottom of a frying pan and add the crushed garlic. Add the rice and cook, stirring, for several minutes. Remove from the heat.

Grease the mould and pack in the rice and vegetables in alternating layers as follows: rice, tomatoes, rice, green peppers, rice, spring onions, rice. Make sure the mould is packed solidly. Place in the refrigerator with a light weight on top for several hours. When ready to serve, line a large platter with lettuce leaves. Turn the mould onto the centre of the dish and surround with the quartered hard-boiled eggs. Decorate with parsley and serve with a bowl of mayonnaise or aiöli (the French garlic flavoured mayonnaise).

Creamy Salads

for dips and hors d'oeuvres

Pureed vegetables, exotically seasoned with herbs and spices, are served as salads in many countries. I have included in this chapter some of the most popular recipes. You will also find here recipes for dishes like Greek taramasalata and the Turkish cacik, which, though eaten mainly as *meze* or hors d'oeuvres, are considered part of the salad repertoire in their countries of origin.

A selection of these salads served with crudités, biscuits or small slices of toast (pitta bread cut into triangles or strips is excellent for this purpose) makes an excellent pre-dinner or party spread.

148

Skordalia and Tarator are actually sauces, but they are eaten as accompaniments to vegetables and, therefore, belong functionally to this section rather than to the chapter on dressings.

Hors d'oeuvres have always a pathetic interest for me: they remind me of one's childhood that one goes through, wondering what the next course is going to be like — and during the rest of the menu one wishes one had eaten more of the hors d'oeuvres.

Saki

Patlican Salatzi

Serves 4

Turkish aubergine salad

There are many variations of this aubergine paté — often known as 'poorman's caviar' — throughout the Balkan countries and the Middle East. Experiment with the proportions of garlic, oil and lemon juice according to taste preference.

> *2-3 large aubergines*
> *1-2 cloves garlic, crushed*
> *45-60ml (3-4 tbs) olive oil*
> *juice of 1 lemon*
> *salt and freshly ground pepper*
> Garnish
> *a few onion slices*
> *15ml (1 tbs) fresh parsley, chopped*

Lightly score the skin of the aubergines with a knife. Place them on a baking sheet and cook in a moderate oven (180°C/350°F/Gas 4) for 45 minutes or until they are completely soft and in a collapsed state.

When cool enough to handle, halve and scoop out the pulp into a sieve. Allow to stand for 15-20 minutes to drain off the bitter juice. Turn the pulp into a large bowl and pound or mash until fairly smooth. Stirring continuously, trickle in the oil, then the lemon juice. Add the crushed garlic and season to taste with salt and pepper. Chill for at least an hour and stir again before serving.

Raw onion slices and a sprinkling of parsley make an attractive garnish.

Note This recipe can be prepared quickly in a blender. Add the oil and lemon juice gradually, as above.

Baba Ghanoush

Serves 4-6

Aubergine salad with tahini

A Middle Eastern favourite, combining two distinctive flavours. More or less tahini may be used, according to taste.

149

3 large aubergines
2 cloves garlic, peeled
salt
juice of 2 small lemons, strained
2.5ml (½ tsp) ground cumin
150-300ml (¼-½ pt) tahini paste (p 246), to taste
Garnish
   a few black olives and thin tomato slices

Lightly score the skin of the aubergines with a knife. Place them under the grill and cook for 20-30 minutes, turning frequently, until the skins have blistered and charred and the flesh is soft (in the Middle East, they would be cooked over an open charcoal fire, giving a distinctive smoky flavour to the dish). When cool enough to handle, cut them in half and scoop out the pulp into a sieve. Allow to drain for 20 minutes to remove the bitter juice.

In the bottom of a large bowl, crush the garlic with salt. Add the aubergine and pound or mash until fairly smooth. Add more salt, if desired, and the ground cumin.

Gradually add the tahini, alternating with drops of lemon juice, and blending after each addition. The exact quantities of tahini and lemon juice are very much a matter of personal taste.

Chill for an hour before serving and garnish with black olives and tomato slices.

Guacamole   *Serves 3-4*

Mexican avocado salad

2 large ripe avocados
2 small tomatoes
15ml (1 tbs) grated onion
1-2 green chilli peppers, chopped (see p 243)
30ml (2 tbs) lemon juice
15ml (1 tbs) olive oil
salt and freshly ground pepper

Immerse the tomatoes in boiling water for several seconds to loosen the skins. When cool enough to handle, peel and chop, discarding the seeds and as much juice as possible. Set aside.

Halve the avocados lengthwise, remove the stones and scoop out the flesh into a large bowl. Mash, but make sure the consistency remains lumpy. Add the chopped tomatoes, onion and chopped chillis. Gradually stir in the lemon juice and olive oil. Season with salt and freshly ground pepper. Cover and chill for about an hour. Before serving, stir again.

This is excellent with crisps, corn or taco chips.

150

Humus Me'Tahini

Serves 6

Chick peas with tahini

> *225g (8 oz) dried chick peas*
> *30ml (2 tbs) tahini paste*
> *150ml (¼ pt) (maximum) cooking liquid from peas*
> *juice of 1 lemon*
> *30-45ml (2-3 tbs) olive oil*
> *2 cloves garlic, peeled*
> *salt and freshly ground pepper*
> *15ml (1 tbs) fresh parsley, chopped*

Wash the chick peas and soak overnight in cold water. Drain and re-wash, then cover with fresh cold water in a deep saucepan. Bring very slowly to the boil and simmer until tender, at least 1½ hours, possibly more. Replenish the water as necessary. The peas are cooked when they can be easily crushed between the fingers.

Drain the chick peas, reserving 150ml (¼ pt) of the cooking liquid. Push the peas through a medium-mesh sieve (discarding any coarse fibres which remain in the sieve) or a food mill. Set aside.

Put the tahini in a small bowl and slowly add *no more* than 150ml (¼ pt) of the cooking liquid to dissolve the tahini to a smooth paste. Beating briskly with a whisk, add the tahini mixture — a teaspoonful at a time — to the chick peas, alternating with lemon juice and olive oil. Crush the garlic over the mixture, blend, and season to taste with salt, pepper and chopped parsley.

Tuica

Serves 4-5

Israeli bean purée

This tasty bean salad was brought to Israel by Romanian immigrants.

> *225g (8 oz) dried white broad beans*
> *1 clove garlic, crushed*
> *juice of 1 lemon, strained*
> *45ml (3 tbs) olive oil*
> *salt and freshly ground pepper*
> optional
> *1 small onion, peeled and finely chopped*
> Garnish　　　　　•
> *paprika*
> *15ml (1 tbs) fresh parsley, chopped*

Soak the beans in cold water for several hours. Drain, cover with plenty of fresh water, and cook for 1-1½ hours, or until the beans can be crushed

151

easily between the fingers. Replenish with water, if necessary, during the cooking.

Drain the beans and pass them through a sieve (discarding any coarse fibres which remain in the sieve) or food mill. Add the crushed garlic and chopped onion, if desired. Gradually whisk in the oil and lemon juice. Season to taste with salt and pepper and serve garnished with a sprinkling of paprika and chopped parsley.

Taramasalata
Serves 4-6

Greek fish roe salad

150g (6 oz) tarama (smoked cod or carp roe)
2-3 slices white bread, crusts removed, soaked in milk, and squeezed to
  remove excess moisture
90ml (6 tbs) olive oil
30ml (2 tbs) lemon juice
1 clove garlic, crushed
freshly ground pepper
optional
  2.5ml (½ tsp) onion juice
Garnish
  black olives and 5ml (1 tsp) fresh parsley, finely chopped

This salad, which should have a uniform creamy consistency, is best prepared with an electric blender.

Place the fish roe, soaked bread and lemon juice in the blender and mix at high speed for 1 minute. Add the garlic and blend for a further 30 seconds. Continue blending at medium speed while gradually trickling olive oil into the mixture. Add onion juice, if desired.

Turn the purée into a serving dish, season with freshly ground pepper and chill until ready to serve. Garnish with black olives, a sprinkling of parsley and a trickle of oil.

Cacik
Serves 4

Turkish herbed yoghurt and cucumber salad

Also known by its Greek name, *Tzaziki*, this refreshing salad is a ubiquitous favourite throughout the Middle East. Most commercial yoghurt is not as thick as the homemade variety and should be strained see page 246 for method.

450g (16 fl oz) plain yoghurt
1 large cucumber
2 cloves garlic, peeled
pinch of white pepper

45ml (3 tbs) fresh mint, finely chopped, or *15ml (1 tbs) dried mint*
coarse salt
Garnish
a pinch of dried mint
black olives

Peel the cucumbers and chop into small dice. Place in a sieve, lightly salt, and allow to drain for 20 minutes.

In a large bowl, crush the garlic with a little coarse salt. Add a few tablespoons yoghurt and blend with a pinch of white pepper. Add the remaining yoghurt, chopped mint and cucumber. Season with salt to taste and mix well. Chill for several hours before serving so that the mint can fully permeate the salad. Garnish with a few black olives and a sprinkling of crushed dried mint.

Salata De Castrareti

Serves 4-6

Romanian cucumber salad

> *2 medium-sized cucumbers*
> *3 slices white bread, crusts removed*
> *1 clove garlic, crushed*
> *60-90ml (4-6 tbs) olive oil*
> *15-30ml (1-2 tbs) wine vinegar*
> *salt and freshly ground black pepper*
> Garnish
> *15ml (1 tbs) chopped chives*

Peel the cucumbers, cut in half and place in a bowl of iced water for approximately 20 minutes. Remove from the water, drain and pat dry. Cut crosswise into paperthin slices (a food processor is a great boon in achieving uniformly thin pieces), and place these in a sieve. Salt lightly and leave for half an hour, pressing occasionally with a small plate or wooden spoon, to remove as much water as possible.

In a small bowl, combine the bread, which has been soaked in water then squeezed to remove excess liquid, with the crushed garlic. Gradually trickle olive oil into the mixture, stirring constantly with a wire whisk or fork. After 60ml (4 tbs) have been added, blend in 15ml (1 tbs) of wine vinegar. This mixture should have a semi-liquid consistency; add more olive oil and vinegar if the paste is either too lumpy or too thick.

Place the well-drained cucumbers in a shallow serving dish and pour on the garlic mixture. Season with plenty of freshly ground pepper and a little salt. Blend carefully with a wooden spoon and garnish with chopped chives (or chopped spring onion tops if chives are unavailable) and a trickle of olive oil.

Now bolt down these cloves of garlic. Well primed with garlic, you will have greater mettle for the fight.

Knights, Aristophanes

Skordalia

The use of garlic, *skordo*, in Greek cooking, dates back to Ancient times when it was probably valued more for its medicinal and magical powers than as a flavouring.

I have given two typical recipes for this sauce, which is often served with cold vegetables as *mezethaki*, or with halved hard-boiled eggs. The important skill in preparing these recipes is knowing how much oil and vinegar or lemon juice the garlic can absorb as it is being pounded and beaten.

Version I

> *2 medium-sized potatoes*
> *salt and freshly ground black pepper*
> *2-3 cloves garlic*
> *300ml (½ pt) olive oil*
> *60ml (4 tbs) vinegar*

Cook the potatoes in boiling salted water until tender. Drain and peel when they are cool enough to handle. Mash very finely.

Crush the garlic and mix well with the potatoes. Gradually add small, alternating amounts of oil and vinegar, beating constantly with a whisk. The right consistency has been achieved when the sauce is thick and smooth like mayonnaise.

Version II

> *4-6 cloves garlic*
> *2 egg yolks*
> *50g (2 oz) ground almonds*
> *140ml (¼ pt) olive oil*
> *45-75ml (3-5 tbs) freshly chopped parsley*
> *50g (2 oz) fresh white breadcrumbs*
> *lemon juice*

First pound the garlic in a mortar. Then add the egg yolks, followed by olive oil in the drop-by-drop method used for making mayonnaise (see p 30). When a smooth, firm consistency has been achieved, stir in the ground almonds and breadcrumbs. Add lemon juice and chopped parsley to taste.

This keeps well for several days in the refrigerator.

Tarator

A popular sauce throughout the Middle East. Ground almonds may be substituted for pine nuts; in Turkey, it is usually made with walnuts or hazel nuts.

Serve the sauce with cold raw or par-boiled vegetables such as cauliflower, courgettes or runner beans which have been lightly dressed with oil and lemon juice.

> *100g (4 oz) pine nuts*
> *1 clove garlic*
> *juice of 1 lemon*
> *cold water*
> *2 slices of white bread, crusts removed*

Soak the bread in water and squeeze dry. Grind the pine nuts and add them to the bread, pounding to a pasty consistency. Thin with a little cold water and lemon juice. Add the crushed clove of garlic and blend until a thick, mayonnaise-like consistency is achieved. (*Note* This process can be speeded up by putting the ingredients through a sieve or into an electric blender.)

Serve with cold vegetables or as an hors d'oeuvre.

A Selection of Mixed Vegetable Salads

Les Crudités

Crudités make one of the simplest mixed salads, but fresh raw vegetables in the hands of an *artiste* can become a beautifully composed plate of contrasting colours and textures.

Crudités are frequently served at cocktail parties or as a dinner appetiser in pieces which can be eaten with the fingers and dipped into a creamy dressing or paté. Arrange a dish with a selection of vegetables such as carrot and celery sticks, cauliflower florets, button mushrooms, watercress, strips of turnip or celeriac, and cherry tomatoes. Serve with one of the puréed salads in the previous chapter; one of the 'dips' below; or a mayonnaise blended with herbs, anchovy paste, or curry. For something more exotic, serve in the Piedmontese fashion — with *bagna cauda,* made with that region's famous white Alba truffle (p 39).

As an hors d'oeuvre, crudités may be shredded into julienne strips — try cabbage, celeriac and beetroot — and arranged around a mound of watercress, button mushrooms or cauliflower florets. Dress generously with a strongly flavoured garlic or herb vinaigrette.

Whichever way you choose to serve them, crudités should be crisp, fresh and slightly chilled.

Antipasto

In Italy, salads are often served as part of a mixed hors d'oeuvre or *antipasti* (literally, before pasta). A typical selection might include fagioli e tonno (p 135); raw mushrooms dressed with oil and lemon juice; caponata (p 48); slices of cheese and salami; and fresh seafood salads. Combinations vary from region to region, but recipes for many popular antipasti salads are described throughout this book.

Dips

Creamy salads, flavoured mayonnaise or dips blended with cream cheese, sour cream, curd cheese or other bland soft cheeses that combine well with sharper cheeses, herbs, spices or chopped vegetables are frequently served as partners to seasonal raw vegetables.

These recipes illustrate a few of the many combinations for dips. Experiment with your own, but always ensure the dip is thick enough not to dribble and prepared far enough in advance for the flavours to mellow.

Roquefort Dip

100g (4 oz) Roquefort cheese (blue cheese is a less expensive substitute)
225g (8 oz) cream cheese
15-30ml (1-2 tbs) cream
dash of Tabasco sauce
dash of Worcestershire sauce

157

3 spring onions, chopped including 5cm (2 in) of green stem

Allow the Roquefort cheese to soften at room temperature. Crumble with a fork and blend with the cream cheese, adding as much cream as is required to achieve the correct 'dip' consistency. Season with Tabasco and Worcestershire sauce and fold in all but 5ml (1 tsp) of the chopped spring onion. Chill until ready to serve and sprinkle with the remaining onion. Place alongside (or in the middle of) a platter of crudités.

Cottage Cheese with Chopped Herbs and Vegetables

225g (8 oz) cottage cheese
1 carrot, finely chopped
2-3 large spring onions, finely chopped, including 5cm (2 in) of green stem
½ small green pepper, finely chopped
½ small red pepper, finely chopped
15ml (1 tbs) fresh chives, chopped
15ml (1 tbs) fresh parsley, finely chopped
salt and freshly ground pepper
paprika

Mix the chopped vegetables and herbs with the cottage cheese and season to taste with salt and pepper. Chill and sprinkle with paprika just before serving.

Variation For a spicier dip, add 1 large clove of garlic, finely minced, or 1 chopped chilli pepper.

Sour Cream, Bacon and Horseradish Dip

225g (8 oz) sour cream
15ml (1 tbs) horseradish, freshly grated
3 rashers streaky bacon, cooked until crisp and crumbled
5ml (1 tsp) Worcestershire sauce
2 spring onions, finely chopped (optional)

Blend the sour cream, horseradish and bacon with the Worcestershire sauce. If desired, add the spring onion. Chill and serve with a platter of crudités.

Salade de Pepino   *Serves 6*

Portuguese mixed salad

The Portuguese serve a salad with most meals. Tomatoes, peppers and onions are regular features and form the base for this rather festive salad.

1 large Spanish onion (a red one, if available)
2 tart green apples, eg Granny Smiths

1 medium-sized cucumber
2 large green peppers
2 large firm tomatoes
1 clove garlic, halved
90-120ml (6-8 tbs) olive oil
30ml (2 tbs) lime juice, freshly squeezed and strained
salt and freshly ground pepper
Garnish
6 whole chestnuts, 6 strips pimento, 2 hard-boiled eggs

Peel the onion and slice into thin rounds. Peel and core the apple and slice into thin wedges. Without peeling, slice the cucumber into thin rounds. Remove the stem and deseed the peppers; slice into thin strips. Cut each of the tomatoes into 8 wedges, of equal size.

Rub the inside of a large wooden bowl with half the cut garlic and fill it with the apples, cucumber, peppers, onion and tomatoes.

In a separate small bowl, combine the oil and lime juice. Season with salt and pepper to taste — and, if desired, crush the remaining garlic half into the dressing. Whisk to blend. Pour over the salad, toss well and allow to stand for at least an hour, during which the salad should be tossed once or twice again. In the meantime, boil the chestnuts for about 15 minutes; peel and grate while still hot. Set aside.

Separate the hard-boiled egg whites from the yolks and sieve both. Set aside.

Just before serving, garnish the salad as follows: sprinkle the sieved egg yolks in the centre and surround with a ring of grated chestnut, followed by a ring of egg white. Decorate with pimento strips, pinwheel fashion, around the outside of the bowl.

Horiatiki Salata   *Serves 4-6*

Greek village salad

This most traditional of Greek salads is served throughout the year, varying only with seasonal vegetables. The ubiquitous summer favourite in tavernas is a combination of cucumbers, tomatoes and onions, green peppers, olives and Feta cheese.

4-5 firm medium-sized tomatoes or *2 large Mediterranean tomatoes*
1 clove garlic, halved
1 large cucumber, peeled and thickly sliced
1 medium-sized Spanish onion or 4 large spring onions
16 Greek olives
2 medium-sized green peppers
150g (6 oz) Feta cheese, broken into bite-sized pieces

15ml (1 tbs) fresh parsley, chopped
7ml (1 heaped tsp) dried oregano
salt and freshly ground pepper
olive oil
optional
wine vinegar or lemon juice, capers

Cut the tomatoes into quarters. Remove the tops from the peppers, deseed and slice into thin rounds. Peel and slice the Spanish onion into thin rounds or slice the spring onions, including at least 5cm (2 in) of green stem, into round pieces.

Rub a large wooden bowl with the cut garlic and add the cucumber, tomatoes, onions, green peppers, half the Feta and 8 olives. Sprinkle with salt and plenty of freshly ground pepper. Toss. Crumble the remaining Feta across the top and sprinkle the parsley and oregano all over. Decorate with the remaining olives and capers, if desired. Then gradually pour on the olive oil, beginning at the outer edges and steadily moving, in circular motion, towards the centre.

The Greeks seem mostly to dress their salads with olive oil alone — usually a flavourful local variety — but a sprinkling of wine vinegar or lemon juice may appeal more to northern palates.

Fattoush and Panzanella

These are both bread salads, the first a Syrian peasant salad; the second an Italian version. They provide a cheap, tasty way of using leftover, slightly stale bread and, served with a soup, are filling enough for a supper main dish.

The quantities given here will serve 6 large portions.

Fattoush

3 pieces of pitta or 6 slices of white bread
*1 large cucumber, chopped into 2.5cm (1 in) pieces**
4 firm tomatoes, chopped into 2.5cm (1 in) pieces
1 medium-sized Spanish onion or 6 spring onions (including 5cm (2 in) of stem), chopped
1 medium-sized green pepper, deseeded and chopped
45ml (3 tbs) fresh parsley, finely chopped
30ml (2 tbs) fresh coriander, finely chopped (or 15ml (1 tbs) extra of parsley, if coriander unavailable)
30ml (2 tbs) fresh mint, finely chopped (or 15ml (1 tbs) dried mint)
2 cloves garlic, crushed
90-120ml (6-8 tbs) olive oil
juice of 1 lemon, freshly squeezed and strained

160

> salt and freshly ground pepper
> optional
> > 15ml (1 tbs) chopped purslane

Panzanella

> 1 small, slightly stale (day old) Italian loaf, diced
> 1 large Spanish onion, peeled and chopped
> 5 firm tomatoes, chopped into 2.5cm (1 in) pieces
> 45ml (3 tbs) fresh parsley, chopped
> 30ml (2 tbs) fresh basil, chopped (or 15ml (1 tbs) dried basil)
> 90ml (6 tbs) olive oil
> 30ml (2 tbs) wine vinegar
> 1 clove garlic, crushed
> salt and freshly ground pepper

*For the fattoush, sprinkle the chopped cucumber with salt and allow to drain in a colander or sieve for about half an hour before adding to the salad.

Place the pieces of bread in a large bowl and moisten with water. Drain off any excess liquid that has not been absorbed by the bread. Add the chopped vegetables and herbs, and season generously with salt and freshly ground pepper. Prepare a dressing with oil, lemon juice or vinegar, and crushed garlic.

Pour on the salad just before serving and toss well.

Haigagan Aghtsan   *Serves 4-6*

Armenian mixed salad

Romaine (or cos) is the choice lettuce for most Armenian salads. It is not uncommon to see an Armenian peasant enjoy a 'snack' of an entire head of romaine, fresh from the field, dressed only with a sprinkling of salt!

This salad uses a large romaine for its base, but a mixture of shredded cabbage, spinach leaves, purslane or watercress may be substituted when romaine is out of season.

> 1 large romaine (cos) lettuce
> 1 large tomato, deseeded and chopped into 2.5cm (1 in) pieces
> 1 green pepper, deseeded and sliced into thin rounds
> 5 spring onions, chopped (including 5cm (2 in) of green stem)
> 30ml (2 tbs) fresh mint, finely chopped or 30ml (2 tbs) fresh basil, finely
> > chopped
> 30ml (2 tbs) fresh parsley, finely chopped
> 60ml (4 tbs) olive oil
> 15ml (1 tbs) lemon juice
> salt and freshly ground pepper

optional
6 radishes, thinly sliced

Wash the lettuce, tear into bite-sized pieces, and dry thoroughly. Place in a large salad bowl with the chopped tomato, green pepper, spring onions, mint (or basil) and parsley. Toss and chill for at least 1 hour.

Meanwhile, prepare the dressing from oil and lemon juice. Season with salt and pepper. Just before serving, pour over the salad, toss gently and garnish with radish slices, if desired.

An interesting Middle Eastern variation of this salad can be made with the addition of 5ml (1 tsp) coriander seeds with the other herbs, substituting a dressing made from fresh *leban* (yoghurt) and a sprinkling of lemon juice.

Meshana Salata   *Serves 6-8*

Bulgarian mixed salad

A simple salad to accompany leftover slices of roast pork, beef or lamb. Choose your herbs according to the type of meat being served.

450g (1 lb) French beans
450g (1 lb) carrots
450g (1 lb) potatoes
90ml (6 tbs) olive oil
30ml (2 tbs) wine vinegar
salt and freshly ground pepper
45ml (3 tbs) mixed fresh green herbs (parsley, chives, marjoram, thyme, mint, basil, etc)

Peel the carrots and cut them into matchstick strips, approximately 7.5cm (3 in) long. Trim the beans but leave them whole (if runner beans are substituted for French beans, halve them). Cook together in lightly salted boiling water for about 8 minutes, or just until tender. Drain and set aside.

Wash and peel the potatoes. Cook in lightly salted boiling water until tender (the time will vary according to the size of the potatoes). Drain and cut into thick slices.

Place the potatoes in the centre of a shallow salad bowl and surround with carrots and beans.

Mix the oil and vinegar and season to taste with salt and freshly ground pepper. Pour over the vegetables and toss gently, being careful not to disturb the decorative arrangement. Chill and garnish with fresh herbs just before serving.

ook Choo Na Mool; *centre:* Chinese Lemon Chicken; *bottom left:*
Root Salad; *bottom right:* Selection of Crudités; *right:* Keundae

(Overleaf)
Left: Morrocan Carrot Salad; *bottom left:* Michoteta; *bottom:* Ful
Medames; *bottom right:* Tuica; *centre:* Khoshaf; *top right:* Bazargan

Top left: Salade des Champs; *top right:* Ambrosia Mould; *centre:* Wyoming
Bean Salad; with Russian dressing in foreground

Crunchy Belgian Salad   *Serves 4-6*

A cooked salad to be served slightly warm with main-course dishes

> *450g (1 lb) French beans*
> *325g (12 oz) new potatoes*
> *225g (8 oz) streaky bacon*
> *1 medium-sized Spanish onion, finely chopped*
> *15ml (1 tbs) butter*
> *45-60ml (3-4 tbs) wine vinegar*
> *30ml (2 tbs) fresh parsley, chopped*
> *salt and freshly ground pepper*

Cut the bacon crosswise into small strips.

Trim and wash the beans. Wash the potatoes but do not peel. In separate saucepans, cook the beans and potatoes in lightly salted boiling water until just tender.

Meanwhile, fry the bacon over a low heat. When it turns translucent, add the chopped onion and butter. Stirring constantly, fry the onion until it is soft, but do not allow to brown. The bacon should become crisp. When cooking is nearly completed, add the vinegar and reduce to a very low heat.

Drain the vegetables. Slice the potatoes into 5mm (¼ in) pieces and place, with the beans, in a serving bowl. Season to taste with salt and plenty of freshly ground pepper.

Pour the bacon and onion mixture over the warm vegetables and toss gently but thoroughly. Sprinkle with chopped parsley and serve immediately.

Tomate, Escarola y Alcachofas   *Serves 6*

Spanish tomato, batavia and artichoke salad

> *1 small head batavia*
> *4 medium-sized firm tomatoes, peeled*
> *5 tinned artichoke hearts, drained and quartered*
> *salt and freshly ground pepper*
> *1 clove garlic, crushed*
> *3 hard-boiled eggs*
> *1 egg white, whipped to form peaks*
> *90ml (6 tbs) mayonnaise (p 30)*
> *90ml (6 tbs) double cream, whipped*
> *a few sprigs of parsley*

Wash the batavia, drain thoroughly and break into pieces. Place in the centre of a large serving dish. Peel the tomatoes by immersing in boiling water for several seconds. When cool enough to handle, remove the skin and chop coarsely. Mix the artichokes with the tomatoes and turn onto the dish. Surround with quartered egg whites (set aside the yolks for garnish).

To the mayonnaise add the crushed garlic, up to 90ml (6 tbs) whipped cream and a few tablespoons of beaten egg white. Vary the amounts according to taste and desired consistency. Season well with salt and freshly ground pepper. Chill for an hour then pour over the salad.

Just before serving, decorate with the sieved egg yolk and a few sprigs of parsley.

Salade au Paprika   *Serves 6*

Paprika salad

> *1 medium-sized celeriac*
> *3 heads Belgian endive*
> *3 large field mushrooms*
> *1 green apple (eg Granny Smith)*
> *50g (2 oz) almonds, chopped*
> *200ml (7 fl oz) mayonnaise (see p 30)*
> *salt and freshly ground pepper*
> *1 pimento, cut into strips*
> *paprika*

Peel the celeriac and cut into matchstick pieces, about 7.5cm (3 in) long. Parboil in acidulated water for about 5 minutes. Drain and cool.

Wash the endive, drain and chop coarsely. Trim the stalks from the mushrooms, wipe clean with a damp paper towel and slice. Wash and core the apple, but do not peel. Cut into dice.

Place all these ingredients in a large bowl and add the chopped almonds, reserving 15ml (1 tbs) for garnish. Season with salt and pepper and blend in the mayonnaise. Chill for about an hour and just before serving, sprinkle generously with paprika and decorate with the pimento and remaining almonds.

Waldorf Salad   *Serves 4*

Apple, celery and nuts mixed with mayonnaise are the basic components of this well-known American salad, invented by Oscar Tschirky for the very first banquet in 1893 at New York's famous Waldorf Astoria Hotel. Raisins, sultanas or grapes are frequently added; celeriac, parboiled and diced, can be substituted for celery; and the dressing can be blended with whipped cream, if preferred.

> *1 head fresh crisp celery*

50g (2 oz) walnuts, coarsely chopped
225g (8 oz) green grapes, halved and pitted (or 100g (4 oz) raisins,
    currants or sultanas)
1 large crisp apple
juice of ½ lemon, freshly squeezed and strained
60-90ml (4-6 tbs) mayonnaise (see p 30)
salt and freshly ground pepper
optional
    30ml (2 tbs) whipped cream
Garnish
    chopped parsley and a few chopped celery leaves

Wash the celery thoroughly, trim the stalks and cut into 1cm (½ in) pieces. Peel the apple, core and dice.

In a large bowl, combine the celery, apple, chopped walnuts and grapes. Sprinkle with lemon juice and stir. Gradually add the mayonnaise and the whipped cream, if desired, stirring constantly to blend all ingredients. Season with salt and plenty of freshly ground pepper.

Chill until ready to serve and garnish with parsley and celery leaves.

Crunchy Health Salad   Serves 4-6

4 large carrots, peeled and coarsely grated
6 stalks celery, washed, drained and cut into 1cm (½ in) pieces
¼ small white cabbage, shredded
225g (8 oz) beetroot, peeled and diced
1 green pepper, deseeded and diced
45ml (3 tbs) Spanish onion, finely chopped
1 large crisp apple, cored and diced
50g (2 oz) almonds, walnuts or hazelnuts, coarsely chopped
75ml (5 tbs) sunflower oil
30ml (2 tbs) cider vinegar
2.5ml (½ tsp) brown sugar
salt and freshly ground pepper

Place all the chopped ingredients in a large bowl and dress with a mixture of oil, vinegar and sugar. Season to taste with salt and plenty of freshly ground pepper.

Serve with slices of wholemeal bread and fresh butter.

Chinese-style Mixed Salad   Serves 6

450g (1 lb) fresh mangetouts (snowpeas) or 1 lb packet frozen mangetouts
1 small head cauliflower
125g (5 oz) tin water chestnuts, drained and thinly sliced
45ml (3 tbs) chopped pimento

75ml (5 tbs) vegetable oil*
15ml (1 tbs) lemon juice
15ml (1 tbs) wine vinegar
5ml (1 tsp) caster sugar
1 small clove garlic, crushed
2.5ml (½ tsp) salt
30ml (2 tbs) sesame seeds

If fresh mangetouts are used, snap off the tops and remove the strings. Parboil in lightly salted water for 1 minute. Drain and set aside. Wash the cauliflower and break into small florets. Cook in lightly salted water for 3 minutes, or until just tender. Drain.

In a large bowl, combine the mangetouts, cauliflower, water chestnuts and chopped pimento. Cover and chill.

To prepare the dressing, place the oil (*a mixture of 3 parts corn or sunflower oil to 1 part Chinese sesame oil makes a deliciously different dressing for this recipe), vinegar, lemon juice, sugar, crushed garlic and salt in a small jar. Cover and shake well. Set aside.

Toast the sesame seeds under the grill until golden brown, shaking the pan occasionally to avoid burning.

Pour the dressing over the salad, toss to blend thoroughly and, just before serving, sprinkle on the toasted sesame seeds and toss again.

Oriental Salad Bowl *Serves 4-5*

225g (8 oz) bean sprouts, steamed for 1 minute
1 small webb lettuce
½ cucumber (or 1 whole ridge cucumber)
100g (4 oz) melon, diced
2 stalks celery
10 tinned lychees, drained
75ml (5 tbs) vegetable oil
15ml (1 tbs) wine vinegar
5ml (1 tsp) soy sauce (or more, if desired)
5ml (1 tsp) sugar
1.25ml (¼ tsp) prepared mustard
1 clove garlic, crushed
a few slices of red ginger pickle

Peel the cucumber and chop. Place in a sieve or colander, salt lightly and leave to drain for half an hour.

Wash the lettuce, drain and dry thoroughly. Break into bite-sized pieces or shred coarsely.

Wash and dry the celery stalks. Dice.

166

Combine the lettuce, bean sprouts, cucumber, melon, celery and lychees in a large bowl.

In a small jar, mix the oil, vinegar, soy sauce, sugar, mustard and crushed garlic. Shake well and add more soy sauce if desired. Pour over the salad, toss thoroughly and chill. Just before serving, toss again and garnish with red ginger pickle.

Martinique Salad Bowl   *Serves 6*

> *4 green (unripe) bananas*
> *1 large Mediterranean tomato*
> *1 medium-sized cucumber, peeled and coarsely chopped*
> *2 large carrots, peeled and shredded*
> *1 small Webb (iceberg) lettuce, washed and dried*
> *90ml (6 tbs) olive oil*
> *30ml (2 tbs) wine vinegar*
> *5ml (1 tsp) Dijon mustard*
> *1 clove garlic, crushed*
> *salt and freshly ground pepper*

Peel the green bananas carefully, so that they remain whole. Place in a saucepan with enough lightly salted cold water to cover. Bring to the boil and simmer, covered, until tender, approximately 10-15 minutes. Drain, cool and cut crosswise into 1cm (½ in) slices.

Meanwhile, immerse the tomato in boiling water for several seconds. Remove the skin, deseed and chop coarsely. Set aside.

Place the chopped cucumber in a sieve or colander, salt lightly and leave to drain for half an hour.

Prepare the dressing by blending the oil, vinegar, mustard and crushed garlic. Season with salt and pepper.

Line a large bowl with the whole lettuce leaves. In a separate bowl, mix the bananas, cucumber, tomato, celery and shredded carrots. Pour on the dressing and toss thoroughly. Spoon the mixture on to the lettuce leaves; chill for an hour and serve.

This salad should not be prepared too far in advance.

Urap   *Serves 5-6*

Indonesian mixed vegetable salad

To be authentically Indonesian, the dressing should include a small quantity of cooked *trasi*, a paste made from salted and dried shrimps, which have been pounded and rotted, and moulded into cakes. Although *trasi* (or *blachan*) can be bought at many Asian grocery stores, it has a very powerful, slightly unpleasant odour, so I have substituted anchovy or shrimp paste in this recipe.

(For the more adventurous cook, I recommend the recipe for Gado-Gado, p 236).

> *225g (8 oz) bean sprouts, steamed for 1 minute*
> *½ small white cabbage, shredded*
> *225g (8 oz) stringbeans, trimmed and halved*
> *4 stalks celery, chopped*
> *1 clove garlic, finely chopped*
> *flesh from ½ coconut, with brown skin removed, and grated*
> *2.5ml (½ tsp) shrimp or anchovy paste*
> *2 green chillis, deseeded and thinly sliced (p 243)*
> *soy sauce to taste*
> *brown sugar to taste*
> *salt to taste*

Cook the beans in lightly salted boiling water for approximately 8 minutes, or just until tender. Drain and set aside.

In a large bowl, mix the coconut, garlic, shrimp paste and chillis. Sprinkle soy sauce, sugar and salt (if desired) over the mixture, toss and adjust the seasoning. Allow to stand for several minutes then add the vegetables. Toss again and serve immediately.

Russian Vegetable Salad with Satsivi (Walnut Sauce) *Serves 4*

> *1 medium-sized cucumber, peeled and chopped*
> *1 large tomato, deseeded and diced*
> *4 stalks celery, chopped*
> *30ml (2 tbs) fresh parsley, finely chopped*
> *50g (2 oz) shelled walnuts*
> *1 small clove garlic*
> *pinch of cayenne pepper*
> *15ml (1 tbs) wine vinegar*
> *45ml (3 tbs) cold water*
> *30ml (2 tbs) onion, finely chopped*
> *30ml (2 tbs) fresh coriander leaves, chopped or 2.5ml (½ tsp) dried,*
> *   ground coriander*
> *salt*
> *10-12 large cos lettuce leaves*

Place the chopped cucumber in a sieve or colander and salt lightly. Allow to drain for half an hour. In a large bowl, combine the cucumber, tomato and celery. Sprinkle with salt.

Pound the walnuts to a paste with the garlic and cayenne pepper. Gradually stir in the vinegar and water until well blended. Add to the vegetables, toss, add the chopped herbs and onion, and toss again. Chill for at least an hour.

Line a large bowl with the lettuce leaves. Turn the vegetable mixture onto the centre and serve.

Mexican Salad   *Serves 6-8*

'Food goes through the eyes before it passes the mouth' is a Mexican saying, well illustrated by this decorative salad. The selection of ingredients from the serving dish is left to each individual according to his taste. An excellent dish for a party buffet.

> *450g (1 lb) potatoes, scrubbed*
> *4 large carrots, peeled and diced*
> *2 turnips, peeled and diced*
> *1 small cauliflower*
> *6-8 small gherkins*
> *30ml (2 tbs) capers*
> *12 black olives*
> *120ml (4 fl oz) mayonnaise (see p 30)*
> *10ml (2 tsp) Dijon mustard*
> *vinaigrette (see p 25)*

Cook the potatoes in their jackets until tender when pierced with a fork. Set aside.

Cook the carrots and turnips separately in lightly salted boiling water, for 8-10 minutes, until tender but still crisp. Drain and set aside.

Divide the cauliflower into florets and cook in lightly salted boiling water just until tender, about 5 minutes. Drain and set aside.

Sparingly dress each of the above three vegetables, while still warm, with vinaigrette. Arrange on a large serving dish as follows: pile the gherkins in the centre and surround with capers and olives in alternating bunches; follow with a ring of cauliflower, and finally a ring of alternating bunches of carrots, potatoes and turnips.

Blend the mustard and mayonnaise and spread between the rings of cauliflower and mixed vegetables. Serve at room temperature.

Ratatouille Provençale   *Serves 4-6*

This delicious mixture of southern vegetables is usually served cold as an hors d'oeuvre or as a side salad — either way, there should be plenty of crusty bread on hand to soak up the tasty liquid created by the cooking process.

> *2 large aubergines*
> *4 medium-sized courgettes*

2 large green peppers
2 medium-sized Spanish onions
450g (1 lb) tomatoes, peeled (see p 246)
2 cloves garlic
6-8 black peppercorns, crushed
12 coriander seeds
1 bouquet garni
light olive oil
coarse sea salt
Garnish
30ml (2 tbs) chopped parsley
15ml (1 tbs) chopped basil

Peel the onions and chop, or slice into very thin rounds. Cut the aubergines into 1cm (½ in) square dice (do not peel) and place in a colander. Salt lightly and allow to drain for 20-30 minutes. Slice the courgettes into 1cm (½ in) thick rounds. Halve the peppers, remove the seeds and ribs, and slice into strips about 1cm (½ in) wide. Chop the tomatoes coarsely.

Cover the bottom of a large frying pan with a thin layer of olive oil and sauté the onions over a low heat until they become translucent, about 10 minutes. Add the aubergines, peppers, bouquet garni and courgettes. Stir for 2 minutes, then cover and simmer for a further 10 minutes. Uncover, stir again, and add the garlic cloves, chopped tomatoes, crushed black pepper, coriander seeds and season to taste with salt. Continue cooking and stirring until the tomatoes have started to soften. (If necessary, add another 15-30ml (1-2 tbs) of oil, but be careful not to make the mixture too watery, as the vegetables will themselves create a lot of liquid.) Cover and simmer another 10-15 minutes.

Remove from the heat, take out the bouquet garni and allow to cool. Just before serving, garnish with chopped basil and parsley.

Ratatouille Creole   *Serves 6-8*

A dish from the French Caribbean islands, its special feature is the *gros concombre*, a huge light green cucumber about 450g (1 lb) in weight. Ordinary English cucumbers may be substituted in this recipe.

450g (1 lb) aubergines
450g (1 lb) cucumbers
450g (1 lb) courgettes
450g (1 lb) tomatoes, skinned (p 246)
15ml (1 tbs) fresh tarragon, chopped (or 5ml (1 tsp) dried tarragon)
30ml (2 tbs) fresh parsley, chopped
225g (8 oz) green peppers
5ml (1 tsp) sugar

90ml (6 tbs) olive oil
salt and freshly ground pepper
12 coriander seeds

Wash all the vegetables and drain.

Halve the peppers, deseed and cut into 1cm (½ in) slices. Trim the courgettes and cut into 1cm (½ in) slices. Peel the cucumbers and cut into 2.5cm (1 in) crosswise slices; salt lightly and place in a sieve or colander to drain for 20 minutes. Peel the aubergines and cut into crosswise slices 1cm (½ in) thick. Place in a colander, sprinkle with salt and leave to drain at the same time as the cucumbers. Skin the tomatoes and chop coarsely.

Heat the oil in a large earthenware or enamel casserole. Place the aubergines on the bottom, then add the cucumbers, courgettes, tomatoes and peppers. Season with sugar and plenty of freshly ground pepper, coriander seeds and half the parsley and tarragon. Cover and cook gently for 15 minutes.

Uncover and check the seasoning, adding salt and more pepper, if desired. Stir well and continue to cook, uncovered, for a further 15 minutes, or until most of the liquid has evaporated. If there is too much liquid when the cooking time is completed, remove the vegetables with a slotted spoon to the serving dish, increase the heat under the casserole and reduce the liquid to the desired quantity. Pour over the vegetables and chill until ready to serve. Garnish with the remaining chopped herbs.

Schlada L'filfil

Serves 5-6

Moroccan relish salad

A finely chopped Middle Eastern salad, perfect with cous cous or other hearty casserole dishes.

> *2 cucumbers*
> *1 large Mediterranean tomato*
> *1 large Spanish onion, peeled*
> *2-3 red chilli peppers, deseeded (p 243)*
> *45ml (3 tbs) olive oil*
> *15ml (1 tbs) wine vinegar*
> *salt to taste*

Chop each of the vegetables into very small dice. If desired, peel the cucumbers and tomato first.

Place all the ingredients in a large glass bowl and add oil, vinegar and salt. Chill for 1-2 hours before serving — this allows the 'hotness' of the chilli peppers to permeate the other vegetables.

Pesadumbre   *Serves 6*

Mexican chilled vegetable salad

'Pesadumbre', which literally means 'sadness', is a traditional Lenten dish
— spicy and vinegary — served as an accompaniment to meat and beans.
According to the prescriptions of the *curandero* (herb doctor), the use of
cumin strengthens the heart; laurel or bayleaf stimulates the affections;
thyme reinforces the veins and firms the breasts; and the small vegetables
fortify and relax the stomach.

> *900g (2 lb) courgettes*
> *450g (1 lb) petits pois*
> *30ml (2 tbs) chilli powder*
> *1 clove garlic*
> *2.5ml (½ tsp) cumin*
> *5ml (1 tsp) dried thyme (or 15ml (1 tbs) fresh thyme)*
> *150ml (¼ pt) red wine vinegar*
> *120ml (4 fl oz) water*
> *2 stalks celery*
> *1 bay leaf*
> *salt*
> *120ml (4 fl oz) olive oil*
> optional
> *freshly ground black pepper*

Trim the ends off the courgettes and cut into 1cm (½ in) circles. If using
frozen peas, cook in boiling water for 2-3 minutes; if tinned peas are used
(buy only the best French petits pois), drain off the liquid.

Mash the garlic, chilli powder and herbs, and place in a bowl with the
vegetables. Boil the water and vinegar and pour over the vegetables. Add
the bay leaf and season with salt. Cover the bowl with a plate and leave
the pesadumbre to stand in a cupboard for 48 hours.

Before serving, chill for at least 2 hours then gradually stir in the olive
oil. Remove the bay leaf and season with additional salt and a few grinds
of black pepper, if desired.

Salads with Poultry, Meat and Seafood

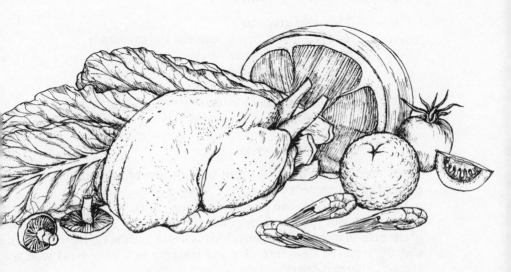

Honesalat   *Serves 4*

Danish chicken salad

425g (12 oz) diced cooked chicken (or turkey)
150g (6 oz) celeriac, peeled and cut into julienne strips or 6 stalks celery,
*   trimmed and chopped*
300ml (½ pt) double cream
2.5-5ml (½-1 tsp) mild mustard
salt and freshly ground pepper
30ml (2 tbs) capers
1 tomato, thinly sliced
a few large lettuce leaves

If using celeriac, parboil the strips in acidulated water (water to which a

173

few drops of vinegar or lemon juice have been added) for 3-4 minutes. Drain.

In a large bowl, combine the diced meat and celeriac (or celery). Whip the cream in a separate bowl with a wire whisk until it has slightly stiffened. Fold in the mustard and salt and pepper. Add to the chicken along with 15ml (1 tbs) of drained capers. Gently mix until all ingredients are well blended.

Line a large platter with lettuce leaves. Turn the chicken salad onto the platter, sprinkle with the remaining capers and garnish with tomato slices. Chill and serve.

Salade aux Avocats et Poulet   *Serves 6*

> *3 firm ripe avocados*
> *juice of 1 lemon, freshly squeezed and strained*
> *50g (2 oz) diced cooked chicken (or turkey)*
> *30ml (2 tbs) chopped celery*
> *30ml (2 tbs) chopped cucumber*
> *150ml (¼ pt) double cream*
> *12.5g (½ oz) slivered almonds*
> *paprika*
> *salt and freshly ground pepper*

Toast the almonds under the grill until golden brown, shaking the pan occasionally to prevent burning.

Halve the avocados and remove the stones. Sprinkle lightly with lemon juice, which will prevent discoloration of the flesh. Gently remove some of the pulp to increase the cavity, leaving about 1.25cm (½ in) in the shell. Cut the removed flesh into dice and combine in a large bowl with the chicken, chopped celery and cucumber.

Whip the cream with a wire whisk until slightly stiffened and add lemon juice, salt and pepper, to taste. Add to the chicken mixture along with the toasted almonds and gently stir until all ingredients are well blended.

Fill the avocado halves with the chicken salad and sprinkle paprika on top of each one. Chill until ready to serve.

Mrs Glasse's Salamongundy   *Serves 6+*

'You may always make Salamongundy of such things as you have, according to your fancy.'

The Art of Cookery, Hannah Glasse

This English favourite, later known simply as salamagundy, was intended to form a centrepiece for a supper table. It was always served on a large platter with all the ingredients — shredded and minced in different ways

— arranged in separate rings of contrasting colours.
The size of your chicken will determine the number of servings.

1 small cold roast chicken
1 crisp lettuce, washed whole and dried
1 tin anchovy fillets, drained and rinsed
4 hard-boiled eggs
1 lemon
a few sprigs of parsley, plus 15-30ml (1-2 tbs) fresh parsley, finely chopped
12-18 small pickled onions
150ml (¼ pt) vinaigrette (p 25)
100g (4 oz) large white grapes, skinned and pitted
150g (6 oz) stringbeans, trimmed and halved

Cook the green beans in a little boiling salted water for 6-8 minutes, or until just tender. Drain and set aside. Remove the skin from the chicken and cut all the white meat into thin strips, about 7.5cm (3 in) by 5mm (¼ in). Cut the dark meat into dice.

Peel the lemon and chop into small dice, removing all the pith and pips. Mash the egg yolks and chop 4-6 anchovies into small pieces. Cut the remaining anchovies in half lengthwise. Finely chop the egg whites.

In a large bowl, mix the diced dark meat, chopped lemon, parsley, egg yolks and chopped anchovies. Blend with half the vinaigrette and mix well.

Shred the lettuce very finely and spread it about 1cm (½ in) thick across a large serving dish. Pile the chicken mixture in the centre in a loaf shape and decorate with one or two onions and a few grapes. Surround with strips of white meat, leaving spaces between the strips and an empty ring around the circumference of the chicken mixture. In this ring scatter the chopped egg whites and the green beans. In between the strips of chicken, put the remaining chopped grapes and place the anchovy strips in between the chicken strips and the grapes. Decorate the outer edge of the platter with the white onions and a few sprigs of parsley.

Chill and just before serving, pour the remaining vinaigrette over the undressed chicken and garnishes.

American Chicken Salad, Southern Style   *Serves 4-6*

2 hard-boiled eggs
5ml (1 tsp) dry mustard
5ml (1 tsp) caster sugar
15-30ml (1-2 tbs) white flour
240ml (8 fl oz) chicken broth (with fat skimmed)
275-325g (10-12 oz) cooked chicken, diced
15ml (1 tbs) olive oil

15ml (1 tbs) chicken fat or *30ml (2 tbs) butter*
salt and freshly ground pepper
45-75ml (3-5 tbs) mayonnaise (p 30), strongly flavoured with lemon juice
15ml (1 tbs) fresh parsley, chopped
paprika
optional
15ml (1 tbs) fresh chives, chopped

Mash the egg yolks and blend with the sugar, mustard and the flour. Chop the whites and set aside. Gradually add the chicken broth, stirring constantly with a wooden spoon until smooth.

In a saucepan, heat the olive oil and chicken fat (or butter). When hot but not bubbling, slowly add the broth and seasoning mixture. Cook over low heat until the mixture is the consistency of mayonnaise. Remove from the heat and sieve to remove any lumps. Chill for 1 hour, then add the mayonnaise and mix well.

In a large bowl, place the diced chicken, chopped egg whites and fresh herbs. Season with salt and pepper and add the dressing. Blend thoroughly and chill. Just before serving, sprinkle with paprika.

Salade de Poulet aux Amandes

Serves 10

Chicken salad with toasted almonds

1 1.35-1.80kg (3-4 lb) chicken, roasted or boiled
100g (4 oz) raisins
1 bunch watercress
4 stalks celery
37g (1½ oz) slivered almonds
1 orange
120ml (8 tbs) olive oil
30ml (2 tbs) wine vinegar
salt and freshly ground pepper
optional
45-60ml (3-4 tbs) mayonnaise (see p 30)

Soak the raisins in hot water for approximately 1 hour. Drain. Toast the almonds under the grill until golden brown, shaking the pan occasionally to prevent burning.

Remove the skin from the chicken and carve the meat into julienne strips or dice.

Wash the watercress, dry and discard any damaged leaves and thick stems. Clean the celery and chop into small pieces.

In a large bowl, mix the chicken, celery, toasted almonds and raisins.

Mix the oil, vinegar and juice of half the orange. Season with salt and pepper to taste and pour over the chicken salad. Toss to blend all

ngredients and turn onto a large serving dish. Surround with watercress
and decorate on top with the remaining half orange, cut into thin slices.

If a creamy chicken salad is preferred, add a few tablespoons, according
to taste, of mayonnaise to the chicken mixture, and half the amount of
vinaigrette.

Chill for several hours before serving.

Hawaiian Chicken Salad in Tomato Petals   *Serves 6*

> *200ml (1/3 pt) mayonnaise (p 30)*
> *10ml (2 tsp) curry powder*
> *salt and freshly ground pepper*
> *275-325g (10-12 oz) diced cooked chicken*
> *1 eating apple, peeled and diced*
> *3 stalks celery, diced*
> *100g (4 oz) large green grapes, pitted and quartered*
> *50g (2 oz) slivered almonds (or chopped walnuts or chopped hazelnuts)*
> *10ml (2 tsp) grated onion*
> *6 very large firm tomatoes (Mediterranean or US beefsteak)*
> *6 sprigs parsley*

Blend the mayonnaise with the curry powder and season to taste with salt
and pepper.

Toast the almonds under the grill until golden brown, shaking the pan
occasionally to prevent burning. If walnuts or hazelnuts are used, no
toasting is necessary.

In a large bowl, combine the chicken, apple, celery, grapes, nuts and
grated onion. Add the curried mayonnaise and stir until well blended.
Chill.

When ready to serve, cut the tomatoes into sixths *almost* but not all the
way through and gently separate to form petals. Scoop out some of the
flesh and seeds to create a larger cavity and fill with chicken salad. Place a
sprig of parsley in the centre of each and serve on individual plates.

Duck and Orange Salad   *Serves 6*

> *225g (8 oz) duck meat, skin removed and diced*
> *75g (3 oz) dry roasted peanuts*
> *30ml (2 tbs) vinaigrette (see p 25)*
> *225g (8 oz) fresh shelled green peas (or frozen peas), cooked al dente*
> *60ml (4 tbs) mayonnaise (see p 30)*
> *celery salt*
> *salt and freshly ground pepper*
> *1 bunch watercress*
> *2 oranges, peeled and sliced into rings*

177

Wash and dry the watercress, discarding any damaged leaves and thick stems. Season the duck with celery salt and sprinkle with vinaigrette. Add to the duck the peas and peanuts, and blend the entire mixture with *up to* 60ml (4 tbs) mayonnaise, according to taste. Adjust seasoning with salt and plenty of freshly ground pepper.

Turn the mixture onto a large serving dish and surround with watercress and orange slices, reserving a little of both to decorate the top. Chill until ready to serve.

Nôm Ga   *Serves 4*
Vietnamese Chicken Salad

2 large chicken breasts
1 thick slice belly pork
6 large prawns, peeled
1 ridge cucumber or ½ telegraph (long) cucumber
3 small carrots
60ml (4 tbs) wine vinegar
5ml (1 tsp) sugar
salt
50g (2 oz) shelled roasted peanuts

Boil the chicken breasts and belly pork over medium heat until tender and thoroughly cooked. Remove from the heat, drain and allow to cool. Peel the cucumber and cut into small dice. Place in a sieve or colander, sprinkle with salt, and leave to stand 10-15 minutes. Rinse and drain thoroughly.

Peel the carrots and grate coarsely. Grind the peanuts (this can be done quickly with an electric coffee grinder). Set both aside.

Shred the chicken into fairly large pieces. Cut the pork into thin strips, cutting *across* the meat. Slice the prawns into 1cm (½ in) pieces.

In a large bowl, combine the chicken, pork, prawns, grated carrots and cucumber. Add the vinegar which has been sweetened with 5ml (1 tsp) sugar. Mix well and correct the seasoning with salt. Chill. Just before serving, add all but 15ml (1 tbs) of ground peanuts to the salad. Toss and sprinkle the remaining peanuts across the top.

Chinese Lemon Chicken   *Serves 6-8*

This dish takes time to prepare but it makes a delicious and most unusual salad.

1 1.35-1.80kg (3-4 lb) chicken
10 dried black mushrooms
4 lemons
45ml (3 tbs) vegetable or peanut oil
60ml (4 tbs) finely shredded fresh ginger

178

4-5 fresh green chilli peppers, deseeded and cut into julienne strips (see p 243)
25g (1 oz) caster sugar
5-10ml (1-2 tsp) lemon extract
salt

The authentic way to prepare the chicken is to steam it over boiling water for at least an hour, or until tender. Alternatively, it can be boiled gently until cooked, but do not overboil as the meat will become tough and rubbery.

While the chicken cooks, prepare the other ingredients: cover the mushrooms with boiling water, allow to stand for 20 minutes, then drain and squeeze to extract moisture. Cut off and discard the tough stems. Set aside.

Carefully peel one of the lemons into long continuous strips, avoiding as much of the pith as possible. Cut each strip into the thinnest possible shreds and set aside. Grate another lemon to make about 15ml (1 tbs) of grated rind. Set aside. Squeeze enough lemons to make about 120ml (4 fl oz) of juice, making sure to remove all pips.

Leave the cooked chicken to cool in the cooking liquid. Then remove; strain and reserve the broth. Gently remove the breast meat and cut into small cubes. Chop the wings, legs and thighs into small pieces (leave in the bone if you have a sharp butcher's knife).

In a Chinese wok or large enamel frying pan, heat the oil over a high flame and add the mushrooms and ginger. Cook for about 1 minute, then add the chilli peppers and lemon shreds. Stir and cook for a further minute, then add the sugar and stir again. Add 180ml (6 fl oz) of the chicken broth, bring to the boil and add the lemon juice and salt, to taste. Add the chicken pieces and cook for another minute, maximum. With a slotted spoon, transfer the pieces to a large shallow bowl, arranging them neatly and symmetrically. To the liquid in the pan, add the grated lemon and lemon extract. Reboil and continue cooking to slightly reduce the quantity. Pour over the chicken and let stand to room temperature. (If prepared in advance and chilled, allow to return to room temperature again before serving.)

Chef's Salad   *Serves 4-5*

This great American favourite is now finding devotees across the Atlantic. The original chef salad may have been the creation of Louis Diat, the late chef of the bygone Ritz-Carlton Hotel in New York; his use, however, of watercress as the *only* green has certainly been supplanted by the use of lettuce, generally iceberg (Webb), in combination with other seasonal greens according to the whim, as the name suggests, of the chef.

This is a basic recipe, but it may be garnished and varied in many ways.

Chef salad should be prepared in a large glass or wooden bowl and served with a selection of dressings. American favourites are Russian, Roquefort or oil and vinegar.

1 large iceberg (Webb) lettuce
225g (8 oz) cooked turkey or chicken (preferably white meat), cut in
  julienne strips
225g (8 oz) cooked ham, cut in julienne strips or 225g (8 oz) ox (beef)
  tongue, cut in julienne strips
225g (8 oz) Emmental, Gruyère or Jahlsberg cheese, julienne or cubed
2-3 hard-boiled eggs, quartered
2 firm tomatoes, quartered
Suggested garnishes
  olives, parsley, croutons, crumbled bacon, capers, spring onions, pickled
  onions, tinned artichoke hearts, asparagus tips, watercress, etc

Wash and dry the lettuce. Break it into bite-sized pieces and line the salad bowl, forming a thick bed for the other ingredients.

Arrange the julienne strips of meats and cheese, pinwheel fashion, in rotating bunches around the centre. Along the outer edge of the bowl, arrange the egg and tomato wedges.

Decorate with any of the suggested garnishes and serve slightly chilled. Some chefs toss, dress and arrange the salad on individual plates — but only after first displaying the carefully arranged creation to be admired before eaten!

Chef Salad, Italian-Style *Serves 4-6*

1 head batavia (escarole)
75g (3 oz) Italian salami, cubed or cut into julienne strips
75g (3 oz) Fontina or Mozzarella cheese, cubed or cut into julienne strips
4 anchovy fillets, drained and chopped
2 small spicy Italian sausages
45-60ml (3-4 tbs) red wine
75ml (5 tbs) olive oil
15-30ml (1-2 tbs) wine vinegar
pinch of oregano
salt and freshly ground pepper

Wash and dry the lettuce then place in a large bowl.

Brown the sausages in the red wine, ensuring they are well cooked before removing to drain and cool. Cut into 1cm (½ in) rounds and set aside.

In a glass jar, put the oil, vinegar, chopped anchovies, a dash of salt, plenty of freshly ground pepper and a pinch of oregano. Cover tightly and shake to blend all ingredients. Pour about a third of the dressing onto the lettuce leaves and toss lightly. Arrange in the bottom of a salad bowl.

Arrange the sausage, cheese and salami pinwheel fashion in rotating bunches around the centre. Chill for about an hour.

Bring to the table for display before adding the rest of the dressing. Toss and serve with crusty Italian bread.

Dannevang Salad
Serves 6

Danish stuffed tomatoes

6 large Mediterranean (or beefsteak) tomatoes
1 small round lettuce
225g (8 oz) Danish Samsoe cheese, cubed (Edam, Gouda or Fontina may be
   substituted)
150g (6 oz) cooked ham, cubed
150g (6 oz) cooked chicken, cubed
90-120ml (6-8 tbs) olive oil
30-45ml (2-3 tbs) tarragon vinegar
5ml (1 tsp) salt
freshly ground pepper
5ml (1 tsp) dry mustard
15ml (1 tbs) fresh parsley, chopped
Garnish
parsley, green olives
optional
15ml (1 tbs) fresh chives, chopped

Wash the lettuce, removing any bruised or rough dark green outer leaves, but leave whole. Shred and dry thoroughly in a lettuce basket or colander.

In a small bowl, blend the oil, vinegar, fresh herbs, salt, dry mustard and plenty of freshly ground pepper.

Combine the shredded lettuce, cheese and meat with the dressing and toss well.

Cut a large slice off the top of the tomatoes and carefully scoop out enough flesh to form a large cavity. Fill the tomatoes with the salad mixture, then arrange them in a circle on a large serving dish, placing any leftover salad in the centre. Decorate with parsley and green olives.

Russian Mixed Vinigret
Serves 4-5

225g (8 oz) cold roast beef, cubed
225g (8 oz) cooked beetroot, peeled and cubed
225g (8 oz) potatoes, boiled and cubed

181

3 large carrots, diced and boiled for 8-10 minutes, or until just tender
4 small gherkins, chopped
60ml (4 tbs) (or less, according to taste) mayonnaise (see p 30)
1 small tin baby shrimps, drained
a few large lettuce leaves
salt and freshly ground pepper
Garnish
8-10 black olives
2 hard-boiled eggs, quartered

Place all the ingredients in a large bowl and add enough mayonnaise to bind the mixture. Season with salt and pepper, to taste, and turn onto a large serving dish which has been lined with lettuce leaves. Decorate with black olives and quartered eggs and chill for several hours before serving.

Huzarensla   *Serves 4-5*

This is a Dutch version of Russian vinigret, similar to the recipe above. It is purported to originate from the small garrison towns where the hussars were stationed. Army food being nearly inedible, the young soldiers were encouraged to find kitchen maids as girlfriends — preferably ones that served rich families. After the dinner hour, the soldier would sneak round to his sweetheart's kitchen and charm her into preparing a salad of leftovers.

225-275g (8-10 oz) cooked veal or pork, cubed
2 Granny Smith apples (or any tart variety), peeled, cored and diced
1 medium-sized cooked beetroot, peeled and diced
2 hard-boiled eggs
4 small gherkins, chopped
45-75ml (3-5 tbs) mayonnaise (see p 30)
2 spring onions, chopped (including 5cm (2 in) of green stem)
8-10 small new potatoes, boiled and quartered
75ml (5 tbs) olive oil
15-30ml (1-2 tbs) vinegar
salt and freshly ground pepper
a few large lettuce leaves
1 medium-sized firm tomato, thinly sliced

Chop one of the hard-boiled eggs and set aside the other for garnish.

In a large bowl, combine the meat, apples, beetroot, chopped eggs, gherkins, spring onions and potatoes.

Prepare a dressing of oil and vinegar and season with salt and freshly ground pepper.

Pour over the salad mixture and toss to coat thoroughly. Turn the salad onto a large serving dish lined with lettuce leaves. Arrange in a boat shape and spread a thin layer of mayonnaise right across the top. Decorate with tomato slices and the remaining egg, quartered.

Salade Bagration
Serves 6-8

A variation on one of Alice B. Toklas's recipes, this is an extremely decorative salad for a party buffet.

6-8 tinned artichoke hearts, drained and sectioned into thirds
1 small celeriac
100g (4 oz) macaroni (approx 5cm (2 in) in length)
5 large hard-boiled eggs
6-8 thick slices of boiled beef tongue or baked ham
salt and freshly ground pepper
150-200ml (5-7 fl oz) mayonnaise (see p 30)
45ml (3 tbs) tomato purée
30ml (2 tbs) fresh parsley, finely chopped

Peel and shred the celeriac, then parboil (3-4 minutes) immediately in lightly salted water to which a few drops of lemon juice or vinegar have been added. Drain and set aside.

Add the macaroni to approximately 1 litre (2 pts) rapidly boiling salted water. Whe the water comes back to the boil, reduce the heat and cook gently for 10-15 minutes, or until the macaroni is tender but not too soft. Drain in a colander, refresh with cold water, drain again and set aside.

Chop the egg whites and yolks in 2 separate bowls. Set aside. Cut the meat into julienne strips and set aside.

Place the macaroni in a large bowl with the artichokes and celeriac. Season with salt and pepper and blend in the mayonnaise to which the tomato purée has been added.

Turn this mixture on to the centre of a large serving dish and surround first with a ring of egg yolk, then meat strips, and finally egg whites. Sprinkle the parsley on the centre mound and chill for at least 2 hours before serving.

Salvador Dali's Red Salad
Serves 4-5

In *The Artist's Cookbook*, published by the Museum of Modern Art in New York, it says of Dali: 'He does not have time to entertain as much as he would like, but when he does, he has dinners for 20-25 friends. His table is always exquisitely presented and always white — white porcelain, white damask, and white flowers in crystal vases'. This beautiful red salad makes a striking contrast to that background.

225g (8 oz) cooked beetroot, peeled and diced

225g (8 oz) smoked tongue (or smoked ham, if tongue unavailable) diced
325g (12 oz) red cabbage, finely grated
45ml (5 tbs) double cream, chilled
45ml (3 tbs) lemon juice, freshly squeezed and strained
15ml (1 tbs) tomato purée
1 large shallot, finely chopped
5ml (1 tsp) sugar
dash cayenne pepper
1 small webb (iceberg) lettuce, washed, dried and broken into pieces
salt and freshly ground pepper

Make the dressing by combining the cream, tomato purée, sugar, chopped shallot and cayenne pepper. Beat with a wire whisk until light and foamy (approximately 3 minutes). Gradually beat in the lemon juice.

Put the beets, red cabbage and tongue in a large bowl. Add the dressing and toss to blend thoroughly. Cover and chill for at least 2 hours.

Just before serving, line a large serving dish with lettuce leaves. Season the salad mixture with salt and pepper and arrange in the centre of the platter. Serve with crusty French bread and full-bodied red wine.

Brazilian Beef Salad   *Serves 4*

A friend who lived for many years in Rio de Janeiro says this is a popular and simple salad recipe for using up leftover meat.

325-400g (12-14 oz) cooked beef
1 large Spanish onion
salt and freshly ground pepper
120ml (8 tbs) olive oil
juice of ½ lemon, freshly squeezed and strained
1 clove garlic, minced
optional
15ml (1 tbs) chopped green chilli pepper (p 243)

Slice the beef into thin strips. Peel and slice the onion into thin rounds. Place both in a shallow serving bowl.

Prepare a dressing from the oil, lemon juice and garlic. Pour over the salad and season well with salt and plenty of pepper. If desired, add the chopped chilli pepper. Toss to cover all ingredients with dressing and marinate in the refrigerator for at least 2 hours, stirring occasionally, before serving.

Hawaiian Crabmeat and Pawpaw Salad   *Serves 6*

Pawpaws (also known as papayas or tree melons) are a popular tropical fruit. Often available from the West Indian markets of Great Britain, they are also cultivated in the warmer parts of America and shipped to supermarkets all over the country.

> *3 pawpaws*
> *450g (1 lb) crabmeat (flesh only)*
> *60ml (4 tbs) mayonnaise (p 30)*
> *60ml (4 tbs) (or less, according to taste) sour cream*
> *3 stalks celery, chopped*
> *30ml (2 tbs) chilli sauce (Tabasco)*
> *30ml (2 tbs) lime juice*
> *scant 5ml (1 tsp) caster sugar*
> *1.25ml (¼ tsp) salt*
> *45ml (3 tbs) fresh chives, chopped*
> *few large lettuce leaves*

Using a potato peeler, carefully remove the skin from the pawpaws; halve them and scoop out the seeds and some of the flesh with a spoon.

In a large bowl, mix the mayonnaise, sour cream to taste, chilli sauce, lime juice, sugar, salt and 30ml (2 tbs) chives. Blend and add more salt or sugar if desired. Add the crabmeat and celery and stir until thoroughly coated with dressing. Arrange the pawpaw halves on a large dish lined with lettuce leaves. Fill each with the crab mixture and sprinkle a few chopped chives on top. Chill until ready to serve.

The following mixture also makes a delicious filling for pawpaws.

> *450g (1 lb) cooked jumbo prawns, chopped into 1cm (½ in) pieces*
> *3-4 stalks celery, chopped*
> *50g (2 oz) slivered almonds, toasted golden brown*
> *salt and freshly ground pepper*
> *5ml (1 tsp) curry powder*
> *90ml (6 tbs) mayonnaise (p 30)*
> *15-30ml (2-3 tbs) sour cream*
> *juice of ½ lime*
> *½ lime cut into 4-6 thin slices*

In a large bowl, blend the mayonnaise, sour cream, curry powder and lime juice. Season with salt and pepper. Add the chopped celery, toasted almonds and shrimp, and mix well.

185

Fill pawpaw halves (as described in previous recipe) and garnish with a slice of lime.

Crab Salad Louis

This is a San Francisco favourite, said to have originated at Solari's restaurant. Estimate the amount of crabmeat required according to the number being served and whether the dish is to be served as an appetiser or main course — but always use fresh crabmeat, if available.

The dressing can be poured over the crabmeat just before serving or brought to the table in a sauceboat, for the portions to be dressed individually, as desired.

120ml (8 tbs) mayonnaise (p 30)
60ml (4 tbs) double cream
15ml (1 tbs) paprika (or, for extra spicy dressing, use 15ml (1 tbs) chilli sauce)
5ml (1 tsp) Worcestershire sauce
5 spring onions, chopped (including 5cm (2 in) of green stem)
30ml (2 tbs) lemon juice
Garnish
lemon wedges, 2 hard-boiled eggs, quartered, a few sprigs of parsley, a few large lettuce leaves.

Line a large platter with the lettuce leaves and pile the crabmeat on top. Decorate with lemon wedges, quartered eggs and parsley. Prepare the dressing by mixing all the above ingredients, stirring until thoroughly blended. Chill for at least an hour before using and serve in one of the ways described above.

Vinigret Olivier

Serves 6-8

A special variation of the basic well-known Russian vinigret; a salad of mixed boiled vegetables, seafood and mayonnaise.

6 medium-sized potatoes, peeled and boiled
2 medium-sized cooked beetroot
450g (1 lb) fresh or frozen green peas, boiled or steamed al dente
1 small cucumber
450g (1 lb) green beans, trimmed, halved and boiled al dente (approx 8 minutes)
100g (4 oz) button mushrooms
225g (8 oz) crabmeat (or 1 large tin best salmon, drained)
5 spring onions, chopped (including 5cm (2 in) green stem)
90ml (6 tbs) mayonnaise
salt and freshly ground pepper

15ml (1 tbs) lemon juice

Peel the cucumber, cut into large dice and place in a sieve or colander. Salt lightly and allow to drain for approximately half an hour. Dice the potatoes and beetroot. Clean the mushrooms with a damp paper towel, trim the stalks and cut into quarters.

In a large bowl, mix all the vegetables and the crabmeat (or salmon). Gently fold in up to 90ml (6 tbs) mayonnaise. Add the lemon juice and season to taste with salt and pepper. Chill for at least an hour before serving.

Oriental Mussel Salad   *Serves 6-8*

> *1 540g (1 lb 4 oz) tin bamboo shoots*
> *1 large red pepper*
> *6 stalks celery*
> *12 black olives*
> *45ml (3 tbs) fresh parsley, chopped*
> *30ml (2 tbs) capers*
> *1 large, approx 550g (20 oz) tin mussels in brine*
> *30ml (2 tbs) sesame oil*
> *15ml (1 tbs) vegetable oil*
> *15-30ml (1-2 tbs) lemon juice, to taste*
> *10ml (2 tsp) light soy sauce*
> *salt and freshly ground pepper*
> optional
> *2.5ml (½ tsp) sugar*

Grill the red pepper until all sides are charred. Cool; skin, remove the core and seeds. Chop into small dice.

Drain the bamboo shoots and cut into pieces about 1cm (½ in) thick. Chop the celery and the black olives, discarding the stones.

Drain the mussels and place them in a large glass bowl with the various chopped ingredients. Add the capers and parsley.

To prepare the dressing, mix the oils, lemon juice and soy sauce. Add sugar if a sweeter dressing is preferred. Pour over the salad, toss well and season with salt and pepper to taste. Chill for 2-3 hours, stirring occasionally, before serving.

Insalata di Frutti di Mare

Italian seafood salad

This delicious salad, a standard appetiser in most Italian restaurants, should be made with the best quality olive oil, a generous amount of

187

crushed garlic, freshly ground pepper, a sprinkling of lemon juice and fresh chopped parsley.

The selection and proportions of seafood can vary; see what is available from your fishmonger, but use as many fresh ingredients as possible. Prawns or scampi, scallops, squid, octopus, crabmeat and mussels are all excellent. Where cooking is required, stew the fish in lightly salted boiling water to which a slice of onion and lemon peel have been added, for about 5 minutes, or until tender.

Drain the seafood and mix in a large bowl with crushed garlic, oil, lemon juice, salt, pepper and chopped parsley. Add a dash of oregano, if desired, and leave to stand for 1-2 hours, stirring occasionally, so that the seafood is well marinated.

Bow Yee *Serves 2-3*

Chinese Abalone salad

There are many species of this large univalve mollusk which is such a popular ingredient in Chinese cookery. Fresh abalone needs tenderising. The Chinese often purchase it dried and then soak it, but for Westerners approaching abalone for the first time, I recommend the tinned pre-cooked variety which requires no special preparation.

> *1 227g (8 oz) tin pre-cooked abalone*
> *4-5 stalks celery*
> *5ml (1 tsp) sugar*
> *15ml (1 tbs) peanut or Chinese sesame oil*
> *15ml (1 tbs) light soy sauce*
> *salt, to taste*

Drain the abalone and slice very thinly. Wash the celery, dry and cut crosswise into diagonal strips. Place both ingredients into a serving bowl and add the oil, soy sauce and sugar. Stir to coat the abalone and season with salt. Chill, stirring occasionally, until ready to serve.

Yam Koong *Serves 6-8*

Thai shrimp salad

> *240ml (8 fl oz) fresh milk*
> *75g (3 oz) fresh coconut, grated*
> *900g (2 lb) fresh raw jumbo prawns or shrimps*
> *10ml (2 tsp) salt*
> *1 bay leaf*
> *15ml (1 tbs) olive oil*
> *1 large green pepper, coarsely chopped*

2 cloves garlic, finely chopped
2 shallots, finely chopped
30ml (2 tbs) light soy sauce
1 green apple, peeled and grated
45ml (3 tbs) chopped peanuts

In a small saucepan, combine the milk and coconut. Bring slowly to the boil, remove from the heat and leave to stand for 30 minutes. Pass the mixture through a sieve, pressing out all the milk from the coconut. Discard the pulp and set aside the liquid.

De-vein the shrimps and wash thoroughly. Place them in a good-sized saucepan with enough water to cover, salt and the bay leaf. Bring to a boil and simmer for 5-8 minutes, or until the shrimps have cooked through. Drain, peel, and split them lengthwise in half. Chill for 1 hour.

Heat the olive oil in a large frying pan. Add the garlic and shallots and fry gently for 2 minutes, stirring constantly. Remove from the heat and when slightly cooled, place in a bowl with the green peppers, soy sauce, apple and peanuts. Toss thoroughly and add the coconut milk. Chill for at least an hour.

Arrange the shrimps in a shallow dish, pour over the chilled dressing and serve at once.

Salade Niçoise   *Serves 6-7*

'There are', writes Elizabeth David, 'as many versions of [salade niçoise] as there are cooks in Provençe, but in whatever way it is interpreted, it should be a simple and rather crude country salad. The ingredients should be put in the bowl with each category kept separate, in large pieces, nicely arranged so that the salad looks colourful and fresh. The dressing should be mixed in at the table.'

1 head cos (romaine) lettuce, washed, dried and broken into bite-sized pieces
225g (8 oz) potato salad (see basic potato salad I, p 104)
225-325g (8-12 oz) French beans
15-30ml (1-2 tbs) fresh seasonal herbs, chopped
5ml (1 tsp) Dijon mustard
3 medium-sized firm tomatoes, quartered
2 hard-boiled eggs, quartered
6 anchovy fillets
1 200g (7 oz) tin tuna fish
½ medium-sized Spanish onion
12 black olives
1 large clove garlic, crushed
120ml (8 tbs) olive oil

30-45ml (2-3 tbs) wine vinegar or lemon juice
salt and freshly ground pepper

Cook the beans in lightly salted boiling water for approximately 6-8 minutes, or just until tender.

Drain the tuna fish and anchovy fillets. Peel the onion and slice into thin rounds.

Line a large wooden salad bowl with a bed of lettuce leaves. Place chunks of tuna fish in the centre and surround, pinwheel fashion, with alternating bunches of green beans, spoonfuls of potato salad and tomato wedges. Spread the quartered eggs around the outside to form a border and place strips of anchovies or olives between each quarter. Sprinkle onion rings and freshly chopped herbs across the top.

Prepare a dressing of olive oil, vinegar or lemon juice, mustard, crushed garlic, salt and plenty of freshly ground pepper.

Bring the dressing to the table in a sauceboat, to be poured over the salad just before serving — and there should always be plenty of crusty French bread to accompany a salade niçoise.

Tuna Fish Salad   *Serves 2-3*

One of the mainstays of the American home lunch, coffee-shop, drugstore counter and picnic basket.

Canned tuna (tunny fish) is the base and a variety of different ingredients — from chopped fresh vegetables such as peppers or onions, to pickles, olives or even pieces of bacon — are added and blended with mayonnaise, and sometimes sour cream as well. Here are two variations:

> *1 200g (7 oz) tin tuna*
> *2 stalks celery, finely chopped*
> *2 hard-boiled eggs, chopped*
> *a few large lettuce leaves*
> *30ml (2 tbs) onion, finely chopped*
> *30-45ml (2-3 tbs) mayonnaise (see p 30)*
> *salt and freshly ground pepper*
> Garnish
> *tomato wedges, lemon slices*

Drain the tuna and place in a mixing bowl. Flake, and add the celery, chopped onion and eggs. Blend with as much mayonnaise as desired (use more for a creamier salad). Season with salt and freshly ground pepper. Turn onto a serving dish lined with lettuce leaves and decorate with tomato wedges and lemon slices. Chill for at least an hour before serving.

Tuna Salad II   *Serves 6*

2 200g (7 oz) tins tuna, drained and flaked
30ml (2 tbs) lemon juice
1 green pepper, cored, deribbed and finely chopped
1 small red pepper, cored, deribbed and finely chopped
2 stalks celery, chopped
3 spring onions, chopped (including 5cm (2 in) of green stem
dash of cayenne pepper
30ml (2 tbs) each mayonnaise and sour cream (use more for a creamier
*   consistency)*
salt and freshly ground pepper
a few large lettuce leaves
1 tomato, quartered
a few sprigs of parsley
30ml (2 tbs) capers

In a large bowl, mix the tuna, lemon juice, chopped peppers, celery and spring onions. Add the mayonnaise and sour cream, stirring constantly to blend thoroughly. Season with cayenne, salt and pepper. Turn the mixture onto a large serving dish lined with lettuce leaves and garnish with tomato wedges, capers and a few sprigs of parsley.

Insalata di Patate Con Tonno   *Serves 2*

Italian-style tuna fish salad

2 medium-sized potatoes
1 200g (7 oz) tin tuna fish
1 small onion
15ml (1 tbs) fresh parsley, chopped
15ml (1 tbs) capers
salt and freshly ground pepper
45ml (3 tbs) olive oil
sprinkling of wine vinegar

Boil the potatoes in their skins until tender. Drain, peel and cut into chunks while still warm. Season with salt and freshly ground pepper. Slice the onion into thin rounds and mix with the potatoes. Add the olive oil and a sprinkling of wine vinegar. Stir and allow to stand for about an hour. When ready to serve, turn the potato salad onto a shallow serving dish and flake the drained tuna fish on top. Garnish with chopped parsley and capers.

Fagioli e Tonno

Another Italian favourite, see p 135

Sardine Salad *Serves 2*

> 1 tin sardines preserved in oil
> 30ml (2 tbs) lemon juice
> 15ml (1 tbs) oil from sardines
> 1 spring onion, chopped (including 5cm (2 in) of green stem)
> 2 hard-boiled eggs, finely chopped
> 10ml (2 tsp) fresh parsley, chopped
> 1 small dill pickle, chopped
> salt and freshly ground pepper
> a few large lettuce leaves

Garnish
> radishes and tomato wedges

Drain the sardines, reserving 15ml (1 tbs) oil. Place them in a bowl and mash; gradually blend in the lemon juice and oil. Add the chopped eggs, onion, parsley and pickle. Season to taste with salt and pepper and turn onto a serving dish lined with lettuce leaves. Decorate with radishes and tomato wedges.

Ensalada à Bilbainita *Serves 6*

Spanish codfish salad

> 1 smoked cod, approx 675g (1½ lb)
> 1 head curly endive
> 1 large green pepper, chopped
> 8 large Spanish olives (stuffed with almonds or pimento)
> 2 hard-boiled eggs, coarsely chopped
> 1 clove garlic, crushed
> 90ml (6 tbs) Spanish olive oil
> 30ml (2 tbs) wine vinegar
> dash of cayenne pepper
> salt and freshly ground pepper
> 4-6 anchovy fillets, drained and chopped
> 1 pimento, thinly sliced
> milk

Soak the cod overnight (or for at least 8 hours) in milk. Drain and place in a saucepan with enough milk and water, in equal proportions, to cover. Simmer until tender (the fish should separate easily). Drain, remove any bones and flake. Set aside and chill.

Separate the lettuce leaves and wash carefully; drain and dry.

In a large bowl, mix the chopped green pepper, olives, chopped eggs, lettuce and fish.

Make a dressing from the oil, vinegar, crushed garlic and a dash of cayenne. Blend and season with salt and pepper to taste. When ready to serve, pour the dressing over the salad mixture and toss well to coat all ingredients. Sprinkle the top with chopped anchovies and arrange the pimento strips, pinwheel fashion, around the centre of the bowl.

Serve with hot garlic bread.

Maqueraux aux Asperges   *Serves 4-6*

French mackerel and asparagus salad

> *3 fresh mackerel, cleaned and gutted*
> *450g (1 lb) new potatoes*
> *450g (1 lb) young green or white asparagus*
> *1 clove garlic, finely chopped*
> *60-75ml (4-5 tbs) olive oil*
> *30ml (2 tbs) lemon juice*
> *5ml (1 tsp) Dijon mustard*
> *court bouillon (see p 244)*
> *pinch of nutmeg*
> *5ml (1 tsp) fresh thyme leaves or 1.25ml (¼ tsp) dried thyme*
> *15ml (1 tbs) fresh parsley, chopped*
> *15ml (1 tbs) fresh chives, chopped*
> *1 sprig chervil*
> *1 egg yolk*

Boil the potatoes in their skins in lightly salted water (do not peel) until quite tender. Drain.

Prepare the asparagus as in recipe, p 46. Drain, dress and set aside.

Simmer the court bouillon for 20 minutes, then poach the mackerel for approximately 8-10 minutes. Drain, and when cool enough to handle, skin and bone them. In a large bowl, flake the fish and add the potatoes. Mash well with a fork while adding the lemon juice, oil, mustard, nutmeg, herbs and chopped garlic. Season to taste with salt and pepper and fold in the egg yolk. Mix well and chill.

When ready to serve, turn the mixture onto a large flat platter and surround with asparagus.

Herring Salad

A favourite of Eastern Europeans and Scandinavians, herring makes a delicious luncheon salad, dressed with vinaigrette, or a creamy sauce — a recipe is given for each type.

Version I   *Serves 6*

> *2 salted herring fillets*

2 medium-sized potatoes, peeled and cooked
1 medium-sized cucumber
100g (4 oz) cooked beetroot
2 spring onions
1 large eating apple
2 hard-boiled eggs
5ml (1 tsp) Dijon mustard
60ml (4 tbs) olive oil
30ml (2 tbs) wine vinegar
15ml (1 tbs) fresh dill, chopped (or parsley, if dill unavailable)
salt and freshly ground pepper

Peel the cucumber, slice into 1cm (½ in) slices, and halve each slice. Place in a sieve or colander, lightly salt and allow to drain for half an hour. Rinse and drain again. Chop the herring fillets into pieces about 2.5cm (1 in) long. Slice the potatoes into 1cm (½ in) pieces and halve each slice. (They should be roughly the same size as the cucumber.)

Peel the beetroot and cut into large dice; peel and core the apple and dice. Chop the onions, including 5cm (2 in) of green stem. Place all the above ingredients in a large bowl, reserving 30ml (2 tbs) chopped beetroot for garnish.

Mash the hard-boiled egg yolks and separately crumble the whites. To the egg yolk, add mustard and salt (a pinch or two to start). Gradually blend in the oil, followed by the vinegar. Pour over the chopped ingredients and mix well. Turn onto a large serving dish and garnish with chopped dill, beetroot and egg white.

Chill before serving.

Version II   *Serves 4-5*

2 jars of pickled herrings (in vinegar)
1 large beetroot, cooked
1 medium-sized onion
salt and pepper
1 medium-sized gherkin, chopped
15ml (1 tbs) vinegar
30-45ml (2-3 tbs) sour cream
30-45ml (2-3 tbs) mayonnaise (p 30)
optional
5ml (1 tsp) dried dill
Garnish
chopped egg; parsley

Drain the herring and chop into 2.5cm (1 in) pieces. Peel and chop the beetroot into coarse chunks. Peel the onion and slice into thin rounds.

Place these ingredients in a large bowl and sprinkle with vinegar. Add the mayonnaise, sour cream, chopped gherkin, salt and plenty of freshly ground pepper. If desired, flavour with dill and garnish with chopped egg and parsley. Chill before serving.

I'A Ota   *Serves 4*

Tahitian fish salad

This raw fish salad is actually anything but raw — it completely 'cooks' in the acid of the lime juice. In Tahiti, it is appreciated as an antidote, 'for the man who has looked too long upon the flowing bowl the night before'.

1 raw fish (large enough for 4), boned and filleted
240ml (8 fl oz) freshly squeezed lime juice (lemon juice may be substituted)
2 medium-sized onions, peeled and thinly sliced
90ml (6 tbs) vegetable oil
30ml (2 tbs) vinegar
salt and freshly ground pepper
Garnish
15ml (1 tbs) chopped parsley
15ml (1 tbs) chopped red pepper (or 5ml (1 tsp) chopped red chilli)

Cut the fish into pieces about 2.5cm (1 in) square and 1.25cm (½ in) thick. Place in a large deep bowl and add the lime (or lemon) juice. Toss gently to thoroughly cover the fish and leave to 'cook' for about 1½ hours.

Drain off all the juices and dress the fish with a mixture of oil and vinegar, seasoned to taste with salt and freshly ground pepper. Toss well, add the onion, and turn the salad onto a large platter. Garnish with chopped parsley and chopped red pepper.

Japanese Raw Fish Salad   *Serves 4*

450g (1 lb) mackerel, filleted
225g (8 oz) cucumber
300ml (½ pt) vinegar
salt
Dressing
75ml (5 tbs) vinegar
30ml (2 tbs) light soy sauce
20ml (4 tsp) mirin *(or medium dry sherry)*
10-15ml (2-3 tsp) caster sugar
Garnish
*15ml (1 tbs) freshly grated Japanese horseradish (*wasabi*), which is slightly*
stronger than the European variety. It can also be made from a powder
which is blended with water to a mustard-like consistency.

195

Salt the fish fillets, making sure to thoroughly cover the skin side. Allow to rest, skin-side up, for 20 minutes, or until the salt has dissolved and the skin is wet.

In the meantime, wash and scrub the cucumber but do not peel. Cut into julienne strips, place in a sieve or colander and sprinkle with salt. Allow to stand for 20 minutes, then drain on kitchen towels or a clean tea towel.

Place the fish in a shallow bowl and cover with vinegar. Turn and leave for a further 20 minutes. When ready, the fish will be firm. Remove the fish and carefully peel off the skins. Cut into bite-sized pieces.

Prepare the dressing by mixing together the vinegar, soy sauce, sugar to taste, and *mirin* (or sherry).

Arrange the fish around the outside of a shallow serving dish; place the cucumber in the centre and pour the dressing over the whole salad. Garnish with small dollops of horseradish.

Fruit and Nut Salads

Fruits are used in many recipes throughout this book, but outside this chapter, their use is mainly as garnish or as contrast to a predominantly savoury salad.

Here, I have selected recipes using fruits from several countries, as they are characteristically served in their native lands. Other recipes combine exotic fruits from different countries that are seasonally available here. There are also recipes of historical interest and examples of different styles of serving fruit salad, in particular, the use of melon and citrus shells as 'baskets' for filling with fruit combinations.

Although a 'fruit cocktail' is a popular appetiser on American menus, most cuisines place fruit salads in the 'side salad' or 'dessert salad' category. As a 'side salad', fruits often appear in combination with nuts or cheeses — grated hard cheese or curd and cottage cheese — and with certain vegetables to which they seem to have a natural affinity: for instance, grapefruit and avocado; chicory and orange; apple and celery. Dessert salads made with assorted fruits — fresh, dried or tinned in syrup — are usually dressed with a sweetened vinaigrette, fruit juices, or some creamy concoction made from yoghurt, sour cream or fresh whipped dairy cream (see the chapter on Dressings). Fruits can be turned into luxurious after-dinner salads by macerating them in liqueurs such as Kirsch, Cassis, port or Sauternes; and the addition of essences, such as orange flower water or rose water, can create an exotic perfumed delicacy.

Garnish fruit salads in contrasting colours with sprigs of fresh mint or parsley, fresh bay leaves, rose petals, strips of orange or lemon rind, pomegranate and sesame seeds, bits of dried fruit, crystallised fruit, a sprinkling of chopped nuts or dessicated coconut.

The pure taste of the apple is as much a contact with the beauty of the universe as the contemplation of a picture by Cézanne. And more people are capable of savouring a compote of apple than of contemplating Cézanne.

Simone Weil

Golden Apple Salad
Serves 6

This recipe originates from the kitchens of West Virginia, where the Golden Grime apple was first cultivated. French Golden Delicious may be used with equal success. The hickory is related to the walnut family, so if hickory or pecan nuts are not available, substitute walnuts.

> *450g (1 lb) yellow apples, washed and cored*
> *juice of ½ lemon*
> *75g (3 oz) shelled hickory nuts*
> *100g (4 oz) stoned dates, quartered*
> *105ml (3½ fl oz) double cream, whipped to peaks*
> *105ml (3½ fl oz) mayonnaise (p 30)*
> *60ml (4 tbs) orange (dark cut) marmalade*
> Garnish
> *lettuce leaves; 15ml (1 tbs) grated orange rind*

Cut, but do not peel, the apples into large dice. Place in a large bowl and sprinkle with lemon juice. Add the dates and hickory nuts and toss.

In a separate bowl, blend the mayonnaise and whipped cream; then fold in the orange marmalade. Add this mixture to the salad and mix well to thoroughly blend all ingredients.

Turn onto a platter lined with lettuce leaves and garnish with grated orange rind. Chill for several hours and serve with cold duck or goose.

In the seventeen-seventies Londoners developed a craving for Jesse Fish oranges. These had thin skins and were difficult to peel, but the English found them incredibly juicy and sweet, and Jesse Fish oranges were preferred before all others in the making of shrub, a drink that called for alcoholic spirits, sugar, and the juice of an acid fruit — an ancestral whiskey sour . . . It hardly mattered to the English who Jesse Fish was, and it didn't seem to matter to Jesse Fish who his customers were. Fish was a Yankee, a native of New York and by sympathy a revolutionary. Decades before the Revolution, he had retreated to an island off St. Augustine to get away from a miserable marriage, and he became Florida's first orange baron.

Oranges, John McPhee

Oranges are a lovely fruit for salads. John Evelyn described them as 'moderately dry, cooling and incisive', sharpening the appetite and refreshing the palate. In addition to these recipes, try Salade d'Endives à l'Orange p 17, English mushroom and Walnut Salad p 92, and Fennel with Orange Salad p 85.

Morroccan Oranges with Black Olives

Serves 4-6

> *3-4 large navel oranges*
> *75g (3 oz) ripe black olives (pitted)*
> *1.25-2.5ml (¼-½ tsp) cayenne*
> *large pinch of cumin*
> *salt*
> optional
> *15ml (1 tbs) parsley, coarsely chopped*

Peel the oranges and cut away all the white membrane from the flesh. Carefully remove each section with a sharp knife and place in a large shallow bowl. Squeeze any remaining juice from the membrane over the sections and add the cayenne and cumin. Toss, add the olives, and toss again. Season to taste with salt and sprinkle with chopped parsley if desired. Serve chilled.

'The Emir's Pearls'

Serves 4-6

The dramatic contrasts of orange, black and white, reminiscent of kingly

199

jewels, probably gave this salad its name. It was introduced to Europe by Anatole France.

> *4 large navel oranges*
> *2 large sweet onions, thinly sliced*
> *50g (2 oz) black olives, pitted and coarsely chopped*
> *olive oil*
> *lemon juice*

Peel the oranges and cut away the white membrane and pith from the flesh. Slice crosswise and place in a large shallow dish. Place a thin slice of onion on top of each orange and sprinkle with chopped olives. Chill for at least 2 hours, and just before serving, trickle the oil and lemon juice over the salad.

Moroccan Oranges with Dates and Almonds   *Serves 6-8*

> *6 large navel oranges*
> *8 dates, pitted and chopped*
> *25g (1 oz) blanched and slivered almonds*
> *15ml (1 tbs) orange flower water*
> *juice of ½ lemon*
> *5ml (1 tsp) icing sugar*
> *cinnamon*

Peel the oranges and cut away the white membrane and pith from the flesh. Cut into crosswise slices and place in a shallow bowl with the dates and almonds.

In a small separate bowl, blend the lemon juice, orange flower water and sugar, to taste. Pour this over the oranges and chill for at least 2 hours. Just before serving, sprinkle with cinnamon.

Orange Salad with Poppy Seed Dressing   *Serves 4-5*

> *4 large oranges*
> *60ml (4 tbs) corn or safflower oil*
> *15ml (1 tbs) lemon juice, freshly squeezed and strained*
> *2.5ml (½ tsp) poppy seeds*
> *1.25ml (¼ tsp) dry mustard*
> *2.5ml (½ tsp) caster sugar*
> *salt and freshly ground pepper*

Peel the oranges and cut away the white membrane and pith from the flesh. Slice crosswise and place in a large shallow dish.

Place the remaining ingredients in a small jar, cover and shake well. Pour this dressing over the oranges, toss and chill for at least an hour before serving.

Orange Salad with Sesame Seeds   *Serves 4-6*

> *1 bunch of watercress*
> *4 large navel oranges*
> *25g (1 oz) sesame seeds*
> *45ml (3 tbs) corn or safflower oil*
> *15ml (1 tbs) lemon juice, freshly squeezed and strained*
> *1.25ml (¼ tsp) dry mustard*
> *1.25ml (¼ tsp) caster sugar*
> *salt and freshly ground pepper*

Wash the watercress, removing any damaged leaves and stems. Drain and dry thoroughly.

Toast the sesame seeds in a dry frying pan or under the grill, shaking occasionally to avoid burning. Remove from the heat when the seeds begin to pop and turn golden brown.

Peel the oranges and cut away the white membrane and pith from the flesh.

In a large shallow bowl, make a bed of watercress leaves. Place a layer of oranges on this and sprinkle with sesame seeds. Repeat until all the ingredients have been used.

Place the lemon juice, oil, sugar and dry mustard in a small jar. Cover and shake. Season with salt and freshly ground pepper and pour over the salad. Chill for an hour and serve with cold turkey, duck, other poultry or cold lamb.

> What wondrous life is this I lead
> Ripe apples drop about my head;
> The luscious clusters of the vine
> Upon my mouth do crush their wine;
> The nectarine and curious peach
> Into my hands themselves do reach.
> Stumbling on melons, as I pass,
> Ensnared with flowers, I fall on grass.

Thoughts in a Garden, Andrew Marvell

Nheam Krauch Thlong   *Serves 4*

Cambodian grapefruit salad

Serve as a first course to grapefruit lovers. The garnishes add a savoury flavour to this popular citrus fruit.

> *2 large grapefruit*
> *60ml (4 tbs) grated and toasted coconut*
> *4 jumbo prawns, peeled and chopped*

30ml (2 tbs) dried prawns
3 rashers streaky bacon

Fry the bacon until very crisp. Drain on paper towels. Peel the grapefruit, remove the pith and membrane, and cut the flesh into sections. Place in a bowl and squeeze any remaining juice onto the fruit. Add the chopped prawns and toasted coconut and toss. Crumble the bacon and dried prawns into the salad and chill. Just before serving, toss again. No dressing is required.

See *Stuffed grapefruit salads,* p 213.

Lemon Salad   *Serves 4*

In Thomas Dawson's *The Good Hufvvifes Ievvell,* one of the earliest cookbooks in English, a recipe appears for 'sallet of lemmons' made from the peel, thin slices of the fruit and a generous sprinkling of sugar. This is a somewhat unusual inclusion in a sixteenth century work, as a noted physician of the day had warned against the 'putrid fevers' that might occur from eating raw citrus.

Even today, we value the lemon more for its juice or as a garnish than we do for its use as a food in itself. The following recipe, recommended by Alice B. Toklas, is, indeed, encouragement for a more imaginative use of lemons in the making of salads.

> *4 lemons*
> *4 artichoke hearts, tinned in brine*
> *15ml (1 tbs) lemon juice, freshly squeezed and strained*
> *15ml (1 tbs) clear honey*
> *30-45ml (2-3 tbs) corn or safflower oil*
> Garnish
> *a handful of salted almonds*

Immerse the whole lemons in a large saucepan filled with lightly salted boiling water. Cook until soft; drain and cool. Remove any protruding stems and cut the lemons into slices about 12mm (½ in) thick. Place in a bowl with the artichoke hearts, cut into quarters. Prepare a dressing with the oil, honey and lemon juice. Pour over the lemons and artichokes and toss gently. Scatter the salted almonds across the top and serve at room temperature.

Yam Chomphu   *Serves 3-4*

Thai Mango Salad

Mangoes, a fruit native to Asia and popular in tropical regions all over the world, can be purchased in Britain from many Indian and West Indian

202

greengrocers. They are large kidney-shaped fruits, green when unripe and varying in colour when ripe, from green-skinned to deep rose red. The flesh will be yellow to orange-yellow. Mangoes usually weigh between 275g-675g (10 oz-1½ lb).

3 firm green mangoes (if mangoes are unavailable, substitute 2-3 tart
    green cooking apples)
5-10ml (1-2 tsp) salt
30ml (2 tbs) peanut or other vegetable oil
30ml (2 tbs) shallots, finely chopped
15ml (1 tbs) garlic, minced
75g (3 oz) lean pork, thinly sliced
30ml (2 tbs) dried salted shrimps (see p 244) or 45ml (3 tbs) potted shrimps
30ml (2 tbs) soy sauce, flavoured with 2.5ml (½ tsp) anchovy essence
30ml (2 tbs) peanuts, roasted and coarsely chopped
5ml (1 tsp) soft brown sugar
freshly ground pepper
optional garnish
    1 red chilli pepper, finely chopped (p 243)

Peel the mangoes (or apples) and grate into long strips. Place in a bowl and sprinkle with salt. Use the hands to mix the fruit, making sure the salt is widely distributed. This helps remove some of the sour taste. Rinse under a cold tap, squeeze gently and place in a sieve or colander to drain.

In the meantime, heat the oil in a frying pan and add the garlic. Remove when crisp and golden brown; next, fry the shallots until soft and translucent, about 3-4 minutes. Set both aside and in the same oil, fry the pork over medium heat, stirring constantly. After 2 minutes, add the soy sauce, sugar, crumbled dried shrimp and chopped nuts. Stir and cook for a further minute or so. Remove from the heat.

Turn the fruit into a large bowl, pour in the mixture from the frying pan, along with the garlic and shallots. Toss well and season to taste with salt and pepper, and additional sugar if required. Serve at room temperature with a sprinkling of chopped red chilli across the top.

South African Guava and Orange Salad   *Serves 4*

Guavas are a tropical fruit, small and sweet, with flesh varying in colour from white to pale pink. They are available tinned from many supermarket chains.

    2 large navel oranges
    3 fresh guavas or 1 medium-sized tin, 410g (14½ oz)
    icing sugar
    1 wineglass of sherry
    ½ wineglass Cointreau or brandy

lettuce leaves

Peel the oranges and remove the pith and white membrane from the flesh. Slice crosswise and set aside in a large bowl.

Peel the guavas, if fresh; drain, if tinned. Slice and add to the oranges. Pour over the sherry, Cointreau and a sprinkling of icing sugar. Toss and refrigerate for several hours, turning the ingredients occasionally to ensure that all pieces are well macerated. Arrange on a platter lined with lettuce leaves and spoon over some of the liquid. Serve with venison or roast beef.

Kelaka Raita   *Serves 4-5*

Indian bananas in curd

Raita, a popular Indian relish, is a blend of well-seasoned curd or yoghurt, served as a side dish to refresh the palate between mouthfuls of hot curries.

> *3 large bananas, thinly sliced*
> *600ml (1 pt) curd or yoghurt*
> *salt and freshly ground pepper*
> *1 green chilli, finely chopped (p 243)*
> *30ml (2 tbs) fresh coriander leaves, finely chopped (parsley may be substituted)*

If using yoghurt instead of curd, it is important to partially strain it, so that the raita does not turn out watery. See page 246 for method.

Season with salt and pepper; add the bananas and chopped chilli and mix to thoroughly blend. Chill and garnish with chopped coriander.

Bananas with Chopped Walnuts   *Serves 4*

> *1 bunch watercress*
> *4 large firm bananas*
> *juice of ½ lemon, freshly squeezed and strained*
> *45ml (3 tbs) sour cream*
> *45ml (3 tbs) mayonnaise (p 30)*
> *45ml (3 tbs) fresh parsley, finely chopped*
> *50g (2 oz) coarsely chopped walnuts*
> *sugar or salt, to taste*
> *paprika*

Wash the watercress and remove any damaged leaves and stems. Drain thoroughly. Peel and slice the bananas into thin rounds. Place them in a large bowl and pour in the lemon juice. Toss gently to cover all the pieces.

In a separate bowl, blend the mayonnaise, sour cream and chopped parsley. Add this to the bananas, along with the chopped walnuts and stir.

Season with salt for a savoury salad, or sugar, if sweetness is preferred.

Make a bed of watercress on a large dish and spoon on the banana mixture. Chill for at least an hour and serve garnished with a sprinkling of paprika.

Melons are a wonderfully versatile fruit, and although prices fluctuate throughout the year, during the summer months many kinds may be bought at a reasonable price. Many coloured, melons of different variety blend beautifully together. Scooped into balls and served in chilled glasses, they make one of the most refreshing of all fruit salads.

Popular varieties of melon include the expensive, small and sweet, juicy green-fleshed ogen melon; the rough, green-skinned Spanish melon — often cheapest in winter months; the musk melon or rough-skinned canteloupe — probably America's most popular variety, with its juicy orange flesh; the Persian melon, looking like an oversized canteloupe, but with a slightly smoother rind and a more fragrant bouquet and flavour; the pumpkin-shaped casaba — a delicate, pale-fleshed summer melon; and the honeydew, a very large, smooth and pale green-skinned melon, with a lovely sweet, green flesh. In a class by itself is the watermelon. Its crisp red flesh literally melts in the mouth, but because of its very high water content, it is not an ideal fruit for salads: it can lose its crispness too quickly and add excessive water to the salad.

To make melon balls, halve the melon and remove all the seeds and membrane. Press the ball cutter (or Paris cutter, as it is sometimes called) firmly into the flesh and rotate until fully embedded. Twist in a full circle and remove the ball.

Melon balls mix well with berries and tropical fruits, such as mangoes, pawpaws and bananas. Grapes (split and deseeded) or cherries also make attractive additions to a bowl of melon balls. Once the flesh has been removed, the melon shells can be saved to make fruit baskets for stuffing (See *Stuffed Fruits* p 214).

Sárgadinnye Saláta   *Serves 4-6*

Hungarian cantaloupe salad

> 2 *medium-sized cantaloupes (or substitute another pink-fleshed melon)*
> 60ml (4 tbs) mayonnaise (p 30)
> 60ml (4 tbs) sour cream
> 2.5ml (½ tsp) salt
> freshly ground pepper

Garnish
> *a few large lettuce leaves; paprika; a few sprigs of parsley*

Cut the melons in half and scoop out the seeds. Cut away the outer skins and dice the flesh into 2.5cm (1 in) cubes. Place in a large bowl and set aside.

Blend the sour cream and mayonnaise; season with salt. Mix half this dressing with the melon cubes and toss until well blended. Chill the fruit and the remaining dressing for about an hour.

Line individual chilled salad plates with lettuce leaves and scoop the cantaloupe mixture onto each. Garnish with a sprinkling of paprika, a sprig of parsley and serve with a small bowl of the remaining dressing.

Israeli Melon Salad   *Serves 3-4*

Galia is a lovely sweet melon with pale green flesh, a cross between ogen melon and cantaloupe, which is imported from Israel. If Galia is not available, an ogen melon may be substituted.

> *1 galia, or 1 large ogen melon*
> *225g (8 oz) Chinese cabbage, finely shredded*
> *100g (4 oz) dates, peeled and chopped*
> *1 large navel orange*
> *juice of 1 orange*
> *15-30ml (1-2 tbs) light vegetable oil*
> *nutmeg*
> *cinnamon*
> optional
> *5ml (1 tsp) orange flower water*

Peel the orange and remove all the white membrane and pith. Carefully remove each section and place in a large bowl, along with the peeled dates and the orange juice. Sprinkle with cinnamon and nutmeg, and orange flower water if desired. Stir to blend. Cut the melon in half and scoop out the seeds. Cut out melon balls with a Paris cutter and add to the orange. Stir to mix all ingredients.

Toss the shredded cabbage with the oil and arrange on a large platter or shallow bowl. Pile the fruit mixture on top and chill until ready to serve.

Tropical Fruit Salad   *Serves 4-6*

This is a wonderfully light dessert salad (enhanced by the addition of a little Kirsch), or it may be served as a light lunch, accompanied by a scoop of cottage cheese, curd cheese or a dish of thick yoghurt. Papaya (sometimes known as paw paw) is a native American fruit, varying in size from 15cm (6 in) to well over 30cm (12 in). The colour, too, varies from green skinned when unripe to deep yellow or orange at maturity. The unripe fruit is usually cooked or preserved as a relish. Ripe, papaya is eaten as a melon.

2 ripe papayas
½ fresh pineapple
100g (4 oz) green grapes
juice of 1 lemon
juice of 1 orange
2 large bananas
3 satsumas or tangerines
2 sprigs of fresh mint, coarsely chopped
25g (1 oz) shredded coconut (preferably fresh)
    optional
approx 30ml (2 tbs) Kirsch

Cut the papayas in half, scoop out the seeds and cut away the skin with a paring knife or potato peeler. Cut the fruit into large dice, about 2.5cm (1 in) square, and place in a large bowl.

Cut away the stem and skin of the pineapple, as well as the tough woody core. Cut out cubes about 2.5cm (1 in) square and add to the papayas.

Peel the bananas and cut into thin slices. Halve the grapes and remove the pips. Add both to the fruit bowl.

Peel the satsumas and remove the white membrane. Separate into sections and add to the other fruits. Pour in the orange and lemon juices, add the mint, and toss well. (If Kirsch is to be added, do so now.) Chill for several hours and garnish, just before serving, with shredded coconut.

Russian Pineapple and Celery Salad   *Serves 4*

Excellent with cold pork, veal or poultry

½ fresh pineapple
3 stalks celery
8 large cos or romaine lettuce leaves, washed and dried
1 medium-sized cooked beetroot
45ml (3 tbs) olive oil
15ml (1 tbs) cider vinegar
salt and freshly ground pepper
2.5ml (½ tsp) sugar
    Garnish
sprigs of parsley

Remove the skin from the pineapple and cut away the tough woody core. Cut the flesh into cubes, about 2.5cm (1 in) square.

Wash and dry the celery; cut crosswise into 12mm (½ in) slices. Peel the beetroot and cut into 12mm (½ in) dice.

Prepare the dressing from the oil, vinegar and sugar and season to taste with salt and pepper.

In a mixing bowl, blend the celery and pineapple with the dressing. Toss and turn onto a large platter, lined with cos leaves, leaving a space in the centre for the beetroot.

Chill until ready to serve, garnished with a few sprigs of parsley.

'You have to ask children and birds how cherries and strawberries taste.'

Goethe

Cherries with Cucumber
Serves 3

This simple salad has a stunning contrast of colours and should be well chilled before serving — the perfect accompaniment to cold, cooked meats, poultry and sausages.

> *1 large cucumber, peeled*
> *225g (8 oz) cherries*
> *a few large lettuce leaves*
> *vinaigrette (p 25)*
> Garnish
> *10ml (2 tsp) chopped fresh dill*

Wash and stone the cherries (special gadgets are available for stoning cherries and olives). Cut the cucumber into thin slices, sprinkle with salt and place in a sieve or colander to drain for 15-20 minutes. Mix the cherries, cucumber and vinaigrette in a bowl and turn onto a shallow dish lined with lettuce leaves. Garnish with a sprinkling of chopped dill.

Gay Nineties Salad
Serves 8

A rich summer dessert salad, made with fresh fruits and rose-perfumed port wine and cream. As the fruits need time to macerate, begin preparation well in advance.

> *450g (1 lb) fresh strawberries, washed, drained and hulled*
> *2 large ripe peaches, destoned and cut into eighths*
> *225g (8 oz) fresh black cherries, halved and destoned*
> *2 teacups full of freshly picked rose petals, rinsed clean*
> *240ml (8 fl oz) double cream*
> *100g (4 oz) caster sugar*
> *15ml (1 tbs) icing sugar*
> *240ml (8 fl oz) port wine*

Pour the port into a bowl, add one teacup of rose petals and stir. Pour the cream into another bowl and add to it the remaining rose petals. Place both bowls in the refrigerator for at least 2 hours. Into another large bowl, place the berries and peaches. Sprinkle, while stirring, with caster sugar.

Make sure all the fruit is well covered with sugar, then place in the refrigerator for 2 hours.

Strain the rose petals from the port and pour the liquid into the fruit. Stir gently but thoroughly to moisten all ingredients. Return the fruits to the fridge for a further hour.

Just before serving, strain the rose petals from the cream. Whip the cream until stiff, adding the icing sugar towards the end. Serve in a sauceboat with the fruit. Garnish with a few fresh rose petals, if available, or a few sprigs of fresh mint.

Summer Mixed Berry Salad   *Serves 4-5*

> *100g (4 oz) raspberries*
> *100g (4 oz) loganberries (or blackberries)*
> *100g (4 oz) blackcurrants*
> *100g (4 oz) redcurrants*
> *50g (2 oz) caster sugar*
> *300ml (½ pt) light red wine*
> *sour cream or yoghurt*
> Garnish
> *fresh mint*

Mix the berries in a large bowl with the wine and sugar. Toss gently and chill for several hours.

Serve garnished with mint, and with a sauceboat of sour cream or yoghurt.

Khoshaf   *Serves 6-8*

According to Claudia Roden, author of *A Book of Middle Eastern Food*, this wonderful salad of macerated fruits was traditionally made with only apricots, raisins and mixed nuts. Of the many variations, I like this particular combination. Khoshaf should be prepared well ahead, so that the bouquet has time to fully permeate the fruit.

> *100g (4 oz) dried apricots*
> *100g (4 oz) dried figs*
> *100g (4 oz) dried prunes*
> *50g (2 oz) raisins*
> *15ml (1 tbs) orange flower water*
> *75g (3 oz) blanched almonds*
> *50g (2 oz) pine kernels*
> *50g (2 oz) unsalted, shelled pistachios*
> *30-45ml (2-3 tbs) hymettus honey*
> *orange juice*
> optional garnish
> *30ml (2 tbs) pomegranate seeds, sour cream or thick yoghurt*

209

Wash the dried fruit and soak overnight in cold water. Drain and place in a large mixing bowl. Add the nuts and stir.

In a small separate bowl, blend the honey with the orange flower water and several tablespoons of orange juice. Pour this over the salad and toss gently to cover all ingredients. Cover and chill for several hours.

As a dessert, serve garnished with a sprinkling of pomegranate seeds and a bowl of sour cream or yoghurt. Khoshaf is also delicious served with roasted meats or as an exotic contrasting accompaniment to stews and casseroles seasoned with savoury Middle Eastern herbs and spices.

Maiwa Kachumar   *Serves 4*

Indian fruit and nut salad

150-225g (6-8 oz) walnuts, coarsely chopped
4 dried figs, coarsely chopped
6 dates, stoned and quartered
18g (¾ oz) fresh shredded coconut
15ml (1 tbs) ghee (clarified butter p 243), melted
25g (1 oz) raisins
1 large green apple, peeled, cored and coarsely grated
6 sprigs watercress, cleaned and coarsely chopped
45ml (3 tbs) olive oil
15ml (1 tbs) white wine vinegar
salt and freshly ground pepper
Garnish
    a few large lettuce leaves, a few sprigs of coriander, 1 large tomato, cut
      into wedges

Soak the raisins in very hot water for 15 minutes. Drain.

Place the melted ghee in a large bowl and add the chopped nuts, figs, dates, raisins, chopped walnuts, watercress, apple and coconut. Mix well.

In a small separate bowl, prepare a dressing of oil, vinegar, salt and freshly ground pepper. Pour over the salad and toss carefully, but thoroughly, to cover all ingredients.

Turn onto a large serving dish lined with lettuce leaves and garnish with tomato wedges and coriander leaves.

Two hazel nuts I threw into the flame,
And to each nut I gave
    a sweetheart's name.
This with the loudest bounce
    me sore amazed,
That in a flame
    of brightest colour blazed.
As blazed the nut

so may thy passion grow,
For 'twas thy nut
   that did so brightly glow.

Spell, John Gay

Salade aux Noisettes

Serves 6

Hazel nut salad

The wild hazel nut is one of the most common nuts of the countryside. Also known as cobnuts and filberts, they are abundant throughout the British Isles.

> *450g (1 lb) French beans, washed and trimmed*
> *225g (8 oz) dried haricot beans*
> *2 stalks celery, cleaned and chopped*
> *125g (5 oz) roasted hazel nuts*
> *90ml (6 tbs) vinaigrette (p 25) (with a pinch of nutmeg added)*
> *salt*

Soak the haricot beans for 2 hours, then cook in plenty of boiling water, over medium low heat for about 45 minutes, or until tender but still whole. (Add salt about 10 minutes before cooking is completed.) Drain and cool.

Cook the French beans in a little lightly salted boiling water for approximately 8 minutes, or until just tender. Drain, refresh with cold water and drain again.

In a large bowl, mix the two beans with the chopped celery and nuts. Add the vinaigrette and toss to thoroughly blend. Serve at once.

Nougada

Serves 4

References to the almond are numerous in early records. The Bible alone mentions this nut over seventy times and the Greek philosopher, Theophrastus describes its singular quality of producing blossoms before leaves. The Hebrews called it 'shakod' (the awakening) for it blooms in Palestine as early as May.

This Middle Eastern salad of ground almonds is an excellent accompaniment to poultry, or as part of a vegetarian supper.

> *225g (8 oz) ground almonds*
> *5ml (1 tsp) caster sugar*
> *1 clove garlic, crushed*
> *juice of 1 large lemon, freshly squeezed and strained*
> *salt and white pepper, to taste*
> *90ml (6 tbs) olive oil*
> *45ml (3 tbs) fresh parsley, chopped*

211

Garnish
a few sprigs of parsley, slivered almonds

Put the ground almonds and chopped parsley into a bowl. Add the sugar, a sprinkling of salt and a pinch of white pepper. Stir, then add the garlic. Gradually add the oil and lemon juice, in alternating trickles, while mixing constantly with a fork. Correct the seasoning with additional salt and pepper and turn the mixture onto a shallow serving dish. Garnish with slivered almonds and a few sprigs of parsley.

Pecan and Pomegranate Salad   *Serves 5-6*

The pecan is a truly American nut. Even its name is derived from the Cree Indian word *paccan* meaning 'nut having a hard shell to crack'. This salad makes an unusual accompaniment for roasted game. If pecans are difficult to find, substitute shelled walnuts.

> *225g (8 oz) shelled pecans*
> *3-4 hard sweet apples, approx 450g (1 lb)*
> *30ml (2 tbs) dark rum*
> *2.5ml (½ tsp) sugar (optional)*
> *60ml (4 tbs) olive oil*
> *30ml (2 tbs) lemon juice*
> *salt and freshly ground pepper*
> *a few large lettuce leaves*
> *60ml (4 tbs) pomegranate seeds*

Peel and core the apples and cut into thin wedges. Sprinkle with 15ml (1 tbs) of the lemon juice. Place in a large bowl with the pecans and add the rum; stir. Make a simple dressing from oil, lemon juice, salt and pepper and sugar, if desired. Pour over the apples and pecans and toss gently but thoroughly, to blend all ingredients. Turn onto a serving dish lined with lettuce leaves and sprinkle all over with pomegranate seeds. Chill for an hour before serving.

Stuffing Fruits for Salads

Certain fruits — apples, melons, oranges and grapefruits — when hollowed, make lovely edible 'bowls' for presenting fruit salads. The flesh from the fruit itself is removed, cut or sectioned, and usually combined with other ingredients — fruits, nuts, cheeses, seafood, vegetables, dressings and even sorbets.

As this sort of presentation is contrived to appeal to the eye as much as the palate, special emphasis should be placed on the choice of garnishes. Flowers, herbs, grated coconut, berries and candied peel are favourites.

Here are a few ideas:

Apples

Choose large, firm apples. Slice off the top 1/5 of each apple and reserve these 'lids' for garnish. Rub exposed areas of the flesh with a drop of lemon juice to prevent discoloration. Using a small Paris cutter, take out small balls from the apple and immediately immerse in a bowl of cold water with 15ml (1 tbs) of lemon juice. Discard the seeds and core. When as many balls as possible have been removed, trim the flesh so that it forms a shell approximately 5mm (¼ in) thick.

Suggested fillings: Waldorf Salad (p 164)
Golden Apple Salad (p 198)
Salade de Poulet aux Amandes (p 176)
Curd or cottage cheese mixed with diced apple,
raisins and nuts

Grapefruit

Choose large grapefruit; Florida pinks are juicy and sweet, as well as pretty to look at. Halve and remove the sections with a serrated grapefruit knife. Place in a bowl. When all the sections have been removed, carefully cut out the core and membranes, so that a neat hollow shell remains. For added decorative effect, the edges can be fluted by making small triangular incisions around the entire rim.

Suggested fillings: Salade des Champs (p 13)
avocado slices, grapefruit sections and olives, dressed
with vinaigrette
prawns and celery, dressed with mayonnaise, and
grapefruit sections
grapefruit sections, orange sections and strawberries
Gruyère and ham cubes, grapefruit sections with
vinaigrette

Oranges

Choose large navel oranges with thick skin. Cut about 1/3 from the top and then remove the sections in the manner described for grapefruit.

Suggested fillings: any of the orange salads on pp 199-201
Fennel with Orange Salad (p 85)
Raw Mushroom and Orange Salad (p 92)
Duck and Orange Salad (p 177)
cottage or curd cheese mixed with orange sections
and redcurrants

Melons

Use small melons, such as ogen, for shells to be used as individual portions. Watermelon, honeydew and other larger melons make beautiful buffet table centrepieces. Halve the melon, remove the seeds, and scoop out as much flesh as possible with a Paris cutter. Using a sharp knife, trim any remaining flesh from the shell so that only a neat hollow remains. (This is especially important with watermelons, where the high water content of the flesh, if not totally removed, may disrupt the balance of the dressing or, possibly worse, create an excess flow of liquid onto your table top.) As with grapefruit shells, the rim can be decoratively trimmed.

Suggested fillings: three types of melon balls — honeydew, cantaloupe and watermelon
honeydew, fresh mint and blueberries or blackberries
melon mixed with prawns and a mayonnaise dressing
melon, lychees and mangoes
fennel, watercress and melon
Cacik (p 152)
Cucumber and Cherry Salad (p 208)

Grape and Melon Salad   Serves 4

1 medium-sized honeydew melon (or other green melon)
225g (8 oz) green grapes
juice of 1 lime
juice of 1 lemon
juice of 1 orange
30ml (2 tbs) Crème de menthe or Kirsch
Garnish
6 sprigs fresh mint; a few lettuce leaves

Halve the melon and proceed as described above.

Cut the grapes in half and deseed. In a large bowl, mix the melon balls, grapes, liqueur and fruit juices. Toss and chill for several hours, turning occasionally to macerate all the fruit.

When ready to serve, line a large serving dish with lettuce leaves and place the melon shells on top. Fill with fruit, garnish with mint and pour some of the fruit juice over the top.

Brandied Fruit Salad   Serves 6

1 medium-sized pink fleshed melon
2 small tart apples, peeled, cored and sliced
2 firm pears, peeled, cored and sliced
1 large juicy orange, peeled and sectioned

225g (8 oz) stoned cherries
150ml (¼ pt) Sauternes, or other medium dry wine
75ml (⅛ pt) brandy
30-45ml (2-3 tbs) caster sugar, to taste
Garnish
   grated orange peel or candied orange peel; lettuce leaves

Cut the melon in half and follow the instructions on p 214. Place the melon balls and other fruits in a large bowl. Add the sugar, wine and brandy and mix well to blend all ingredients. Chill for several hours, stirring occasionally to fully macerate the fruit.

When ready to serve, spoon the fruit into the melon shells, pour over some of the liquid and place the two shells on a large platter lined with lettuce leaves. Garnish with grated orange rind or candied peel.

Stuffed Cherry Salad   *Serves 6*

An unusual and refreshing green salad to serve after game or cold ham.

100-150g (4-6 oz) large ripe cherries
1 cos lettuce
75g (3 oz) cream cheese
sour cream or double cream
25g (1 oz) toasted almonds, finely chopped
3 drops almond essence
vinaigrette (made with 75ml (5 tbs) oil, 15ml (1 tbs) vinegar, 15ml
   (1 tbs) sweet vermouth)
Garnish
   a few slices of fennel and some of the feathery tops

Wash the lettuce; break into bite-sized pieces and place in a lettuce basket to drain. Wash the cherries and remove the stones.

Mash the cream cheese with a small amount of sour cream or double cream to soften to a pasty consistency. Add the almond extract and toasted almonds and mix well.

Carefully stuff the cherries with this mixture. (If necessary, create larger hollows in the cherries by gently scooping out the flesh with the point of a sharp paring knife.)

Place the lettuce and cherries in a large wooden salad bowl and dress with the vermouth-flavoured vinaigrette. Toss well and garnish with slices of fennel and some of the feathery fennel leaves.

Moulded Salads

Moulded salads, as distinct from aspics and mousses, seem for the most part to be an American culinary speciality, unparalleled in any other national repertoire. They make decorative additions to a buffet spread — especially refreshing in summer — and can be prepared well beforehand.

As there are excellent specialist cookbooks devoted entirely to moulds, mousses and aspics, I have included here only a few representative salads with some general tips on their preparation.

216

Note The brands of gelatine most common in the United Kingdom and United States are Davis and Knox, respectively. As both of these come in envelopes designed to set 1 pt of liquid (20 fl oz British but only 16 fl oz American), it is essential to follow the American cup measures when using Knox gelatine, but the Imperial or metric when using Davis. This means that the solid ingredients will be less concentrated in the British versions of these recipes.

Preparation

1. Always use sufficient liquid or mould will have a rubbery consistency.

2. Unflavoured gelatine is best for vegetable salads; fruit salads blend well with fruit-flavoured jellies.

3. Always adjust seasoning while gelatine is in a liquid state.

4. Dissolve gelatine according to instructions on the packet, or your recipe. To speed-up setting time, stir 7-10 ice cubes into gelatine which has already been dissolved in hot water. Stir rapidly and when the mixture begins to thicken, remove any unmelted ice cubes.

5. Allow adequate time for a mould to set. Clear gelatine may take as little as 2 hours; layered moulds and moulds with added solid ingredients should stay in the refrigerator overnight.

6. Some foods 'sink', some 'swim' when added to gelatine. Chopped cooked meats and vegetables, tinned fruits, stewed fruits, grapes and most citrus fruits 'sink'; celery, apples, pears, bananas, avocados, peaches and nuts 'swim'. To ensure even distribution of solid ingredients throughout the mould, do not add them until the gelatine has turned syrupy.

7. Never add fresh or frozen pineapple to a mould.

8. Drain all foods thoroughly before adding them to gelatine, or the liquid balance may be upset.

9. Choose the right size mould; if the ingredients do not reach the top, there will be problems when you come to unmould the salad. Metal moulds speed up setting time. Use simply shaped moulds for complicated salads!

10. Do not grease mould; rinse with cold water and chill while the mixture is being prepared.

11. Unmould salad just before serving. Hold a pointed knife under a hot running tap for several seconds, then run around the edges of the mould. Dip the mould into a basin of warm water for a few seconds. Place a large serving dish upside down over the mould, hold both together and invert. Shake the mould gently to release the salad; if it resists, wrap a hot damp cloth around the top for several seconds.

Perfection Salad   *Serves 6*

Generally served on a bed of fresh crispy lettuce with well-seasoned mayonnaise, this traditional American salad was 'invented' in 1905 by Mrs John E. Cooke of Newcastle, Pennsylvania, for a competition sponsored by Mr Charles Knox of Knox gelatine fame. A $100 sewing machine was Mrs Cooke's third prize — plus a permanent place in the standard American culinary repertoire.

1.2 litre (1 quart) mould, chilled
1 envelope unflavoured gelatine
450ml (¾ pt) (1½c) water
50g (2 oz) (¼c) caster sugar
30ml (2 tbs) lemon juice
15ml (1 tbs) cider vinegar
1.25ml (½ tsp) salt
12 green olives, pitted and coarsely chopped
115g (4 oz) (1c) Dutch white cabbage, finely shredded (or white and red
  cabbage, mixed)
2 large stalks celery, diced
1 medium-sized carrot, finely grated
1 small red or green pepper, minced
Garnish
  large lettuce leaves; mayonnaise (p 30); parsley; pimento strips or thin
    slices of lemon

Place 150ml (¼ pt) (½c) of water in a saucepan and sprinkle in the gelatine slowly to soften. Stir, add sugar and remaining water and place over a moderate heat until the gelatine is dissolved. Remove from the heat and add lemon juice, vinegar and salt. Stir, and chill until the mixture is syrupy (the consistency of unbeaten egg whites). Fold in the chopped and grated vegetables. Spoon into the mould and set in the refrigerator for several hours.

Unmould onto a bed of large lettuce leaves and garnish with parsley, strips of pimento or lemon slices. Serve with a bowl of mayonnaise.

Ambrosia   *Serves 8*

Ambrosia is a speciality of the American south — a sweet and frivolous combination of fruit, nuts and shredded coconut. Finely grated carrot may be substituted for the coconut to make a more savoury main course salad.

1.2 litre (1 quart) mould, chilled (p 217)
75g (3 oz) packet orange gelatine
240ml (8 fl oz) (1c) boiling water
376g (1 small tin) (1c) undrained crushed pineapple
240ml (8 fl oz) (1c) sour cream
45-90ml (3-6 tbs) caster sugar, to taste

100g (4 oz) (1c) coarsely chopped pecans (use walnuts if pecans
   unavailable)
312g, 1 small tin (1c) mandarin orange segments, drained
50g (2 oz) (½c) shredded coconut (or grated carrot)
Garnish
   lettuce leaves; grated orange rind; 15ml (1 tbs) shredded coconut

Dissolve the gelatine in boiling water, and add the undrained pineapple.
Cool and fold in the sour cream. Add caster sugar to desired sweetness.
Add the remaining ingredients, blend well and turn into a chilled mould.
Place in a refrigerator for at least 4 hours, or until firm.

   Unmould on to a bed of lettuce leaves and decorate with grated orange
peel and a sprinkling of coconut.

Ginger Ale Salad   Serves 6-8

An unusual summer salad to accompany cold poultry dishes. It can be
served with sweetened sour cream or yoghurt.

   1.2 litre (1 quart) mould, chilled (p 217)
   1 envelope unflavoured gelatine
   150ml (¼ pt) (½c) cold water
   50g (2 oz) (¼c) caster sugar
   450ml (¾ pt) (1½c) ginger ale
   30ml (2 tbs) lemon juice, freshly squeezed and strained
   1 orange, peeled, deseeded and sectioned
   2 ripe peaches, peeled and cut into slivers
   115g (4 oz) (¾c) white grapes, seeded and halved
   115g (4 oz) strawberries or raspberries, sliced
   15ml (1 tbs) crystallised ginger, finely chopped

In a saucepan, sprinkle the gelatine over the water to soften; stir over low
heat until the gelatine has completely dissolved. Add the sugar and
continue stirring until dissolved. Remove from the heat and pour the
mixture into a large heatproof bowl. Add the ginger ale and lemon juice
and chill until the mixture turns syrupy (the consistency of unbeaten egg
whites). Stir in the fruits and crystallised ginger and pour into the chilled
mould. Cover and refrigerate for at least 4 hours, or until the mould is
thoroughly set.

Reception Salad   Serves 6

The name of Knox is as closely linked to gelatine in the American
homemaker's mind as Heinz is to ketchup or Hershey's to chocolate.
This old recipe comes from the Knox gelatine packet and remains a

popular favourite, usually set in individual moulds, which have been rinsed with cold water and chilled.

1 envelope unflavoured gelatine
75ml (2½ fl oz) (⅓c) cold water
300ml (½ pt) (1c) mayonnaise (p 30)
300ml (½ pt) (1c) double cream, whipped to peaks
1.25ml (¼ tsp) salt
325g (12 oz) (1½c) diced chicken
25g (1 oz) (¼c) chopped blanched almonds
100g (4 oz) (¾c) white grapes, peeled and seeded
Garnish
  a few large lettuce leaves; a few sprigs of parsley; tomato wedges; 6 olives

Soften the gelatine in a few tablespoons of cold water, add the remaining water and place the dish over (or in) boiling water, stirring until the gelatine is completely dissolved. Cool and combine with the mayonnaise, whipped cream and salt. Gently fold in the chicken, almonds and grapes. When well blended, turn into chilled moulds. Place in the refrigerator for several hours to set. When ready to serve, turn onto a dish lined with lettuce leaves and garnish with sprigs of parsley, tomato wedges and olives.

Bing Cherry Mould   *Serves 6*

An American holiday feast wouldn't be complete without some sort of moulded salad to add colour to the spread. This, and the following recipe made with cranberries and walnuts, are traditional favourites, though every family has its own special recipe.

1.2 litre (1 quart) ring mould, chilled
1 large tin pitted black cherries
cold water
1 envelope unflavoured gelatine
225g (8 oz) cream cheese
60ml (2 oz) (¼c) pineapple juice
Garnish
  watercress and a few lettuce leaves

Drain the cherries and reserve the juice. Place the fruit in a ring mould that has been rinsed with cold water and chilled. To the reserved liquid add sufficient cold water to make 600ml (1 pt) (2c). Put 150ml (¼ pt) (½c) in a saucepan over a medium low heat and sprinkle in the gelatine. Stir until it has fully dissolved. Add the remaining liquid, stir again and pour over the cherries. Chill for several hours until firm. Just before serving, whip the cream cheese with the pineapple juice until the mixture is as light as whipped cream. Unmould the cherry ring onto a platter lined with lettuce, place the whipped cream cheese in the centre and decorate with watercress. At Christmas, add a few sprigs of berried holly.

Cranberry-Walnut Mould   *Serves 6-8*

1.8 litre (1½ quart) mould, chilled
450g (1 lb) fresh or frozen cranberries
2 cinnamon sticks, 24 cloves, 1.25ml (¼ tsp) grated nutmeg, tied in a
*   cheesecloth*
600ml (1 pt) (2c) water
150g (6 oz) (3c) sugar
2.5ml (½ tsp) salt
2 envelopes unflavoured gelatine
4 stalks celery, washed and finely chopped
1 small tin crushed pineapple, well drained
100g (4 oz) walnuts, chopped
Garnish
*   a few large lettuce leaves; watercress or parsley*

Place the water, cranberries and spice bouquet in a saucepan over medium low heat and simmer until the cranberry skins begin to crack, about 5-8 minutes. Remove the spices and purée the cranberries with the cooking liquid in an electric blender (at low speed) or by passing through a food mill. They should still be slightly lumpy. Return the mixture to the saucepan and add the sugar and salt. Sprinkle gelatine over the top while stirring the mixture with a wooden spoon. When the gelatine has completely dissolved, remove from the heat and leave to cool. Chill, stirring occasionally, until the mixture turns thick and syrupy. Add the celery, pineapple and nuts, mix thoroughly and turn into a chilled mould.

Refrigerate for several hours (preferably overnight) and unmould onto a bed of lettuce. Garnish with dark greens, such as watercress or parsley.

Creamy Lime Party Mould   *Serves 12+*

1 large ring mould (3 quart capacity), rinsed and chilled
3.75g (3 oz) packets lime flavoured gelatine
240ml (8 fl oz) sour cream
1 large tin, 550g (20 oz) crushed pineapple, well drained
optional
*   2.5ml (½ tsp) mint extract*
Garnish
*   a few large lettuce leaves; sprigs of fresh mint; thin slices of lemon and lime*

In a large bowl, prepare the lime gelatine as instructed on the packet or use the quick-set method, substituting 7-10 ice cubes for 1 cup of cold water. Stir the ice cubes rapidly round the bowl until the mixture begins to turn syrupy. Remove any unmelted cubes. If this method is used, proceed immediately to the next step; otherwise, chill the mixture until it begins to thicken.

Add the sour cream (and mint extract, if desired) and blend thoroughly with the gelatine. Then add the crushed pineapple, stir again and turn into the ring mould.

Chill for 6-8 hours. When ready to serve, turn onto a large dish lined with lettuce leaves and garnish with slices of lemon and lime, and sprigs of fresh mint.

Avocado and Tomato Ring with Prawns   *Serves 8*

    1 large (3 pt) ring mould, rinsed and chilled
    15ml (1 tbs) unflavoured gelatine
    60ml (4 tbs) cold water
    300ml (½ pt) boiling water
    15ml (1 tbs) caster sugar
    2 avocado pears
    15ml (1 tbs) lime juice, freshly squeezed and strained
    100ml (3½ fl oz) mayonnaise (p 30)
    100ml (3½ fl oz) sour cream
    salt and freshly ground pepper
    100g (4 oz) peeled prawns
  Tomato aspic (600ml/1 pt)
    15ml (1 tbs) unflavoured gelatine
    30ml (2 tbs) water
    300ml (½ pt) tomato pulp (from fresh ripe tomatoes which have been peeled and cored
    150ml (¼ pt) vegetable stock
    2.5ml (½ tsp) tabasco sauce
    15ml (1 tbs) sherry
    1.25ml (¼ tsp) Worcestershire sauce
    10ml (2 tsp) lemon juice
    15ml (1 tbs) fresh tarragon, finely chopped
    15ml (1 tbs) fresh parsley, finely chopped
    salt to taste
  Garnish
    a few large lettuce leaves, parsley, prawns, ½ an avocado pear

To prepare the avocado mousse which forms the crown of this mould, dissolve the gelatine in cold water in a large bowl. Add boiling water, stir, then blend in the sugar and leave to set (after about 20 minutes, place in the refrigerator).

Mash the avocado pears, reserving half for garnish, and sprinkle with

222

lime juice to prevent discoloration. Blend in the mayonnaise and sour cream, season to taste with salt and pepper and add to the gelatine when it has reached a syrupy state (like the consistency of unbeaten egg whites). Mix well with a wooden spoon and pour into a chilled ring mould. Refrigerate.

Start the tomato aspic by dissolving the gelatine in the water. Place in a large saucepan with the tomato pulp and stock. Put on a low heat and blend in the tabasco sauce, parsley, tarragon, Worcestershire sauce, lemon juice and sherry. Stir and adjust the seasoning with salt and pepper. When the liquid begins to boil, remove from the heat immediately and strain through a cloth. Leave to cool.

When the avocado mixture has set, pour the tomato aspic into the mould and dot a few prawns around the centre.

Chill for several hours. When the tomato aspic is completely firm, turn the mould onto a large dish lined with lettuce leaves and garnish with slices of avocado and lime, a few sprigs of parsley and any remaining prawns.

Expensive, Exotic and Eccentric Salads

The 'first service' from the credenza consists of salads decked out with various fantasies such as animals made of citron, castles of turnips, high walls of lemons; and variegated with slices of ham, mullet roes, herrings, tunny, anchovies, capers, olives, caviar, together with candied flowers and other preserves.

Description of a Rennaissance banquet, from
The Horizon Cookbook

224

Now for sallets for shew only, and the adorning and setting out of a Table with a number of dishes, they be those which are made of carret roots of sundry colours, well boyled, and cut into many shapes and proportions, as some into Knots, some in the manner of Scutchions, and Arms, some like Birds, some like Wild-Beasts, according to the Art and cunning of the Workman; and these for the most part are seasoned with vinegar, oyl, and a little Pepper.

The English Housewife, Gervase Markhan

This chapter is dedicated to the element of serendipity in salad making. Although it began as a collection of novelties and otherwise unclassifiable recipes, it grew to include as well, both eccentrically amusing relics from outmoded cookery books and salads made with ingredients either too expensive or too difficult to obtain to be regular features of the ordinary culinary repertoire. Also, there are two recipes designed for salubrious, rather than decorative effect: one from the ancient Roman cookbook of Apicius, and the other, a modern speciality of one of England's most exclusive health hydros, Grayshott's One Day De-Toxicating Salad: a splendid sweet and sour combination of finely chopped fruits and vegetables.

If your purse can afford them and you have the time and palate for experimentation, these recipes will bring much delight and fantasy to your salad making.

Bird's Nest Salad

A turn-of-the-century favourite in America, here is a version from *The Century Cookbook* (1895).

Rub a little green colouring paste into cream cheese, giving it a delicate color like bird's eggs. Roll it into balls the size of bird's eggs, using the back or smooth side of butter pats. Arrange on a flat dish some small well-crimped lettuce leaves; group them to look like nests, moisten them with French dressing; and place five of the cheese balls in each nest of leaves. The cheese balls may be varied by flecking them with black, white and red pepper.

Translated into a practical method, this decorative dish — suitable for children's parties or holiday buffets — can be prepared by adding 2 drops of green food colouring to every 75g (3 oz) package of cream cheese. The flavour of the cheese 'eggs' can be varied by the addition of different chopped herbs — chives (or spring onion tops) and parsley are especially good. For even greater variety, mash or mince some garlic into the cream cheese or blend with 25g (1 oz) of Roquefort cheese. Decorate the 'eggs' with sprinklings of paprika and black pepper — or try rolling some in finely chopped nuts.

225

Multi-coloured Swap Shop Salad

The early nineteenth century cookbook where this recipe was discovered (the name is mine) suggests four separate dishes — one for each colour — set at each corner of the table; alternatively, the salads can be arranged in a line down the centre.

Part of the fun in recreating this salad is in balancing the selection of ingredients to please your own eye and palate. Each should be dressed lightly with vinaigrette and sprinkled generously with fresh chopped seasonal herbs. (The 'white' bowl could be dressed with creamy vinaigrette, p 28 or mayonnaise, p 30, if preferred.)

white salad

A mixture of blanched, slivered almonds; diced celery; chicory; julienne strips of par-boiled turnip; blanched seakale (if available); apples, peeled, cored, sliced and dipped in acidulated water; chopped whites of hard-boiled eggs.

red salad

A mixture of julienne strips of carrots, cooked *al dente*; finely grated red cabbage; julienne strips of cooked beetroot; firm tomatoes, peeled (if desired) and sliced; red sage (either the leaves of the variegated type or some of the scarlet flowers of pineapple sage).

yellow salad

A mixture of peeled and finely sliced oranges; peeled and sectioned grapefruit; julienne strips of swede and parsnip, both cooked *al dente*; marigold or cowslip flowers; chopped yolks of hard-boiled eggs.

black salad

A mixture of large field mushrooms, sliced, lightly fried and drained; pitted black olives; prunes, soaked, stoned and halved; currants or raisins, soaked and drained.

Stuffed Nasturtium Flower Salad

Introduced from Peru in the seventeenth century, the nasturtium flower, so prominently featured in English gardens, is seen hardly at all in the summer salad bowl — a pity, as the flower not only looks beautiful but also has a delightful bouquet and a pleasantly sweet taste.

The leaves have a spicy, peppery flavour, which may account for the name *nasturtium*, meaning 'nose twister'. A delicious green salad may be made with nasturtium leaves combined with milder greens, dressed with vinaigrette and garnished with nasturtium flowers.

This recipe comes from a collection of Commonwealth recipes and is more an hors d'oeuvre than a salad — the sort to be delicately nibbled in warm weather, with a pre-dinner glass of chilled white wine or a gin and tonic.

> *75ml (5 tbs) Cheddar cheese, finely grated*
> *5ml (1 tsp) fresh parsley, finely chopped*
> *5ml (1 tsp) anchovy paste*
> *15-30ml (1-2 tbs) mayonnaise (p 30)*
> *30ml (2 tbs) sweet gherkins, finely chopped*
> *24 nasturtium flowers*
> Garnish
> > *nasturtium leaves*
> > *vinaigrette*
> > *toothpicks*

Combine the cheese, anchovy paste and parsley. Add the chopped pickle and enough mayonnaise to bind the ingredients. Stir until thoroughly mixed. Fill each flower with a little of the mixture and press down the petals to completely close each flower (if this proves difficult, pierce each one with a toothpick, which can double as an hors d'oeuvre stick).

Arrange the flowers on a glass plate and lightly sprinkle with vinaigrette. Chill for at least 2 hours before serving.

Lotus Root Salad

Chinese delicatessens usually sell lotus root, both fresh and in tins, pre-cooked. It is the underwater root of the water-lily plant and much used in cooking throughout the Far East.

Lotus root is extremely attractive when prepared for serving, or, as cookery writer Robin Howe describes it, 'rather like a transverse section of a bullet-chamber of a six-shooter'.

> *1 lotus root, or 1 540g (19 oz) tin, drained*
> *15ml (1 tbs) white wine vinegar*
> *120ml (4 fl oz) sake*
> *30-45ml (2-3 tbs) caster sugar, to taste*
> *2.5ml (½ tsp) (or more) salt*
> *2 small red peppers, deseeded and thinly sliced into rings*
> *60ml/4 tbs water*
> optional
> *1.25ml (¼ tsp) monosodium glutamate*

Note If tinned lotus is used, this first step is unnecessary.

Clean and peel the lotus root. Cut into 2mm (⅛ in) slices and place immediately in a saucepan filled with acidulated water, to prevent discoloration. Bring to a boil and simmer gently for 2-3 minutes, until the slices are tender but still crisp. Remove from the heat, drain and place in a serving bowl.

In another small saucepan, combine the *sake*, sugar (to taste), water, salt and monosodium glutamate, if desired. Stir, and bring gently to the boil. When the sugar has completely dissolved, remove from the heat and pour over the lotus root slices. Add the red pepper rings, toss to ensure that all ingredients are well-covered with dressing, and chill for at least an hour. Toss again before serving.

Bamboo Shoot Salad

These are the tender shoots of young bamboo cane, collected before they appear above ground. They are an essential ingredient in Chinese cooking and can be purchased fresh from Chinese delicatessens. Although tinned bamboo shoots are an acceptable substitute for most recipes, they lack the crispness of freshly cooked shoots and are, therefore, less suitable for salads.

> *1 fresh bamboo shoot or 1 large tin 540g (19 oz) bamboo shoots*
> *15-30ml (1-2 tbs) white wine vinegar*
> *30ml (2 tbs) mirin (see p 244)*
> *2.5ml (½ tsp) salt*

15-30ml (1-2 tbs) caster sugar
2 small red peppers, deseeded and thinly sliced
optional
1.25ml (¼ tsp) monosodium glutamate

Fresh bamboo shoots should be cleaned, sliced into julienne strips and gently boiled for several minutes, until tender but still crisp. Drain and place in a large glass bowl with the red pepper slices. Tinned shoots need only be drained, and then sliced into julienne strips.

In a small saucepan, mix 15ml (1 tbs) vinegar, 15ml (1 tbs) sugar, mirin, salt and monosodium glutamate, if desired. Heat until the sugar has completely dissolved and adjust the seasoning with either more vinegar or more sugar. Remove from the heat and pour over the bamboo shoots and peppers. Toss to cover all ingredients with dressing and chill, tossing occasionally, for several hours before serving.

West African Breadfruit, Plantain or Yam Salad   *Serves 4-6*

These vegetables, rarities on the European dinner table, form part of the staple diet in many parts of Africa and the West Indies. Nowadays, it is possible to find them throughout Great Britain, especially in areas where large immigrant populations have their own greengrocery shops. In the USA, these vegetables appear in Southern cooking and have gained a somewhat trendy popularity with the advent of 'soul food' cuisine.

The *yam* is a type of sweet potato — more oily and orange in colour — which originated in Africa and is said to have been introduced to Europe by Christopher Columbus. To prepare, scrub well under cold water and peel. Place in a large saucepan of cold water and bring to a boil; 15 minutes cooking is probably sufficient — the yams should be tender, but crisp (*al dente*).

Breadfruit, a bumpy, green-brown fruit, has flesh resembling white bread in colour and texture. It is available in tins, but for use in salads is better boiled from its fresh state.

Scrub well under cold water, halve and peel to remove all outer green skin. Cut around the hard, stringy core and remove. Cook in lightly salted water for about 1 hour, or until tender.

Plantains are another starchy fruit, shaped like bananas. The Caribbean islanders have as many ways to cook them as we have for potatoes. To prepare, peel like a banana and parboil in lightly salted water for 10-15 minutes (less if the plantains begin to disintegrate).

2 medium-sized breadfruit or *3 large plantains* or *3 medium-sized yams*
1 medium-sized green pepper, coarsely chopped
1 small green chilli pepper, finely chopped (p 25)
4 stalks celery, coarsely chopped
90ml (6 tbs) vinaigrette
3 hard-boiled eggs
salt and freshly ground pepper
mayonnaise (p 30)

Prepare the vegetables or fruit as described above. Drain and when cool enough to handle, cut into 2.5cm (1 in) dice. Place in a large bowl and pour on the vinaigrette. Let the mixture marinate, tossing from time to time, for about an hour.

Dice the eggs and add them, along with the pepper, celery and chilli, to the marinated mixture. Toss gently, add enough mayonnaise to bind the ingredients, season to taste with salt and pepper, and toss again. Chill for an hour before serving.

Baingan Bhurta *Serves 4*

Garam masala is the unusual spice which gives this typical Indian salad its distinctive flavour. It is a condiment made with cardamoms, cumin and cloves, all dry roasted and ground or pounded to a fine powder. It can be purchased from Indian delicatessens but for the ambitious cook who wishes to prepare garam masala at home, the proportions are: 25g (1 oz) dark cardamom seeds, 50g (2 oz) cumin seeds, 25g (1 oz) cloves (some Indian cooks also add cinnamon to garam masala). When ground, store in a tightly sealed container until ready to use.

Ghee is clarified butter which can be made at home (see p 243) or purchased in tins at most Indian delicatessens.

Baingan bhurta, a pureed salad, closely resembles the 'poor man's caviar' of the Balkans (see p 149).

2 aubergines, approx 450g (1 lb)
30ml (2 tbs) ghee or other vegetable fat
3ml (2/3 tsp) black cumin seeds
5ml (1 tsp) white cumin seeds
3ml (2/3 tsp) chilli powder
15ml (1 tbs) coriander seeds
1.5ml (1/3 tsp) garam masala
salt

Pierce the aubergine skins with a fork and place under a hot grill until the skin burns and the vegetable starts to shrivel (about 30 minutes). Turn occasionally to cook all sides. Allow to stand for 5-10 minutes, then

230

squeeze gently to remove the bitter juices. Peel, and mash the pulp (or purée in an electric blender at low speed). Heat the ghee and fry the cumin seeds until they turn brown; add the aubergine pulp, chilli powder, coriander, salt and garam masala. Cook until the pulp has absorbed all the flavours and turns nicely brown.

> Let's drink the health
> of truffles black;
> In gratitude we must not lack,
> For they assure us dominance
> In all erotic dalliance
> As an aid to lovers' bliss
> Fate pleasurably fashioned this
> Rarity, divine godsend
> To use forever without end.

anonymous French rhyme

If fashioned by fate to be used 'forever without end', hardly a crueller trick has ever been perpetrated on the management of the kitchen purse. Almost prohibitively expensive nowadays (at the time of writing a 50g (2 oz) tin of truffles costs at least £15 in Harrods Food Hall), the most highly esteemed of all truffles is a black fungus which grows on the subterranean roots of trees in France, mainly in the region of the Perigord. Defying attempts to be cultivated (the best that can be done is to plant the trees under which they like to grow in the chalky soil in which they thrive), truffles are found and rooted out by specially trained dogs and pigs.

Brillat-Savarin described the black truffle as 'the diamond of the kitchen', observing its beautiful glossy surface and its mysterious penchant for enhancing the flavours of other foods. In itself, it has little distinctive taste.

In Great Britain and America, truffles can be bought in tins, the peelings being a good deal cheaper than the whole fungus.

Salade Françillon

Salade Françillon was introduced in Alexandre Dumas's play *Françillon* and achieved international fame when adapted for the Paris Exposition of 1900. The recipe is first given from the actual dialogue of the play (my own notes and suggestions for preparation are in brackets), and then again, according to the version popularised at the Exposition.

Annette: Cook some potatoes (1.125kg/2½ lb) in bouillon (600ml/1 pt), cut them in slices as for an ordinary salad, and while they are still warm season them with salt, pepper and a very good fruity olive oil (90ml/6 tbs) and vinegar (30ml/2 tbs).

Henri:	Tarragon?
Annette:	Orléans is better, but that is not of great importance. What is important is a half glass of white wine, Château Yquem if it is possible. A great deal of herbs finely chopped (45ml/3 tbs). At the same time cook very large mussels (450g/1 lb) in a court bouillon (600ml/1 pt) with a stalk of celery; drain them well and add them to the potatoes.
Henri:	Less mussels than potatoes?
Annette:	A third less. One should taste the mussels little by little. One should not foretaste them, nor should they obtrude when the salad is finished, lightly turned, cover it with slices of truffles; a real *calotte* for the connoisseur.
Henri:	And cooked in champagne? (Truffles were poached in champagne, or champagne mixed with stock, for 15 minutes.)
Annette:	That goes without saying. All this, two hours before dinner, so that the salad is very cold when it is served.
Henri:	One should surround the salad with ice.
Annette:	No, no, no. It must not be roughly treated; it is very delicate and all its flavours need to be quietly combined.

Salade Françillon II   *Serves 4*

This version is made doubly inaccessible to the ordinary cost-conscious consumer by the substitution of oysters for mussels and the large quantity of truffles required.

> *450g (1 lb) new potatoes, scrubbed*
> *480ml (16 fl oz) consommé*
> *12-18 small raw oysters*
> *115g (4 oz) truffles, drained and thinly sliced*
> *120ml (4 fl oz) dry sherry*
> *1 thick slice of large Spanish or Bermuda onion*
> *salt and freshly ground pepper*
> *90ml (6 tbs) best olive oil*
> *30ml (2 tbs) white wine vinegar*
> *30ml (2 tbs) champagne or Sauternes*
> *1.25ml (¼ tsp) paprika*
> Garnish
> *fresh parsley, coarsely chopped*

Cook the potatoes in gently simmering consommé for approximately 10 minutes, or just until tender. Drain and cool.

Parboil the oysters in their shells, or steam over moderate heat for 10-12 minutes, or until the shells open. Drain and chill.

Cover the sliced truffles with sherry in a small saucepan, add the onion and poach gently for 5 minutes. Drain and cool.

In a large shallow salad bowl, place the oysters, truffles and potatoes. Make a dressing from the oil, vinegar, paprika, salt and pepper, and pour over the salad. Add the wine or champagne and toss gently, but thoroughly, to cover all ingredients. Refrigerate for several hours, tossing occasionally, and serve in individual chilled salad plates with a sprinkling of chopped parsley.

Victorian Mixed Salad   *Serves 8*

> *6 potatoes, approx 900g (2 lb), washed and peeled*
> *1 medium-sized celeriac*
> *30ml (2 tbs) lemon juice*
> *75ml (5 tbs) mayonnaise (p 30)*
> *45ml (3 tbs) beetroot juice*
> *5ml (1 tsp) salt*
> *freshly ground pepper*
> *6 artichoke bottoms, fresh or tinned, cut into strips*
> *12 cooked asparagus tips, approx 7.5cm (3 in), fresh or tinned*
> *2 black truffles, drained and sliced*

Boil the potatoes in lightly salted water until just tender when pierced with a fork. Drain, and when cool enough to handle, cut into 2.5cm (1 in) dice. Peel the celeriac and cut in same-sized dice, dropping the pieces into a saucepan of water plus 30ml (2 tbs) lemon juice as they are cut. Parboil for 3-5 minutes. Drain and cool.

Blend the mayonnaise with the beetroot juice and season to taste with salt and freshly ground pepper.

In a large bowl, place the potatoes, celeriac and artichoke strips. Pour over the dressing and toss gently.

Arrange this mixture on a large platter and garnish with asparagus tips and truffles. Chill until ready to serve.

Japanese Pork with Bean Curd Dressing   *Serves 4-6*

Tofu, or soy bean curd, is a soft, white, custard-like cake made from the cooking, pounding and filtering of white soy beans. It is very high in protein and is, therefore, a staple element is many Oriental diets. *Tofu* is available fresh from Chinese delicatessens; the dried variety, used by the Chinese only for cooking (featured in the second recipe below) is purchased in flat sheets or twists.

> *450g (1 lb) lean pork*
> *325g (12 oz) French beans, washed and trimmed*
> *450g (1 lb) piece of bean curd*
> *75ml (5 tbs) white sesame seeds*

233

15-30ml (1-2 tbs) sugar (to taste)
30ml (2 tbs) light soy sauce (shoyu, see p 245)
15-30ml (1-2 tbs) stock
optional
1.25ml (¼ tsp) monosodium glutamate

Cut the pork into julienne strips, about 3.5cm (1½ in) by 5mm (¼ in). Drop into boiling salted water and simmer for 4 minutes, or until the meat has cooked. Drain and set aside.

Cook the beans in lightly salted boiling water for about 8 minutes, or just until tender. Drain and mix with the pork slices.

Roast the sesame seeds in a dry frying pan or under the grill, shaking the pan to ensure that all sides are toasted. The seeds should then be crushed in a mortar (or Japanese *suribachi*), or put through a coffee or nut grinder. Add the crushed seeds to the bean curd along with the sugar, soy sauce, salt and monosodium glutamate. Add stock gradually, while stirring, to thin out the sauce. Pour over the pork and beans, toss gently and serve at once.

Coriander and Dried Bean Curd Salad   *Serves 6-8*

1 square of dried brown bean curd
240ml (8 fl oz) peanut or other light vegetable oil
100g (4 oz) raw shelled, fresh unsalted peanuts
325g (12 oz) fresh coriander leaves, washed and trimmed
45ml (3 tbs) light soy sauce
45ml (3 tbs) sesame oil
15-30ml (1-2 tbs) sugar
optional
1.25ml (¼ tsp) monosodium glutamate
2.5ml (½ tsp) salt

In a small saucepan, place the bean curd and enough water to cover. Bring to the boil and simmer gently for about 15 minutes. Drain, and when cool enough to handle, slice and shred finely into uniformly-sized pieces. Place in a large bowl and set aside.

Heat the oil until it starts to smoke, then turn off the heat and add the peanuts. Stir continuously with a wooden spoon until they turn golden brown — probably no more than a minute. Remove with a slotted spoon and drain off excess oil on paper towels.

Blanch the coriander leaves in boiling water for several seconds, then place in a sieve and refresh under running cold water. Drain and squeeze out excess water. Chop finely and add to the bean curd, along with half the peanuts.

Mix the soy sauce, sesame oil, monosodium glutamate (if desired) and 15-30ml (1-2 tbs) sugar, according to taste. Pour over the salad and toss well. Chill for at least an hour, and just before serving, scatter the remaining peanuts across the top.

Salad Berthault   *Serves 6-8*

A very expensive way of preparing a niçoise-style salad — perfect for parties and holiday buffets. (Use the leftover champagne for a festive punch.)

900g (2 lb) new potatoes
450g (1 lb) tender French beans
4 hard-boiled eggs
1 tin anchovy fillets
1 tomato, cut into wedges
12 green olives, pitted
12 black olives, pitted
1/3 bottle chilled dry champagne
30ml (2 tbs) cognac
90ml (6 tbs) best olive oil
5ml (1 tsp) prepared French mustard
juice of ½ lemon, freshly squeezed and strained
salt and freshly ground pepper

Scrub the potatoes and boil for 15 minutes, or until tender but not mushy. Drain and cool. Peel and slice into thin rounds. Divide into 4 equal portions and set aside.

Wash and trim the beans. Cook uncovered in lightly salted boiling water for 8-10 minutes, or just until tender (*al dente*). Drain and cool.

Slice the eggs into rounds.

In a large glass bowl, layer the ingredients as follows: potatoes, beans, potatoes, egg slices and anchovy fillets (reserve one or two for decoration), potatoes, olives (reserve 4-5 for garnish), potatoes. Decorate the top with anchovy fillets, olives and tomato wedges.

Pour the champagne over this and chill for several hours.

Just before serving, sprinkle the salad with cognac and pour on a dressing made from the oil, mustard, lemon juice, salt and pepper.

Dried fish is a popular ingredient in Eastern and Oriental cooking. The Indian version, Bombay duck, is found mainly in the south. It is served as a side dish, rather than a condiment or chutney. Bombay duck is dried *bummelo* fish: small transparent fish which are hung out to dry and with a

235

rather powerful smell which can be quite overwhelming to the uninitiated. Bombay duck can be purchased in packets from Oriental grocers.

Bombay Duck Salad   *Serves 2-3*

6 Bombay duck
1 green chilli pepper, finely chopped (p 243)
2 spring onions, finely chopped (including 5cm (2 in) of green stem)
15ml (1 tbs) thinly sliced fresh ginger
15-30ml (1-2 tbs) white wine vinegar (or rice vinegar)

Roast the Bombay duck under the grill or in a hot oven until crisp and crumble into small pieces. Mix with the chilli pepper, ginger and chopped onion. Toss with a little vinegar and serve.

Pipinge Sambal   *Serves 3-4*

Sambals are the Southeast Asian version of side salads, served with rice. This Sri Lankan cucumber sambal is garnished with *maldive fish*. The islanders claim there is no equivalent for this dried fish, but as it is extremely difficult to find in Western shops, Bombay duck is a reasonable substitute.

1 cucumber
10ml (2 tsp) grilled and crumbled maldive fish
1 small onion, finely chopped
2 green chillis, minced (p 243)
45ml (3 tbs) coconut milk (see p 243)
salt to taste
sharp vinegar to taste

Peel the cucumber and halve. Deseed and cut into long thin strips. Immerse in cold, lightly salted water for a few minutes, then squeeze out all the liquid, cut the strips in half, and put into a glass bowl. Add the chopped onion, crumbled fish and chilli. Pour in the coconut milk and sprinkle with salt and vinegar (coconut vinegar would be used in Sri Lanka) to taste.

Gado-Gado   *Serves 6*

This is an Indonesian cooked vegetable salad, dressed with a spicy peanut sauce. The choice of vegetables can vary — beansprouts, green beans and cabbage generally form the base — but they must be arranged in an attractive pattern, usually layered for maximum authenticity.

The recipe for sauce given here is a less exotic version than others I have seen. *Trasi*, a rather unpleasant smelling shrimp paste; *copha*, a coconut oil; *laos* powder, made from a root somewhat like ginger; curry leaves and tamarind juice may be standard larder items in an Indonesian kitchen, but their cumulative cost, unless one wishes to try other South East Asian delights (for those who do, I recommend Rosemary Brissenden's *South East Asian Food*, Penguin, 1975) is excessive for the average cook. A judicious substitution of these traditional ingredients will produce a tasty and perfectly acceptable dressing as described below.

> *peanut oil*
> *225g (8 oz) French beans, cut into 2.5cm (1 in) lengths and cooked*
>   *al dente*
> *225g (8 oz) spinach, washed and chopped or 225g (8 oz) dark green*
>   *cabbage, shredded and blanched for 1 minute*
> *100g (4 oz) beansprouts, blanched for 45 seconds*
> *2 medium-sized potatoes, scrubbed, boiled and sliced*
> *2 hard-boiled eggs*
> *1 small onion, thinly sliced*
> Garnish
> *prawn crackers*

Arrange the vegetables on a large serving dish, and sprinkle with crumbled hard-boiled egg and onion rings, crisply fried as follows. Allow the slices to stand and dry on some paper towels for a couple of hours. Heat a little peanut oil in a frying pan and when it is very hot add the onions. Reduce the heat and cook until quite brown and crisp on one side. Turn and carefully brown the other side. (If the onions begin to burn, remove the pan from the heat.) Drain thoroughly on paper towels before adding to the salad. Dress with peanut sauce:

> *peanut oil*
> *1 small onion, minced*
> *salt*
> *150ml (5 fl oz) peanut butter*
> *15ml (1 tbs) tamarind water or lemon juice*
> *2 red chilli peppers, minced (p 243)*
> *3 cloves garlic, minced*
> *1.25ml (¼ tsp) grated fresh ginger*
> *300ml (½ pt) coconut milk (p 243)*
> *brown sugar, to taste*

Heat a little peanut oil in a pan and gently fry the onion, minced chillis and garlic. Add the peanut butter and coconut milk, and season to taste with salt. Bring to a boil and add the tamarind water and enough brown sugar to create a sweet and sour flavour. Pour over the vegetables and serve with prawn crackers.

Gado-Gado sauce can be bought ready-made in a concentrated form which needs only the addition of boiling water

237

Nam Prik Pak

Raw vegetables with Thai hot sauce

Nam Prik is a hot spicy sauce, served throughout Thailand in many varieties and accompanying many different types of food. Robin Howe describes it as 'a cross between the French hors d'oeuvre and a salad served with a pungent sauce'. It is usually eaten, he goes on to say,

with everyone sitting around the table or on the floor, with a plate of rice in front of each person. A bowl of *nam prik* is placed in the centre of the table with all the side dishes around it. The food is eaten with a little of the *nam prik*, followed by a spoonful or handful of the rice. Each one selects the item of food he likes and the combinations can be made by placing different bits of food on a lettuce leaf, adding a few drops of the *nam prik* sauce, then folding the leaf into a bite-size package. This is placed whole in the mouth.

Far Eastern Cookery, Robin Howe

Nam prik pak should include a large selection of vegetables and flowers, varying in size, colour, texture and taste. In Thailand, there would most certainly be slices of tart green mango but if this is difficult to find, a crisp tart cooking apple or raw gooseberries will provide the necessary sour ingredient.

For a really authentic nam prik, blachan (dried shrimp cake) and fish sauce should be used, but shrimp or anchovy paste can be substituted for blachan and soy sauce for fish sauce. Dried prawns are available, as are the other oriental ingredients, from specialist grocery stores.

Note Vary these quantities according to taste; no two Thai cooks make *nam prik* the same way.

6 dried prawns, pounded
2-3 cloves garlic
5ml (1 tsp) blachan, roasted in foil or 5ml (1 tsp) shrimp or anchovy paste
hot chillies (deseeded, p 243), to taste
juice of 1 lime (or lemon), freshly squeezed
10ml (2 tsp) sugar
10ml (2 tsp) fish sauce or soy sauce

Place all the ingredients in a blender and mix until a fairly smooth sauce is formed (bits of garlic and chilli should still be visible). Serve the sauce in a bowl, set amidst a large platter of raw vegetables.

Wild Rice Salad

Today an expensive gourmet delicacy, wild rice, just a few decades ago was considered unpalatable by all but the wild mallard and the American Indian.

The Indians of North America introduced this grain (not actually rice, but an aquatic seed which grows in shallow lakes and rivers) to the white traders and trappers. According to an American firm marketing wild rice, the Indians of North America still play a large part in gathering this rice, using the same methods as their ancestors:

When the crop is ready to harvest, the workers — two in each canoe — shore into the rice beds. The man in front of the boat uses a pole to bend the grain over the side of the boat. Using another stick he then beats the grain so the ripened kernels drop into the boat bottom. The other person provides the locomotion for the canoe. In good years, a couple working together are able to gather several hundred pounds of rice daily. Harvesters sell the green rice to buyers who have it prepared for the market.

North American wild rice is generally cheaper than European varieties, and just as tasty. I have seen both available in gourmet food shops (Harrods and Fortnum and Mason usually stock S & W brand, currently priced at just over £5.00 for a 225g (8 oz) box).

Although traditionally served as an accompaniment to game and roast meats, wild rice makes a delicious salad — and because of its high cost and the time it takes to prepare properly (always follow the exact instructions on the package), it makes sense to know some tasty ways of using any leftovers. Here are two suggestions for wild rice salads.

Note Instructions for boiling vary. Always follow the method described on the packet. In general, better results are obtained when the rice has been soaked overnight and washed in several waters before cooking.

Spicy Wild Rice Salad   *Serves 6-8*

A superb accompaniment to cold duck, turkey, pheasant, pork or veal.

> *225g (8 oz) uncooked wild rice (it will treble in size)*
> *1 medium-sized onion, finely shredded*
> *150g (6 oz) blanched almond slivers*
> *50g (2 oz) butter*
> *150g (6 oz) raisins, plumped up in cold water and drained*
> *20 whole cloves*
> *1 large green pepper, deseeded and coarsely shredded*
> *30ml (2 tbs) vegetable oil*
> *15ml (1 tbs) wine vinegar*
> *salt and freshly ground pepper*

239

Garnish
parsley

Boil the rice and set aside. Melt the butter in a large frying pan and sauté the onions and green peppers for 5 minutes over a low heat. Add the almonds and the raisins and continue cooking until both the onions and nuts have turned golden brown. Add the boiled rice and the cloves. Stir with a wooden spoon to thoroughly blend all ingredients. Remove from the heat and turn the mixture into a large serving bowl. Allow to cool and dress with a little vinaigrette, seasoned to taste with salt and pepper. Garnish with a few sprigs of parsley.

Savoury Rice with Bacon and Mushrooms   *Serves 6*

225g (8 oz) uncooked wild rice
6 bacon rashers
1 medium-sized onion, finely shredded
225g (8 oz) button mushrooms, cleaned and sliced
15ml (1 tbs) fresh marjoram, chopped or 2.5ml (½ tsp) dried marjoram
10ml (2 tsp) fresh thyme or 2.5ml (½ tsp) dried thyme
2.5-5ml (½-1 tsp) dried oregano
salt and freshly ground pepper
30ml (2 tbs) olive oil
15ml (1 tbs) wine vinegar
optional
25g (1 oz) butter

Boil the rice and set aside. Fry the bacon in a large frying pan until very crisp. Remove and drain on a paper towel. Next sauté the onion in the bacon fat, adding butter only if the pan becomes dry. After 5 minutes add the mushrooms and continue cooking over a fairly low heat for a further 2-3 minutes. Finally, add the rice and herbs, stir well and season with salt and pepper.

Turn the mixture into a large serving bowl and allow to cool. Just before serving, crumble the bacon into the mixture, dress with a little vinaigrette and toss lightly.

The De-Toxicating Salad

Grayshott Hall Health Centre near Hindhead, Surrey, has developed a marvellous one day salad diet, the perfect antidote to over-indulgence and prolonged holiday excesses. Although the de-toxicating effect depends on following a strict regime, the salad itself is delicious — a blend of sweet and sour flavours, crunchy and moist textures — as a pleasant and healthy light meal at any time:

Commence the day with a glass of hot water with a little lemon juice added. For

240

the rest of the day drinks may be lemon juice in hot water or not more than three cups of tea with lemon — no sugar or sweetening of any kind — and no milk. The drinks should be taken between the meals.

The meals consist of three equal parts of the special salad mixture given below. All the ingredients should be chopped up in the morning and well shaken together in a container. The total is then divided into three portions — one for each meal. With the mixed salad a cup of yoghurt flavoured with a little lemon juice may also be taken — no sweetening.

If this regime is carried out for one day per week, or following any day on which a little 'dissipation' has been unavoidable — the weight will be kept down and toxic accumulation from ordinary meals will be considerably reduced.

3 medium-sized and well cleaned carrots
3 apples, well scrubbed or peeled
3 sticks of celery (if celery is not available, use endive or chicory and in addition take approximately 6 oz of Biotta celery juice. This can be bought from health food stores).
handful of raisins — well washed
¼ cucumber — wash but do not peel
small green pepper, deseeded
2 pears
1 orange (if subject to liver troubles or migraine take ½ grapefruit instead of orange)

Ne Lactucae Laedant

A suitable way to end a book of salads: for those who eat too much lettuce, the first century Roman Apicius created this infusion to deter the harmful effects:

[And in order that the lettuce may not hurt you take (with it or after it) the following preparation: 2 oz of ginger; 1 oz of green rue; 1 oz of meaty dates; 12 scruples of ground pepper; 1 oz of good honey and 8 oz of either Aethiopian or Syrian cumin. Make an infusion of this in vinegar, the cumin crushed, and strain. Of this liquor, use a small spoonful and mix it with stock and a little vinegar: you may take a small spoonful after the meal]

Glossary

Acidulated water — water to which a drop of vinegar or lemon juice has been added to prevent discolouration of peeled fruits and vegetables when soaked.

À la grecque — refers to a method of poaching vegetables in an aromatic broth made from olive oil, white wine, water and herbs. When cooked, the vegetables are generally removed to a serving bowl with a slotted spoon while the broth is reduced to intensify the flavour. It is then poured over the vegetables and cooled.

Al dente — the best way of cooking vegetables, tender but still firm. *Al dente,* from the Italian phrase 'to the tooth', means neither raw nor overcooked: a perfect state of flavourful, crunchy, slightly underdoneness.

Anchovy essence — a concentrated anchovy paste and useful substitute in Oriental cooking for *blachan* or fish sauce when mixed with soy sauce.

Bamboo shoots — the young shoots of the bamboo tree, used frequently in oriental cooking. There are winter and summer varieties, the former being considered the greater delicacy. Available fresh in Far Eastern markets, the tinned variety (pre-cooked) is often the only type available to us. All parts of the tinned bamboo are usable, but once opened the shoots should be covered with water and stored in the refrigerator in a covered container.

Bean curd (see p 233) — a much-featured ingredient in oriental cooking made from curdled and coagulated soy bean. Resembling a soft but firm white cheese, it is sold in a variety of forms — from a watery white custard to a firm, dried cake.

Blachan — see *trasi*

Blanch — to boil various ingredients for 1-2 minutes; a method used to

242

loosen skins (eg almonds), to heighten flavour or to set colour.

Bouquet garni — a bunch of herbs containing 3 sprigs of parsley, 1 of thyme and a small bayleaf, usually sold tied together in a piece of muslin. Used extensively to flavour broths and stews.

Bruise — to partially crush (as a clove of garlic in a mortar and pestle) to release flavour.

Bombay duck (Bommaloe Machee) — a fish caught off the west coast of India, near Bombay (the anglicised name probably refers to the way these small fish skim the surface of the water, rather than swim beneath); it is dried and salted for export.

Cardamom — a pungent Eastern spice, used both as seeds (known as the 'seeds of Paradise') or in a powdered form.

Chapon — a chunk of stale or toasted French bread, rubbed with garlic (and sometimes oil) that is tossed with green salads to add a subtle garlic flavour; sometimes discarded before serving.

Chilli peppers — the fruits of an herbaceous plant belonging to the capsicum family (see p 102). Both the red and green varieties are highly pungent, though varying greatly in strength and flavour. As their oils can make the eyes smart and the skin burn, special caution in handling is advised. If possible, wear rubber gloves and try not to touch your face. Clean the chillis by rinsing under cold running water. If they are to be left whole, break off the stems but do not cut. If the recipe calls for deseeding, pull out the stem and any seeds attached to it, then cut open the pod and brush out any remaining seeds with your fingers. After handling chillis, always wash the hands thoroughly with soap and warm water.

Clarified butter (ghee) — butter from which the milky residue has been removed. Place small pieces of butter in a pan over moderate heat; as soon as the foam subsides, carefully skim it off with a spoon and pour the clear yellow liquid into a clear bowl, leaving the milky residue in the bottom of the pan. This clear liquid will store well in a covered jar in the refrigerator. The type used extensively in Indian cooking is called *ghee* and can be bought in tins at Indian grocery stores.

Clarify — to make cloudy liquid clear.

Coconut milk — in tropical areas where coconuts are indigenous, coconut milk is made by soaking the freshly grated flesh in water and squeezing it out. The white flesh (trimmed of its brown outer crust) is grated into a bowl — a good-size coconut will yield about 3-4 cups. For coconut *cream*, pour 120ml (4 fl oz) of hot water over the flesh and allow to stand for half an hour. Then squeeze it through a cheesecloth or piece of fine muslin. You should get approximately 240ml (8 fl oz) of liquid. For a *thick milk*, use 240ml (8 fl oz) hot water; for thin milk use 480ml (16 fl oz).

An excellent substitute for the fresh liquid can also be made from commercial coconut cream, a packaged concentrate. For a thick liquid, blend 75g (3 oz) of cream with 240ml (8 fl oz) hot water; for a thinner version, mix 25g (1 oz) of cream with 240ml (8 fl oz) hot water. Strain before using, to remove any residue, and stir in a tiny pinch of salt. Alternatively, coconut milk can be made by pouring 600ml (1 pt) of hot water over 225g (8 oz) dessicated coconut, steeping the mixture for 20-30 minutes, then straining through a cheesecloth, squeezing to remove all the liquid.

Court bouillon — aromatised liquid for cooking meat, fish, vegetables, etc — the 'aromatics' can include vegetables, herbs, spices, as well as wines and liqueurs. Here is one basic recipe which can be varied with practice, and according to the type of foods being poached:

300ml (½ pt) water ⎫ *or 450ml (¾ pt) water and a good dash*
300ml (½ pt) dry white wine ⎬ *of dry white vermouth*
1 onion stuck with a clove
1 carrot
a bouquet garni
6 peppercorns
salt

Bring all ingredients to the boil, simmer for 25 minutes and strain.

Croutons — bread cut in dice, fried in oil, often with garlic; toasted under the grill; or dried in the oven.

Daikon (see radishes, p 110) — the enormous white radish of Japan, usually grated for garnish or pickled. Available from oriental grocery stores.
Dice — to cut into small squares.

Dried shrimp — used to provide a sea-like flavour to Oriental dishes, these small dried and salted shrimps are bright pink in colour, about 2.5cm (1 in) long and should be soaked in hot water before adding to other ingredients. After opening the packet, store in a tightly-sealed container.

Fold — to blend gently

Ghee — see clarified butter

julienne — food cut into match-like shreds

Macedoine — a mixture of raw or cooked fruit or vegetables, either hot or cold.
Macerate — to soak fruit in spirits

244

Maldive fish — a dried fish from the Maldive Islands, used in the cookery of Sri Lanka. The closest readily available equivalent in European markets is Bombay Duck.

Marinate — to steep savoury foods — meat, fish, fowl, vegetables — in a spicy liquid for several hours until the food absorbs the flavouring.

Mince — to cut into fine pieces; generally, a smaller, finer cut than chopped ingredients.

Mirin — Japanese rice wine used only for cooking. A reasonably good, dry sherry may be substituted for mirin, but add a pinch of sugar to the recipe as well.

Pare — to cut the peel from fruits and vegetables.

Plump — to soak raisins or other dried fruits in liquid until they soften and expand.

Poppy seeds — the poppy that yields these tiny seeds is not the same poppy that produces opium. Poppy seeds are popular in oriental cooking but they are grown and widely used in Central Europe and North America as well.

Purée — to reduce to a paste, either by pressing through a food mill or whisking in an electric blender.

Reduce — to boil down rapidly until volume is reduced and flavour more concentrated.

Refresh — to plunge hot food into iced water to set the colour and flavour.

Rose water — distilled rose water features regularly in Oriental cooking. It should be stored in a dark cool place to retain its flavour and aroma.

Sake — Japanese rice wine, occasionally used in cooking. An open bottle will not keep forever, so check before adding to your recipe.

Sambal — a generic name for the many different condiments served with curry.

Sauté — a method of browning food in a frying pan with a small quantity of fat.

Score — to make shallow knife cuts over the surface of food, generally in a criss-cross pattern.

Sesame oil — oriental sesame oil has a darker colour and more distinctive flavour than the pale sesame oils that can be purchased from health food stores.

Sesame seeds — these aromatic seeds take on a wonderfully nutty flavour when toasted. Simply place under the grill in a roasting pan or in a dry frying pan on a low heat. Shake occasionally and remove from the heat when the seeds begin to pop.

Soy sauce (shoyu) — a basic oriental flavouring made from barley, soya bean and salt. The Japanese shoyu is much the same as Chinese soy sauce, but Western bottled varieties tend to be saltier than either of the oriental sauces.

Skim — to spoon fat, froth or other residue from the surface of a liquid.

Steam — to cook, covered, over a small amount of boiling liquid so that the steam formed in the pan does the cooking.

Steep — to let herbs, spices, petals, etc stand in hot liquid until their flavour is extracted.

Tabasco sauce — a common American condiment; chilli sauce can be substituted.

Tahini — a sesame seed paste used extensively in Middle Eastern cookery.

Tomatoes, how to peel — when a recipe calls for peeled or skinned tomatoes, choose firm but ripe specimens and immerse them in boiling water for several seconds. To remove, stab them with a sharp knife and lift from the water. When they are cool enough to handle, gently peel off the skin with your fingers.

Trasi — sometimes called the caviar of the Far East, this basic condiment is made from prawns or shrimps, salted, dried, pounded and rotted, then formed into cakes. It has a very strong smell and, once opened, should be stored in a jar with a tight-fitting lid. Westerners who find the smell too offensive, or who do not wish to buy this ingredient for one recipe, can substitute shrimp or anchovy paste.

Turmeric — a bright yellow spice derived from the fleshy root stalk of a tropical plant native to the Far East, Africa and Australia. It is one of the main ingredients in curry and other Indian dishes.

Water chestnuts — available in tins in the West, these crisp, white-fleshed nuts — bearing no resemblance to Western chestnuts — are used extensively in oriental cooking. Drained and chopped, they make a delightful crunchy addition to all sorts of salads.

Yoghurt, straining — as thick yoghurt is nearly always best for salads or as a substitute (when indicated) for curd, shop-bought yoghurt should be strained to remove most of the whey or watery liquid. To do this, line a sieve with a cheesecloth or cotton mesh and place it over a deep bowl. Pour the yoghurt into the sieve and leave to stand for about an hour, squeezing the cloth from time to time to extract the liquid. The curds that remain should be thick and creamy.

Zest — the French term for peel; it actually refers to the oil in the skins of fruit, particularly citrus, which gives them their characteristic fragrance.

Index

247

248

251